Betsy Bruce

SAMS
Teach Yourself
Macromedia®
Dreamweaver™ 4
in 24 Hours

SAMS

201 West 103rd St., Indianapolis, Indiana, 46290 USA

Sams Teach Yourself Macromedia® Dreamweaver™ 4 in 24 Hours
Copyright © 2001 by Sams Publishing

International Standard Book Number: 0-672-30428

Library of Congress Catalog Card Number: 00-110851

Printed in the United States of America

First Printing: December 2000

02   01   4   3   2

Trademarks

Warning and Disclaimer

EXECUTIVE EDITOR
Jeff Schultz

DEVELOPMENT EDITOR
Susan Hobbs

MANAGING EDITOR
Charlotte Clapp

PROJECT EDITOR
Dawn Pearson

COPY EDITOR
Susan Hobbs

INDEXER
Rebecca Salerno

PROOFREADER
Katherin Bidwell

TECHNICAL EDITOR
Ash Patel

TEAM COORDINATOR
Amy Patton

INTERIOR DESIGNER
Gary Adair

COVER DESIGNER
Aren Howell

COPYWRITER
Eric Borgert

PRODUCTION
Cheryl Lynch

Contents at a Glance

Contents

About the Author

Betsy Bruce specializes in technology-based training using Dreamweaver and Authorware. Formerly a senior developer for MediaPro, Inc. in Bothell, WA, she is now an independent consultant and trainer. She is a Macromedia certified instructor for Dreamweaver, CourseBuilder for Dreamweaver, Dreamweaver UltraDev, and Authorware, and she received her B.S. degree from the University of Iowa. She is a frequent speaker at conferences on creating technology-based training. Born and raised in Iowa, Betsy now lives in Seattle, WA. Her Web site is located at `http://www.betsybruce.com/`.

Dedication

This book is dedicated to my father, John Bruce, who was an outstanding educator, man, and father. He touched the lives of so many young people, and I was blessed to be his daughter.

Acknowledgments

I'd like to thank Jennifer Henry and Noah Maas who contributed examples for this book. Seattle Webgrrls has been a wonderful resource for me over the last few years and allowed me to use some examples from their Web site. Thanks go to Craig Kitterman for being my ASP advisor. Thanks to Steve Conrad of MediaPro, Inc., who has been a great mentor over the years. Thanks to the Dreamweaver development team for creating such a great product. Thank you to the wonderful crew at Sams Publishing.

I'd also like to thank my family and friends for helping me through writing this book and supporting me lovingly in all my endeavors.

Tell Us What You Think!

As the reader of this book, *you* are our most important critic and commentator. We value your opinion and want to know what we're doing right, what we could do better, what areas you'd like to see us publish in, and any other words of wisdom you're willing to pass our way.

You can email or write me directly to let me know what you did or didn't like about this book—as well as what we can do to make our books stronger.

Please note that I cannot help you with technical problems related to the topic of this book, and that due to the high volume of mail I receive, I might not be able to reply to every message.

When you write, please be sure to include this book's title and author as well as your name and phone or fax number. I will carefully review your comments and share them with the author and editors who worked on the book.

Email: webdev_sams@mcp.com

Mail: Mark Taber
           Associate Publisher
           Sams Publishing
           201 West 103rd Street
           Indianapolis, IN 46290 USA

Introduction

"Ooooooo, Dreamweaver. I believe you can get me through the night." Remember that song by Gary Wright? OK, some of you weren't born yet. The song brought up memories of seventh grade dances for me. I'm glad that Dreamweaver, the software, came along and replaced that vision in my head. Dreamweaver, the software, has helped me through a number of nights developing Web sites and Web applications!

What Is Dreamweaver?

Dreamweaver is an award-winning HTML editor that is simple to use. Some people do not use the more powerful features of Dreamweaver because they don't know about them. You will not be one of those people with this book in your hand!

Dreamweaver is excellent at quickly creating forms, frames, tables, and other HTML objects. But Dreamweaver really shines when you need to make your Web page *do* something. Dreamweaver excels at Dynamic HTML (DHTML), the more recent Web functionality that enables timeline animation, absolute positioning of content, and the scripting to make it work. Don't know how to script? No problem! Dreamweaver includes behaviors, scripted functionality that you simply click to add to a certain object.

Who Should Use Dreamweaver?

Whether you are creating your very first Web page or have recently decided to try Web editing software after coding by hand for years, you are going to love Macromedia Dreamweaver 4. Dreamweaver gives you the freedom to visually design the look of a Web page and the power to make it act the way you want. Dreamweaver gives you the flexibility to create your own personal Web page or an entire corporate intranet site.

You might have purchased Dreamweaver bundled with either Fireworks or CourseBuilder. There are tips throughout the book about integrating Dreamweaver with Fireworks, an image editor, and an appendix covering CourseBuilder, a tool to create learning interactions. Even if you purchased Dreamweaver by itself, you get an extra HTML editor, BBEdit for the Macintosh, or HomeSite for Windows.

Who Should Use This Book?

This book is for anyone now using Dreamweaver, as well as anyone who is planning to. If you are new to Web development, this book will get you up to speed creating Web pages and Web sites. If you are already a Web developer, you'll find tips, tricks, and instructions to get all you can out of Dreamweaver.

How to Use This Book

Each chapter of this book represents a lesson that should take you approximately an hour to learn. The book is designed to get you productively working in Dreamweaver as quickly as possible. There are numerous figures to illustrate the lessons in the book.

Each lesson begins with an overview and list of topics. The lesson ends with questions and answers, a quiz, and some exercises that you can try on your own. Within the lessons are elements that provide additional information:

Notes give extra information on the current topic.

Tips offer advice or an additional way of accomplishing something.

Cautions signal you to be careful of potential problems, giving you information on how to avoid or fix them.

PART I

Getting Started with Dreamweaver 4

Hour

HOUR 1

Understanding the Dreamweaver Interface

I'm sure you are itching to begin creating gorgeous and dynamic Web sites. First, however, you need to understand the Dreamweaver interface and the numerous functions that are going to help you be successful as a Web developer.

In this chapter, you will learn

- What hardware and software you will need to run Dreamweaver
- How to install Dreamweaver
- How to use the Dreamweaver interface
- How to manage panels, inspectors, and windows

Acquaint Yourself with Dreamweaver

Dreamweaver is an *HTML (Hypertext Markup Language)* editor, authoring tool, and Web site management tool all rolled into one. You can do many things without ever laying your eyes on any HTML. But if you want to get down and dirty with HTML, Dreamweaver makes it easy to do so. If this is your first foray into creating Web pages, you might want to take a peek at the HTML every now and then to get familiar with HTML structure.

HTML is the language of Web pages. This language consists mainly of paired tags, contained in angle brackets (<>). The tags surround objects on a Web page, like text, or stand on their own. Some tags, like the tag used to insert images into Web pages, are single tags. The beginning tag of a paired set looks like <table> and the ending tag begins with a forward slash, </table>. Tags also contain attribute values that alter the way objects look on a page. Dreamweaver inserts all of the HTML tags and attributes for you.

Dreamweaver is a *WYSIWYG* (what you see is what you get) Web page editor that is extremely powerful while also being easy to use. You can create new sites with Dreamweaver, and you can import and edit existing sites. Dreamweaver will not change or rearrange your code. One of Dreamweaver's most popular features has always been that it leaves existing sites perfectly intact; the folks at Macromedia, the company that created Dreamweaver, call this feature *Roundtrip HTML*.

Dreamweaver is also an authoring tool. What do I mean by authoring tool? Dreamweaver can implement Dynamic HTML pages enabling interactivity and animation. Authoring tools enable you to create a complicated application. Even though Dreamweaver can be used as an HTML editor it can also be used to create multimedia applications. So you can, of course, simply edit HTML with Dreamweaver, or you can author an experience for your viewers.

Install the Software

Dreamweaver is installed by a standard Windows or Macintosh installation program. The installation program creates all of the directories and files needed to run Dreamweaver on your hard drive.

1

Hardware and Software Requirements

Table 1.1 lists the hardware and software required to run Dreamweaver.

TABLE 1.1   Hardware and Software Requirements for Dreamweaver

Windows 95/NT	Macintosh
Intel Pentium processor or equivalent 150+ MHz	
Windows 95/98 or NT version 4.0 or later	OS 8.6 or later QuickTime 3.0 or later MRJ 2.2 (for Flash Buttons & Flash Text features)
32MB RAM	32MB RAM
30MB of available disk space	30MB of available disk space
256 color monitor capable of 800×600 resolution	256 color monitor capable of 800×600 resolution
Navigator or Explorer 4.0 or greater	Navigator or Explorer 4.0 or greater

Get the Demo Version

Macromedia is the company that develops and sells Dreamweaver. They offer a demo version of the software that you can evaluate before you decide to purchase Dreamweaver. You can download the demo at `http://www.macromedia.com/software/dreamweaver/ trial/`.

The Installation Process

The easiest way to start the installation program is to pop the Dreamweaver CD-ROM into your CD-ROM drive. The Dreamweaver installation program should launch automatically. If it doesn't launch automatically, you can launch it manually:

1. Open Windows Explorer or click the My Computer icon on the Windows desktop. Macintosh users should click on their CD-ROM drive icon.

2. Find the CD-ROM drive contents. Locate the `Dreamweaver 4 Installer.exe` file (or the demo file that you downloaded from the Macromedia Web site, `dreamweaver4.exe`).

3. Double-click the setup file. Figure 1.1 shows you what the installation program looks like.

FIGURE **1.1**

The installation program installs the directories and files needed to run Dreamweaver.

4. After following the onscreen instructions and entering the serial number that you received with the product you're ready to go!

The Dreamweaver Work Area

When you open Dreamweaver for the first time, you will see an empty window, called the *document window*, with *floating panels* on the top of it. The document window displays your Web page approximately as it will appear in a Web browser.

> When you launch Dreamweaver, an empty document window opens. If you have Web sites set up in the site window, the site window will open along with an empty document window. The Site window is where you will manage your entire Web site. We'll discuss the site window in Hour 3, "Planning and Creating Your Project Using the Site Window."

The Document Window

The document window has a title bar, menu bar, and toolbar at the top of the page. The title bar contains the title of the current Web page. This title will also appear in the title bar of the Web browser. We'll explore page properties and how to title a page in the next hour. The file name is located to the right of the title and is enclosed in parentheses. The title of the Web page is contained within the HTML of the page. The title of the file is the name that you give the page when you save the file to your hard drive.

The Toolbar

The toolbar sits right below the menu bar, giving you quick access to important commands. If the toolbar isn't visible in your document window, select the Toolbar command under the View menu. The three buttons on the left of the toolbar enable you to toggle between the Code view (the HTML Source Inspector), Design view, and a split view with both the code and design views visible (shown in Figure 1.2). When you are in Code view (or split screen view), the Refresh Design View button refreshes the Design view so that you can instantly see the changes you made.

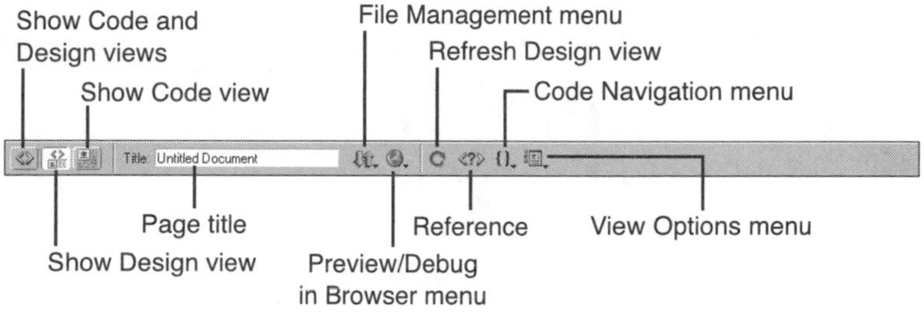

FIGURE 1.2

The toolbar contains commands for commonly used Dreamweaver functions.

Show Code and Design views
Show Code view
Page title
Show Design view
File Management menu
Refresh Design view
Code Navigation menu
Reference
Preview/Debug in Browser menu
View Options menu

Title: Untitled Document

Next to the buttons that control the views is a box where you can create the title of your document. There are also three drop-down menus on the toolbar: the File Management menu, the Preview/Debug in Browser menu, and the View Options menu. The File Management menu lists commands related to file management, such as checking files into and out of the server. We'll explore these commands in Hour 18, "Managing and Uploading Your Projects." The Preview/Debug in Browser menu gives you quick access to a list of browsers that you have set up to preview your Web pages. You can also launch your Web page and debug it in a browser; we'll explore debugging JavaScript in Dreamweaver in Hour 23, "HTML Is Fun! Viewing and Modifying HTML."

The Reference button launches a set of reference books that contain information about CSS (Cascading Style Sheets), HTML, and JavaScript. These complete reference books are available for you to look up tag attributes, JavaScript objects, and CSS styles.

The Code Navigation button is only active when you are in either the Code view or the Code inspector. This menu gives you quick access to debugging commands that you'll explore further when you use the JavaScript debugger in Hour 23. The Options menu enables you to turn on borders, rulers, the grid, and other options in the Design view. In Code view, the Options menu enables you to set the appearance of the code. There is an additional command in the View Options menu that enables you to place the Design view pane on the top or the bottom of the Code view pane.

The Status Bar

The Dreamweaver document window has a status bar along the bottom of the page. It contains the tag selector, the Window Size drop-down menu, download statistics, and the Mini-Launcher, as shown in Figure 1.3. These convenient tools are just some of the nice touches that Dreamweaver offers to help you have a productive and fun experience designing for the Web.

FIGURE 1.3

The status bar contains tools to help you get information about the Web page.

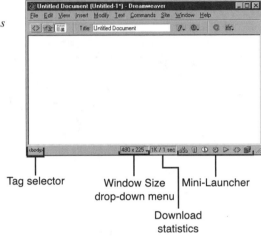

Tag selector   Window Size   Mini-Launcher
                 drop-down menu

                 Download
                 statistics

The tag selector in the lower-left corner of the screen provides easy access to the HTML tags that are involved in any object on the screen. For example, in Figure 1.4 there's an image in a cell in a row in a table. The tag selector enables selection of any of the HTML tags that control an object. The tag that is currently selected is bold.

FIGURE 1.4

The tag selector shows all the HTML tags that affect an object.

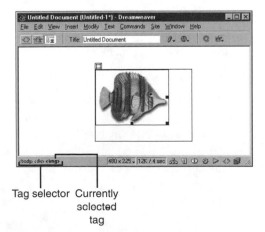

Tag selector Currently
              selected
              tag

The tag selector will be important later when we start using Behaviors in Hour 13, "Inserting Scripted Functionality with Behaviors" and Hour 14, "Adding Advanced Behaviors: Drag Layer." You apply Behaviors to specific tags and sometimes the tags are difficult to select, especially the <body> tag that contains the entire Web page content. The tag selector makes it very easy to select the entire body of the Web page by clicking the <body> tag.

The Window Size drop-down menu helps recreate a certain screen resolution in Dreamweaver, 640×480 or 800×600, for example. You might want to make sure that your design looks good at a low or high screen resolution. You can use the Window Size drop-down to quickly resize the document window to approximate the amount of screen real estate you will have at a certain resolution (see Figure 1.5).

FIGURE 1.5

The Window Size drop-down menu resizes the screen, approximating how the page looks at different screen resolutions.

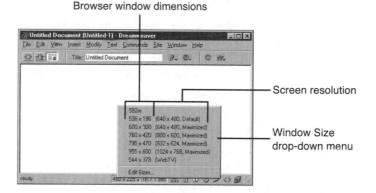

Notice the sizes available in the Window Size menu:

- The dimensions listed on the right (in parentheses) represent the screen resolution.
- The numbers listed on the left are the estimated browser window dimensions. They are smaller than the screen resolution because the browser interface takes up space. For instance, when the viewer's monitor is set to 640×480 the viewable area is only 536×196 pixels.

Create your own custom settings for Window Sizes by selecting the last choice in the Window Size drop-down menu, the Edit Sizes command. This command takes you to the Status Bar category in Dreamweaver Preferences where you can add your custom window size.

Because bandwidth is often an issue when developing for the Web, it's nice to know the estimated file size and download time of your Web page. The estimated download time shown in the status bar is based on the modem setting in the Status Bar category in Dreamweaver Preferences. The default modem setting is 28.8Kbps; you may want to change this setting to 56Kbps.

The last item in the status bar is the Mini-Launcher. The Mini-Launcher is a miniature version of the Launcher that we'll discuss in just a few minutes.

Panels and Inspectors

You set properties, open panels, create animations, and add functionality to your Web page through Dreamweaver's panels and inspectors. Most commands in Dreamweaver are available in several places, usually as a menu command and a panel command. Dreamweaver's panels are *dockable*, which means they can be combined into a common tabbed panel to free up room in the document window.

All of the panels and inspectors are launched from the Window menu. If the panel is open, the command has a check mark beside it in the Window menu, as shown in Figure 1.6. To close a panel or inspector, either click the close box or deselect it in the Window menu. Command names in the Window menu may be slightly different from the names of the panels or inspectors they launch. For instance, launch the Property inspector with the Properties command.

FIGURE 1.6

The Window menu is where you launch Dreamweaver panels and inspectors.

Dockable Panels

Dreamweaver panels initially come docked together, as shown in Figure 1.7. You can change the docking configuration. Undock a panel by selecting its tab and dragging it outside of its current window. To dock a panel, drag-and-drop its tab into a window with another panel or panels. To resize a panel, move your cursor to the edge of the panel and drag the edges of the panel to the desired size.

Docked palettes

FIGURE 1.7

Panels can be docked together in Dreamweaver.

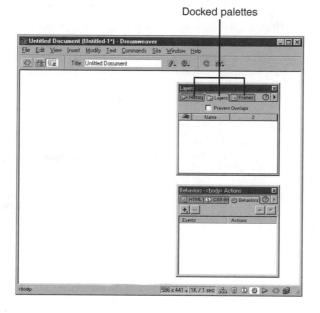

1

The Launcher

The *Launcher* is a panel containing buttons that open and close common Dreamweaver panels and windows. When a panel is open, its button on the Launcher is depressed. Selecting the button while it is depressed will close that panel or window. If the panel is not currently the top panel, clicking the depressed button will first bring it to the top; a second click will close the panel.

You can customize which icons appear in the Launcher in the Panels section of Dreamweaver preferences. Open Dreamweaver preferences by selecting the Preferences command under the Edit menu and select the Panels category from the list on the left side. Simply click the + button to add items to the Launcher. Select an item and click the - button to remove it from the Launcher. To rearrange items, use the up and down arrow buttons. You'll probably want to use Dreamweaver for a while before you know how you want to modify the Launcher to enhance the way you work.

The Launcher, shown in Figure 1.8, can be displayed either horizontally or vertically. Select the orientation icon in the lower-right of the Launcher to change the orientation. Move the Launcher or any of the other panels by dragging them around the screen by their title bar. Sometimes title bars appear vertically on the left side of the panel instead of horizontally at the top.

After you get accustomed to the symbols that represent the Dreamweaver functions, you might want to save some screen real estate by closing the Launcher and using the Mini-Launcher instead. Tooltips appear over the commands in the Mini-Launcher that will tell you to which command the icon corresponds.

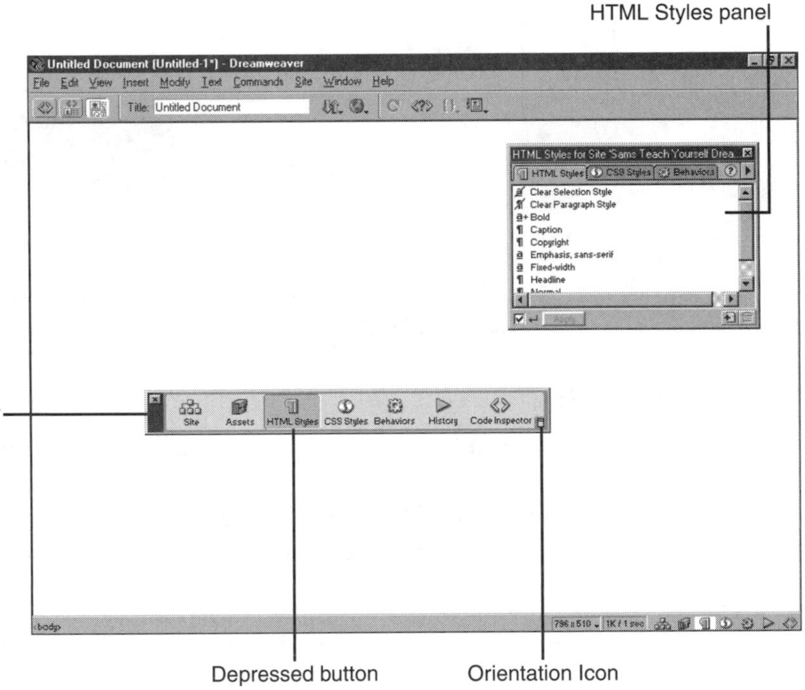

HTML Styles panel

FIGURE 1.8

The Launcher with the HTML Styles panel open.

Launcher—

Depressed button   Orientation Icon

The Property Inspector

The Property inspector displays all the properties of the currently selected object. The Property inspector is chameleon-like; it will look different, displaying appropriate properties, for all the various objects in the Web page. For example, text is selected onscreen and the Property inspector presents text properties in Figure 1.9. In Figure 1.10, an image is selected and image properties are presented.

The default setting for the Property inspector is for the advanced properties expander to be closed. Go ahead and live a little! Expand the properties box so you have access to everything. You can do this by selecting the expander arrow in the lower-right corner of the Property inspector. Notice how the arrow is pointing down in Figure 1.9 and pointing up, with the Property inspector expanded, in Figure 1.10.

FIGURE 1.9
The Property inspector with text selected.

Text selected

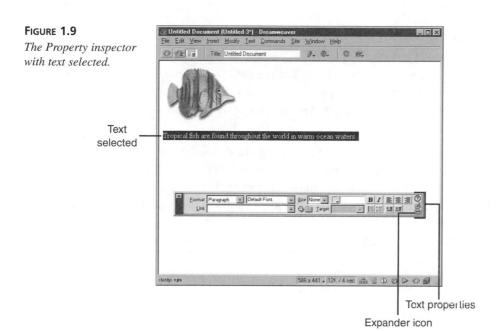

Text properties

Expander icon

FIGURE 1.10
The Property inspector with an image selected.

Image selected

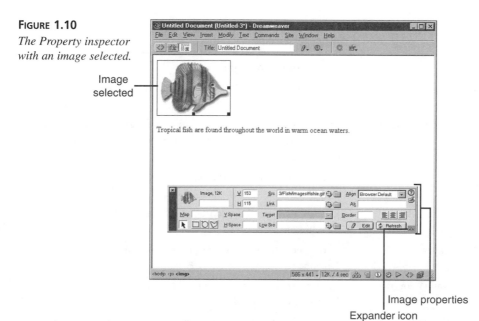

Image properties

Expander icon

The Object Panel

The Object panel contains buttons for inserting common Web page elements, such as images, tables, forms, and hyperlinks. You can either click or drag the button's icon to insert that object into your Web page. The button appears with either an icon, text, or both, depending on the Object panel settings under the General category in Dreamweaver Preferences.

Table 1.2 lists all of the objects, with descriptions, that are available in the Object panel. The Object panel is actually a number of panels rolled into one. There are seven panels in the Object panel by default: Common, Characters, Forms, Frames, Head, Invisibles, and Special. There is a menu in the upper-right corner of the panel that pops up the list of these different categories.

> You'll learn how to create your own objects and panels in the Object panel in Hour 24, "Customizing Dreamweaver."

TABLE 1.2 The Object Panel

Icon	Icon Name	Description
	Common Objects	
	Image	Places an image at the insertion point.
	Rollover Image	Prompts you for two images. One is the regular image and the other is the image that appears when the user puts his or her cursor over the image.
	Table	Creates a table at the insertion point.
	Tabular Data	Creates a table at the insertion point populated with data from a chosen file.
	Layer	Turns your cursor into a marquee tool to draw a layer onto the Document window.
	Navigation Bar	Inserts a set of images to be used for navigating throughout the Web site.
	Horizontal Rule	Places a horizontal rule (line across the page) at the insertion point.
	E-Mail Link	Adds a hyperlink that launches an empty email message to a specific email address when clicked.

TABLE 1.2 continued

Icon	Icon Name	Description
	Common Objects	
	Date	Inserts the current date at the insertion point.
	Server-Side Include	Places a file that simulates a Server-Side Include at the insertion point.
	Fireworks HTML	Places HTML that has been exported from Macromedia Fireworks (an image manipulation and optimization tool) at the insertion point.
	Flash	Places a Macromedia Flash movie at the insertion point.
	Flash Button	Places one of the available prefabricated Macromedia Flash buttons at the insertion point.
	Flash Text	Places editable Flash Text at the insertion point and creates a Flash file.
	Shockwave	Places a *Shockwave movie* (a Macromedia Director movie prepared for the Web) at the insertion point.
	Generator	Places a Macromedia Generator object at the insertion point. Generator enables the creation of dynamic Web images.
	Character Objects	
	Line Break	Places a line break ( ) at the insertion point.
	Non-breaking Space	Inserts a non-breaking space, preventing a line break between two words, at the insertion point.
	Copyright	Inserts the copyright symbol.
	Registered	Inserts the registered-trademark symbol.
	Trademark	Inserts a trademark symbol.
	Pound	Inserts the currency symbol for a pound.
	Yen	Inserts the currency symbol for a yen.
	Euro	Inserts the currency symbol for a euro.

TABLE 1.2 continued

Icon	Icon Name	Description
	Character Objects	
	Left Quote	Inserts a left quote.
	Right Quote	Inserts a right quote.
	Em-Dash	Inserts an em-dash.
	Other Characters	Opens a menu of special characters from which you can choose any of the available characters.
	Forms Objects	
	Form	Places a form at the insertion point.
	Text Field	Inserts a text field into a form.
	Button	Inserts a button into a form.
	Check Box	Inserts a check box into a form.
	Radio Button	Inserts a radio button into a form.
	List/Menu	Inserts a list or a drop-down menu into a form.
	File Field	Inserts a file field, enabling the user to upload a file, into a form.
	Image Field	Inserts an image field, enabling an image to act as a button, into a form.
	Hidden Field	Inserts a hidden field into a form.
	Jump Menu	Creates a jump menu, a common way to allow viewers to navigatate to multiple hyperlinks on the Web.
	Frames	
	Left Frame	Creates an empty frame to the left of the current Document window.
	Right Frame	Creates an empty frame to the right of the current Document window.

TABLE 1.2 continued

Icon	Icon Name	Description
		Frames
	Top Frame	Creates an empty frame on top of the current Document window.
	Bottom Frame	Creates an empty frame on the bottom of the current Document window.
	Left and Top Frames	Creates a grid of four frames. The current Document window stays in the largest, lower-right frame.
	Left and Nested Top Frames	Creates an empty left frame and divides the right side of the screen into top and bottom frames. The current Document window stays in the largest, lower-right frame.
	Top and Nested Left Frames	Creates an empty top frame and divides the bottom frame into left and right frames. The current Document window stays in the largest, lower-right frame.
	Split Frames Center	Creates a grid of four evenly spaced frames. The current Document window stays in the lower-right frame.
		Head
	Meta	Inserts any META tag into the HEAD section of a Web page.
	Keywords	Inserts a Keywords META tag into the HEAD section to help index your Web page.
	Description	Inserts a Description META tag into the HEAD section.
	Refresh	Inserts a Refresh META tag into the HEAD section. This tag sets the number of seconds before the page will automatically jump to another Web page or reload itself.
	Base	Inserts a BASE tag into the HEAD section. This enables you to set a base URL or a base target window.
	Link	Inserts the address of an external file, usually a script or style sheet file.
		Invisibles
	Named Anchor	Places a named anchor at the insertion point. *Named anchors* are used to create hyperlinks within the same file.
	Script	Inserts scripted code at the insertion point.
	Comment	Inserts a comment at the insertion point.

1

TABLE 1.2   continued

Icon	Icon Name	Description
		Special
	Applet	Places a Java applet at the insertion point.
	Plugin	Places any file requiring a browser plugin at the insertion point.
	ActiveX	Places an ActiveX control at the insertion point.

The Object panel has two rows of buttons at the bottom, as shown in Figure 1.11. The bottom row of buttons controls which view you are using, either the Standard view or Layout view. Dreamweaver's Standard view is where you will work most of the time. When you select Layout view the two buttons above the view buttons are no longer grayed out. These are the Draw Layout Cell and Draw Layout Table buttons. We'll explore Layout view in Hour 9, "Designing Your Page Layout Using Tables," and Hour 10, "Using Dynamic HTML and Layers."

FIGURE 1.11

You control the Standard and Layout view with the buttons at the bottom of the Object Panel. In Layout view, you can use the Draw Layout Cell and Draw Layout Table buttons.

Draw Layout Cell

Standard view

Layout view   Draw Layout Table

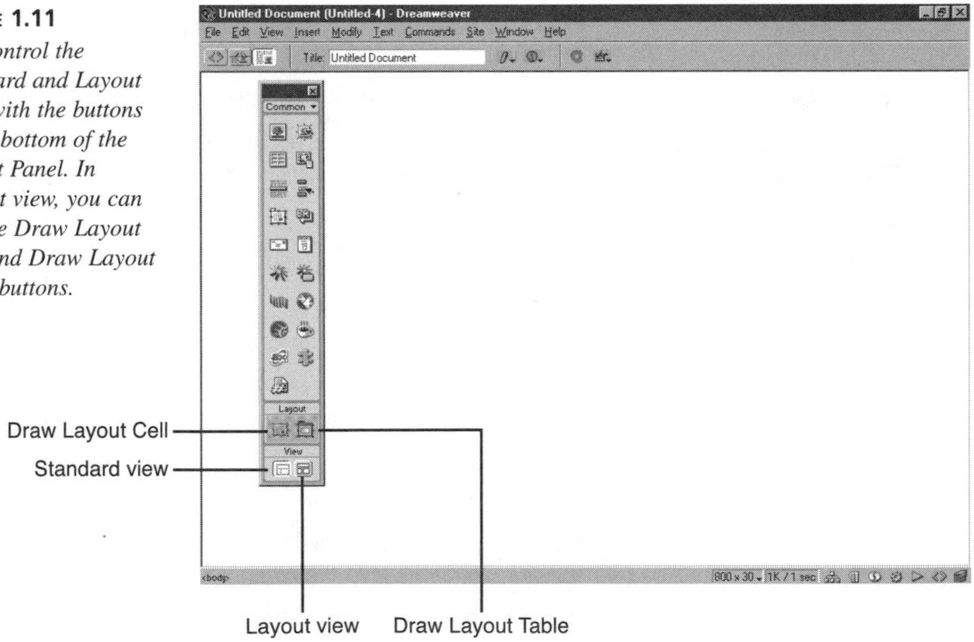

Drop-Down Menus

If you are familiar with other Macromedia products, Dreamweaver's menu bar should look familiar. Macromedia products all have a similar menu structure. The File and Edit menus (see Figure 1.12) are standard to most programs. The File menu contains commands for opening, saving, importing, and exporting files. The Edit menu contains the Cut, Copy, and Paste commands, along with the Select commands, Find and Replace, and the Preferences command. Many elements of the Dreamweaver interface and the way Dreamweaver works can be configured in Preferences.

FIGURE 1.12

The File and Edit menus contain commands that are common to many applications plus a few Dreamweaver-specific ones.

The View menu (see Figure 1.13) turns on and off your view of the head content; invisible elements; layer, table, and frame borders; the status bar; and imagemaps. You can tell whether you are currently viewing one of these elements if a check mark is shown beside it. The View menu also has commands to turn on the ruler and grid, play plugins, and show a tracing image. The Prevent Layer Overlaps command is also located in the View menu. We'll explore layers in Hour 10.

FIGURE 1.13

The View menu houses commands to turn interface elements on and off.

The Insert menu (see Figure 1.14) is roughly equivalent to the Object panel. You can insert all of the items available on the Object panel optionally from this menu. The Modify menu (see Figure 1.14) enables you to modify properties of the currently selected object. The Text menu gives you access to multiple ways of fine tuning the appearance of the text in your Web page.

FIGURE 1.14

The Insert and Modify menus give you control over inserting and changing the attributes of objects.

The Text menu (see Figure 1.15) mirrors many of the properties available in the Property inspector when text is selected. You can indent text, create a list, and modify font properties that we will explore in the next hour. The Commands menu (see Figure 1.15) offers useful commands like Clean Up HTML and Clean Up Word HTML. You can record and play an animation or format and sort a table. You can set up a color scheme and also automatically jump out to Macromedia Fireworks to optimize an image.

FIGURE 1.15

All of the commands necessary to change text elements are in the Text menu. The Commands menu has commands to record animations, clean up the HTML, and format and sort tables. Powerful stuff!

The Site menu (see Figure 1.16) houses the commands that have to do with your entire Web site. We will explore Dreamweaver Web site management in Hour 3 and Hour 18.

FIGURE 1.16

The Site menu commands help you manage your entire Web site.

1

We covered the Window menu when we explored panels and inspectors earlier in this hour. You can refresh your memory by looking at Figure 1.6. We'll discuss the Help system in a couple of minutes. Along with links to the HTML-based help files, the Help menu, shown in Figure 1.17, contains commands to register your Dreamweaver software online. Viewing the About Dreamweaver command may be useful if you need to find out which version of Dreamweaver you are running or your serial number.

FIGURE 1.17

The Help menu launches Dreamweaver's extensive HTML-based help system.

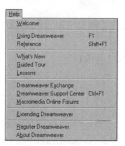

Context Menus

There are multiple ways to access object properties in Dreamweaver. I'm sure you'll find your favorite ways very quickly. Context menus are one of the choices available. These menus pop up when you right-click an object in the document window. The contents of the menu are dependent upon which object you clicked. For instance, Figure 1.18 shows the context menu that pops up when a table is right-clicked.

FIGURE 1.18

The context menu for tables enables you quick access to many table properties.

Table commands

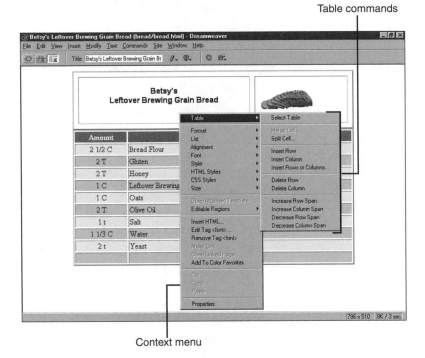

Context menu

Invisible Objects

Some objects that you insert into your Web page aren't designed to be viewable. Because Dreamweaver is a WYSIWYG design tool, Macromedia had to design a way for you to view objects that are invisible. So how can you see invisible objects on the page, like named anchors and forms? You choose the Invisible Elements command from the View menu.

With Invisible Elements turned on, as shown in Figure 1.19, Dreamweaver will show a red dotted outline to represent a form and markers that represent named anchors (they look like little anchors on a gold shield). Select the markers and view or edit the properties for the object that they represent in the Property inspector.

Invisible Elements

FIGURE 1.19
A Web page with invisible elements showing enables you to click markers and edit properties in the Property inspector.

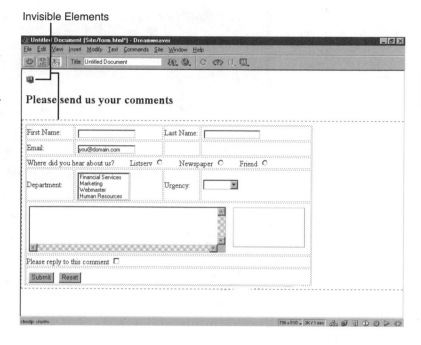

1

Get Help

The Dreamweaver Help menu launches your default browser with the HTML help files. Many of the help files include illustrative Shockwave movies. The lcft side of the page contains a list of topics along with the contents, index, and search buttons. The right side of the page is where the help content files appear. The Next and Previous arrow buttons at the top of the content enable you to page through all of the help topics.

> While you are getting familiar with Dreamweaver, you may want to use the Next and Previous arrow buttons to navigate through the topics. The topics are grouped, so you might get more information on your current topic on the next page. Eventually you will go on to another topic.

The Contents button displays the table of contents. The table of contents is organized in subject categories. Selecting one of the categories expands the list with sub-topics under that category. The Index button shows an alphabetical index of all topics in the help system. There is a field at the top of the topic list where you can type in a topic. Select the Search button to display a Java applet that searches for keywords and displays topic pages related to the keywords, as shown in Figure 1.20.

FIGURE 1.20

The search Java applet searches through every help file for the key-word.

One of the easiest ways to get help on a specific object is to launch context-sensitive help. When you have an object selected (and you can see its properties in the Property inspector), clicking the help icon in the Property inspector shown in Figure 1.21 will take you directly to information about the properties of that object.

The Help icon

FIGURE 1.21

The Property inspector help icon takes you directly to information about the properties of the object currently selected. In this instance you will go directly to help on tables.

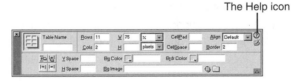

Discover Dreamweaver 4's New Features

It's obvious that Macromedia is tuned in to the wishes of the HTML development community. This might be because Macromedia does a great deal of Web development themselves for their own Web site at http://www.macromedia.com/. Don't be concerned if you don't understand some of the new features. We will cover most of the concepts that you need to understand Dreamweaver in subsequent hours.

1

Dreamweaver 4's many new features include

- **JavaScript Debugger**—The JavaScript Debugger enables you to set breakpoints and watch variables in JavaScript code. You can debug in either Netscape or Internet Explorer.

- **Integrated Text Editor**—When you just need to hand code something, Dreamweaver's new improved text editing capabilities will come in handy. Now you can auto-indent one or many lines of code.

- **Live Syntax Coloring**—Dreamweaver now has live syntax coloring in the HTML Source Inspector. You can select colors in Preferences under the HTML Colors tab.

- **Split View**—Dreamweaver enables you to split the document window to view both the HTML and the WYSIWYG view at the same time. You can edit the HTML and immediately see the results.

- **Reference**—Dreamweaver includes JavaScript, CSS, and HTML online reference books.

- **Edit Non-HTML Documents**—XML or JavaScript files automatically open in Code view where you can edit them.

- **Toolbar**—The new toolbar at the top of the document window enables you to edit the page title, manage the current view of the page, and quickly launch menu options such as Preview in Browser and Design Notes.

- **Code Navigation**—Navigate quickly between JavaScript functions listed in the Code Navigation menu.

- **Layout Mode**—Layout mode enables you to design your Web page visually by drawing table cells. You can draw table cells in the document window and even drag them around the page for positioning.

- **Flash Buttons**—Dreamweaver includes a set of pre-defined, animated Flash buttons that you can include in your Web pages. You can also add your own Flash buttons.

- **Flash Text**—Create editable Flash text right in Dreamweaver. Flash text is small, scalable, and looks great onscreen.

- **Easier Templates**—Dreamweaver 4 makes it easier to visualize the editable regions of templates.

- **Roundtrip Graphics Editing**—If you use Fireworks 4 to create images, you can take advantage of Roundtrip Slicing. After importing images or tables from Fireworks, edit them in Dreamweaver, saving the changes to the original Fireworks file.

- **Easier CSS**—Style sheets have become a little easier to manage in Dreamweaver 4. Define an external styles sheet when you create a new style or easily attach an existing style sheet.

- **Asset Management**—The Asset panel helps catalog, organize, and reuse assets in your Web site. This panel enables you to see lists of all of the colors, images, external URLs, scripts, Flash, Shockwave, QuickTime, Templates, and Library items. You can also save items to a favorites list for quick access.

- **Visual Source Safe**—You can now integrate with Microsoft Visual Source Safe in the Site Management window to check in and out files with version control. You can use any version control system that supports the WebDAV protocol.

- **Configurable Site Window**—You can view Design Notes in the Site Window so you can see if the file has a "Due By" date or any other data you might want to attach.

- **Integrated Email**—When a file is checked out by someone else, you can click their name and send them email right in Dreamweaver.

- **Site Reporting**—Now there is the capability to do site reporting to help with making sure that your Web site doesn't have any problems. Dreamweaver comes with some pre-built reports, such as ones that find untitled documents or missing alt tags. You can also write custom reports. You can even access Web pages that have a problem by clicking on them in the report results window.

- **Extension Manager**—Dreamweaver now integrates an extension manager to install and manage Dreamweaver extensions, such as CourseBuilder or items downloaded from the Macromedia Exchange Web site.

- **Keyboard Shortcuts**—You can now edit keyboard shortcuts. You can edit existing shortcuts, add new ones, or delete ones that you do not want.

- **Common Macromedia Interface**—Dreamweaver takes on the common look and behavior of all the other Macromedia Web Publishing products. Dreamweaver, Fireworks, and Flash have user interface elements in common, making it easier to move from product to product.

Summary

In this hour, you learned about the Dreamweaver document window and its elements, the menus, status bar, and various panels that make up the Dreamweaver interface. You explored launching and docking panels. You saw the commands available in Dreamweaver's menus. You were introduced to the Property inspector and how to get help on Dreamweaver topics. And you learned about Dreamweaver's new features.

Q&A

Q **Why am I having trouble docking a panel? I drag it on top of another panel, but they don't dock.**

A Make sure that you are picking up the panel by its tab and not by its title bar. Sometimes it's easier to get panels to dock if the panel you are docking is smaller than the panel group to which you are adding it. You can easily resize panels by dragging their borders. When the panel group has accepted the panel you are attempting to dock, you will see a dark outline around the panel group. That's your signal to let up your mouse button and drop the panel into place. Also, the Object panel would initially prefer other panels to be docked with it instead of it docking with others.

Q **I clicked the context-sensitive help icon in the Property inspector and nothing happened! Why?**

A You might not have noticed it, but Dreamweaver loaded a new help file into your default browser. The reason you didn't notice was that your browser was already open. If you change applications to your browser, the help file you requested is probably waiting there.

Q **Can I dock the Property inspector?**

A Nope, the Property inspector is a loner. I'll bet that you will be using this panel so much that it will make sense to you to have it stand on its own.

Workshop

The Workshop contains quiz questions and activities to help reinforce what you've learned in this hour. If you get stuck, the answers to the quiz can be found after the questions.

Quiz

1. Which menu do you use to turn on a Dreamweaver panel?
2. What four items are found in the status bar of the document window?
3. Is Dreamweaver an HTML editor, an authoring tool, or a Web site management tool?

Answers

1. The Window menu enables you to turn on and off all of the panels and inspectors. There is a check mark beside a command if it is currently turned on.
2. The status bar contains the tag selector, estimated document size, download time, file size, and the Mini-Launcher.
3. Sorry, this is a trick question! Dreamweaver is all of these things.

Exercises

1. Open up the Behaviors panel from the Launcher or the Mini-Launcher. Undock the panel. Re-dock the panel. Resize the panel until it is narrow and you can no longer see the panel titles. Resize it wider so you can see the panel titles. Close the panel using the Launcher or the Mini-Launcher.

2. Make sure the Object panel is open. Select the Form objects from the drop-down menu. Insert a form into the document window. If you do not see the form, turn on Invisible Elements.

3. Make sure the Property inspector is open. Select the Head Content command from the View menu. Click the items in the window that appears at the top of the screen while looking at the Property inspector.

Hour 2

Creating a Basic Web Page with Text

The most common elements in a Web page are text and images. Get started creating Web pages with Dreamweaver by becoming familiar with adding text and setting text properties.

In this chapter, you will learn

- How to create a new Web page and give it a title
- How to use the Property inspector to change object properties
- How to change fonts and font sizes
- How to create unordered and ordered lists
- How to preview a Web page in different browsers

Create a New Page and Set Page Properties

To create a new Web page, select the New command from the File menu. If a file is already open and you have modified it, Dreamweaver will ask you to save any changes before it opens another window. If you just opened Dreamweaver you will probably have an empty Dreamweaver window already open that you can use. With the Dreamweaver document window open, you are ready to create a Web page with images, text, and other objects.

Enter and Center Some Text

You can simply type into the document window to enter text into your Web page. Type some text for a heading, press the Enter key, and type a couple of sentences. To align your heading in the center of the page, do the following:

1. Open the Property inspector.
2. Select the heading text.
3. Click the Align Center icon in the Property inspector (see Figure 2.1).

Align Center (depressed)

Align Left ——⌐   ⌐—— Align Right

FIGURE 2.1

The Alignment icons in the Property inspector look and act like the alignment commands in your word processing software.

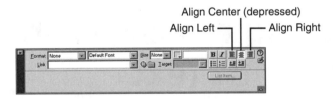

Alternately, with the heading text selected, choose Alignment and then choose the Center command from the Text menu. The Text menu contains all of the text formatting commands that we will use in this hour.

Add a Document Title

The title of your document appears in the title bar of both Dreamweaver and the browser. The document title is saved to a user's browser bookmarks or favorites list, so you should make it meaningful and memorable.

It's important to give your Web page a meaningful title, especially if you want people to be able to find your page using the major search engines. Some search engines rate pages based on the words in the title.

Set the document title in Page Properties. You can access Page Properties in one of two different ways:

- Select the Page Properties command under the Modify menu.
- Right-click an empty part of the document window and select Page Properties from the drop-down menu, as shown in Figure 2.2.

FIGURE 2.2

Select the Page Properties command from the drop-down menu by right-clicking an empty part of the document window.

Page Properties Command

To add a title to your document, do the following:

1. After selecting the Page Properties command, type a descriptive title into the title box at the top of the Page Properties dialog box, as shown in Figure 2.3.

Title

FIGURE 2.3

Enter a title into Page Properties. You can see changes without closing the dialog box by selecting the Apply button instead of the OK button.

Text Color

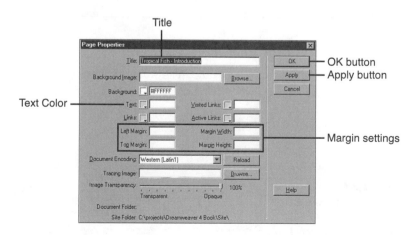

OK button
Apply button

Margin settings

2. Select the Apply or OK button. If you choose the Apply button, the Page Properties dialog box will remain open and ready for your next page edits. If you click OK, the dialog box will close.

> Did you notice that the word "untitled" is still in the title bar? That's because Dreamweaver displays the filename in parentheses alongside the document title. Because the file hasn't been saved, it's still called "untitled" in the Dreamweaver title bar.

You can also set the document title in the Dreamweaver toolbar. If the toolbar doesn't appear under the menu bar, turn it on by selecting the Toolbar command under the View menu. Set the document title in the box next to the Title label.

Set Default Text Colors and Page Margins

The text on the page is black by default. You can change the default text color in Page Properties. If you selected the Apply button after changing the title, the Page Properties box should still be open. If it's not open, re-open it to make text color or page margin changes.

> You can also choose the color that will make your hyperlinks stand out on the page. We'll cover creating hyperlinks in Hour 4, "Setting Lots o' Links: Hyperlinks, URLs, Anchors, and Mailto Links," and you'll have a chance to experiment with changing the link colors.

Use the Color Picker

There are a number of areas in Dreamweaver where you can change a color. When you change the default text color, practice using the Dreamweaver color picker. Change the default text color by first clicking the color box beside Text in the Page Properties dialog box, as shown in Figure 2.4.

FIGURE 2.4
Select a color box to choose a color from the currently selected palette or create a custom color to use.

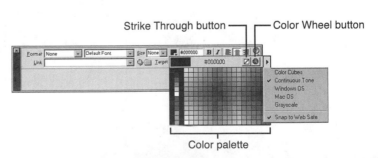

Strike Through button ——————— Color Wheel button

Color palette

You can pick a color using the color picker in a number of ways:

- Pick one of the available colors by clicking it with the eyedropper. You are in eye-dropper mode when the Eyedropper button is depressed in the color picker. There are five panels available: Color cubes, Continuous tone, Windows OS, Mac OS, and Grayscale. Select the Snap to Web Safe from the color picker menu to make sure you select Web safe colors.

- Use the eyedropper to pick up any color onscreen by simply clicking the eyedropper on it. You can pick up any color on the screen, not just colors in Dreamweaver.

- Select the system color button to create a custom color. This opens the system color picker where you can either pick one of the basic colors on the left or click anywhere in the color spectrum on the right. Click the Add to Custom Colors button and then the OK button to use the color.

You can also type the color information directly into the box:

- Colors are represented in HTML by three hexadecimal numbers proceeded by the pound (#) sign. For instance, the RGB value for light blue is represented as #0099FF, where the value for R is 00, the value for G is 99, and the value of B is FF. If you know the hexadecimal values for the color, you can simply type it in.

- Most browsers will display standard color names instead of the hexadecimal values. For instance, you could type in "red" instead of #FF0000.

To clear the current color without picking another color, click the Strike Through button in the color picker. After you've chosen a color, select the Apply button. You should see the text onscreen change color.

> The Dreamweaver Web-safe palette is made up of 212 colors that work in Netscape and Internet Explorer on both Windows and Macintosh operating systems. This is a couple of colors less than the traditional Web-safe palette of 216 colors. Choosing custom colors that are not part of the palette may have an undesirable appearance in some, usually older, browsers.

Set the Background Color

Experiment some more with color selection by changing the background color of the page. The background color is located right above the text color in Page Properties.

Note that the default color is #FFFFFF—white. Make sure that the combination of the background color and the text color doesn't make your Web page difficult to read. If you apply a dark background color, you will need to use a light text color so that the viewer can read the text.

Set the Page Margins

Set the margins for your page in Page Properties. Margins set the amount of space between the contents of your Web page and the left and top edges of the browser window.

There are four settings for page margins: left margin, top margin, margin width, and margin height.

- Internet Explorer uses the left margin and top margin settings.
- Netscape Navigator uses the margin height and margin width settings.

If you want your page to look similar in both browsers, set left margin and margin width to the same number and top margin and margin height to the same number. The default setting for page margins is 10 pixels from the top and 10 pixels from the left. Sometimes you may want to remove the margins by entering a 0 value into all of the margin boxes.

Paste Text from a File

Often, you need to put text that already exists as a word processor document into a Web page. You can easily copy text from another application and paste it in Dreamweaver.

To copy and paste text from a word processor or other program, do the following:

1. Open a document.
2. Select at least a couple of paragraphs so you can see that format retention in Dreamweaver.
3. Copy it to the Clipboard (the keyboard command is usually Ctrl+C).
4. Go to Dreamweaver and place the insertion point where you want to paste the text.
5. Select the Paste HTML command from the Edit menu. The keyboard shortcut is Ctrl+V in Windows or Command+V on a Macintosh.

Understand Paragraph and Break Tags

It's important to understand the difference between paragraph and break tags. Paragraph tags surround a block of text placing two carriage returns after the block. Think of the paragraph tags as a container for the block of text. You create a new paragraph at the end of a line with the Enter key.

The break tag is a single tag rather than a set of paired tags, such as the paragraph tags. The break tag inserts a single carriage return into text. Insert a break into a Web page with the keyboard shortcut Shift+Enter or select the Line Break object from the Object panel. The break tag does not create a container like the paragraph tags.

Formatting applied to a block of text, like the Heading format that we'll explore in a few minutes, will apply to all of the text within a container. That's why it's important to understand the differences between paragraph and break tags.

Apply Text Formatting

Apply standard HTML formatting to text using the Format drop-down menu in the Property inspector. There are four basic formatting options:

- None removes any formatting style currently applied to the selection.
- Paragraph applies paragraph tags, <p></p>, to the selection. This will add two carriage returns after the selection.
- Heading 1 through Heading 6 applies heading tags to the selection. Heading 1 is the largest heading and Heading 6 is the smallest. Applying a heading tag makes everything on the line that heading size.
- The Preformatted format displays text in the fixed, or non-proportional, font. The font is Courier 10 point on most systems.

Select the top line in your Web page and apply Heading 1 formatting, as shown in Figure 2.5. Try applying all the different heading sizes to see what they look like.

FIGURE 2.5

The Format drop-down menu in the Property inspector applies heading, paragraph, and preformatted tags to text.

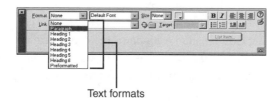

Text formats

Change Text Size

Change the text size by selecting one of the size settings—size 1 through size 7—in the Property inspector size drop-down menu shown in Figure 2.6. The default text size is 3, so sizes smaller than 3 will look smaller than the default text and sizes larger than 3 will look larger than the default text.

FIGURE 2.6

The text sizes drop-down menu in the Property inspector enables you to set the size of the text selected.

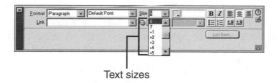

Text sizes

Select size +1 through size +7, listed after size 1 through size 7, to increase the font size. Select size -1 through size -7, listed after size +1 through size +7, to decrease the font size from the default font size. Select None to go back to the default font size.

There is no way to set a specific point size in HTML. Use Cascading Style Sheets (CSS) to set point size and other text properties covered in Hour 11, "Formatting Your Web Pages with Cascading Style Sheets and HTML Styles."

Select a Font

To apply a font, select some text and drop-down the Font Combination box in the Property inspector, as shown in Figure 2.7.

FIGURE 2.7

The Font Combination drop-down menu has several font groups from which to choose.

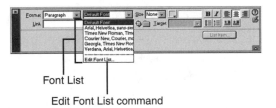

Font List

Edit Font List command

The fonts in the Font Combination drop-down menu are defined in groups. Specifying a group instead of an individual font increases the odds that your viewers will have at least one of the fonts in the group. Dreamweaver has predefined groups to choose from, but you can also create your own groups.

Remember, just because you can see the font and it looks great on your machine doesn't mean that everyone has that font. If a font isn't available, the browser will use the default font—usually Times Roman—instead. The fonts that are in the predefined font combinations in Dreamweaver are commonly available fonts in Windows and on the Macintosh.

The font and font size properties that we've been exploring use the <font> tag. You should be aware that this tag is being deprecated by the W3C, the Web standards organization. *Deprecated* means that the W3C is removing it from the approved tag list and eventually it may not be supported by browsers. It is supported by all the major browsers right now, however; and will probably continue to be supported for a while.

The Cascading Style Sheets (CSS) text specifications are the approved way of applying fonts and font sizes. The problem with CSS, however, is that older browsers don't support them.

There is really no way to guarantee that a Web page will look the same on a viewer's computer as it does on your computer. Browser preferences enable the user to override font settings, size settings, background colors, and hyperlink colors. Don't depend on the page fonts and colors to be exact. If it makes you feel better though, most users don't change the browser defaults.

2

Turn Text into a List and Use Indent Button

You can implement bulleted lists, called unordered lists in HTML, and numbered lists, called ordered lists in HTML. The Unordered and Ordered List buttons appear on the Property inspector when you have text selected.

First, let's create an unordered list:

1. Type three items, pressing the Enter key after each item.

2. Drag the cursor over all three items to select them.

3. Click the Unordered List button in the Property inspector, as shown in Figure 2.8.

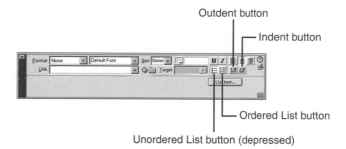

Outdent button

Indent button

FIGURE 2.8

The Property inspector has buttons to control ordered and unordered lists. You can select the Indent and Outdent buttons to nest lists or to indent and outdent text.

Ordered List button

Unordered List button (depressed)

Now each line is preceded by a bullet. Next, add another list nested in the first list:

1. Place the insertion point after the last item.

2. Press the Enter key to make a new line; the new line should be preceded by a bullet.

3. Type three items as you did in the previous list.

4. Drag the cursor over these new items and select the Indent button in the Property inspector.

Now the second list is nested within the third item of the first list. You can tell because it is indented and preceded by a different style of bullet. To turn the nested unordered list into an ordered list, as shown in Figure 2.9, select the three items again and click the Ordered List button from the Property inspector. To bring the nested list back in line with the main list, select the Outdent button.

Unordered list   Nested ordered list

FIGURE 2.9

An unordered list can have another list nested within it. Select the Indent button in the Property inspector to nest a list. Select the Ordered List button to make a numbered list.

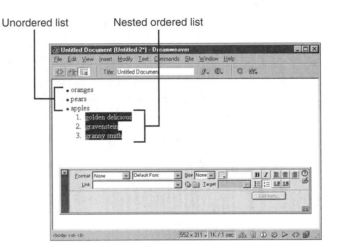

Add a Separator to a Page

A graphical item that has been around since the Web stone age (a few years ago) is the horizontal rule. That little divider line is still useful. Note that you can't place anything else on the same line with a horizontal rule.

Add a horizontal rule to your Web page by selecting the horizontal rule object from the Object panel. Of course, if you're a menu kind of person, you can find the Horizontal Rule command under the Insert menu. In Figure 2.10, the Property inspector presents the properties of a horizontal rule. You can give the rule a name, and you can set width and height values in either pixels or percent of the screen. You can set the alignment and turn shading on and off.

Many objects in HTML have the capability to render width and height in either absolute pixel values or as a percentage of the size of the browser window. If the horizontal rule is set to a certain percentage and the viewer changes the size of the browser window, the horizontal rule will resize to the new window size. If the horizontal rule is set to an absolute pixel size, it will not resize and the viewer will see horizontal scrollbars if the horizontal rule is wider than the screen.

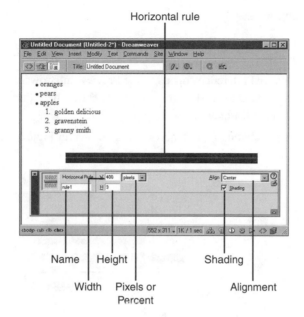

FIGURE 2.10
Horizontal rule properties appear in the Property inspector when the rule is selected.

Horizontal rule

Name   Height   Shading

Width   Pixels or   Alignment
         Percent

Save Your Work and Preview in a Browser

Even though Dreamweaver is a WYSIWYG tool, you'll need to see how your page really looks in particular browsers. It's a good idea to save your work before you preview it. Saving your work lets Dreamweaver set the paths to linked files, such as images, correctly. We'll explore the concept of linked files and paths further in the next hour.

Macromedia says you can define up to 20 browsers for previewing. Good luck finding 20 browsers! I generally have two defined: Microsoft Internet Explorer and Netscape Navigator. You will have to have these programs installed on your computer before you can use them to preview your Web pages. Both browsers are free and available to download over the Internet.

Download Netscape Navigator at `http://home.netscape.com/computing/download/` and download Microsoft Internet Explorer at `http://www.microsoft.com/windows/ie/`.

First, set up a browser.

1. Select the Preview in Browser command under the File menu. Then select the Edit Browser List command.

2. Dreamweaver Preferences opens to the Preview in Browser category. Dreamweaver may have already located a browser and entered it here during the installation process, so the list may not be empty.

3. Click the plus button to add a browser, as shown in Figure 2.11.

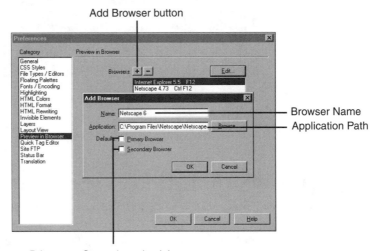

FIGURE **2.11**

Set the browsers you will use to preview your Web pages in the Preview in Browser category in Preferences.

4. Give the Browser a name. Select the Browse button and navigate to the browser program. For computers running Windows, the default installation location for most browsers is in the Programs directory.

5. Click either the Primary or the Secondary check box. This specifies which keyboard shortcut you use to launch the browser. The keyboard shortcut for the primary browser is F12, while the shortcut for the secondary browser is Ctrl+F12.

6. Repeat this procedure until all browsers have been added. Click the OK button when you are done.

After saving your file, select the Preview in Browser command under the File menu. Select the browser you want to use from the menu. If the browser is already open, you may have to switch to the application to see the page. If the browser isn't already open, Dreamweaver will open it and load the requested page to preview.

You are viewing a temporary HTML file (look at the URL and see that the filename starts with TMP). Dreamweaver creates this temporary file when you request Preview in Browser. If you go back into Dreamweaver and make changes to your page, those changes will not be reflected if you jump back over to the browser and click the Refresh button. Why? Because Dreamweaver hasn't yet created a new temporary file, and you will still be viewing the old file.

You will need to select the Preview in Browser command every time you want to see changes. Alternately, you could save your changes and open your Web page with the browser.

2

Summary

In this hour, you learned how to enter and import text into a Web page. You set text properties including headings, fonts, lists, and alignment. You used a horizontal rule to separate the page into sections and then previewed your work in a browser.

Q&A

Q Is there any way I can make sure a font is available on the viewer's computer?

A The only way you can be sure that a font is present on the viewer's machine is to require them to install it. There are browser-specific methods to embed fonts and send them over the Web. Internet Explorer's methods are described at `http://msdn.microsoft.com/workshop/author/fontembed/font_embed.asp`. Netscape Navigator's information is at `http://developer.netscape.com/docs/manuals/communicator/dynhtml/webfont3.htm`.

Q I indented a line of text with the Indent button. I wanted it to act like a tab acts in my word processing program, but it seems to indent both the beginning and the end of the line.

A Oddly enough, there is no way in HTML to tab like in your word processing program. The Indent button actually applies the blockquote tag to the text. This tag, as you noticed, actually indents both the left and the right of the text. The blockquote tag was originally designed for quotes in research type documents.

Workshop

The Workshop contains quiz questions and activities to help reinforce what you've learned in this hour. If you get stuck, the answers to the quiz can be found after the questions.

Quiz

1. What button on the Property inspector do you select to nest a list?

2. Which is the largest heading size—heading 1 or heading 6?

3. What is the usual default font, size, and color for pages viewed in the default browser configuration?

Answers

1. The indent button nests one list within another.

2. Heading 1 is the largest size and heading 6 is the smallest.

3. Times Roman, Size 3, black text.

Exercises

1. Explore changing the alignment, shading, and size of a horizontal rule.

2. Explore the various image alignment properties by adding an image and some text to a Web page. Select the different alignment settings, such as absolute middle, right, and bottom. Place another image next to the text and see how the new image reacts to changes in the alignment properties of the original image.

3. Select one of the color boxes in Page Properties and set up a custom color. Use the eyedropper to pick a color from anywhere onscreen.

HOUR 3

Planning and Creating Your Project Using the Site Window

You use the Site window to plan, create, and manage your projects. Dreamweaver contains richly functioned file management capabilities that enable you to upload files to a LAN (Local Area Network) or use FTP (File Transfer Protocol) to transfer files to a remote server. You can even interface with a resource management system, such as Microsoft Visual SourceSafe.

Dreamweaver enables you to check in and out files to work on them. This capability is especially useful in a multi-user environment where you are not the only person working on the Web site. When you have a file checked out no one else can work on it until you check it back in. In Hour 18, "Managing and Uploading Your Projects," you'll explore additional capabilities that you can use to manage your Web sites.

In this hour, you will learn

- How to define a Web site in the Site window
- How to set up LAN, FTP, and source control transfer methods
- How to import an existing Web site

Define a New Web Site

You open the Site window to define the *root* directory of a Web site. The root of your Web site is the main directory that contains the files and other directories. You'll want to think carefully about which directory defines the root of your Web site. For instance, if you are working on your company Web site, the Web server defines the default Web site directory; that directory would be the root. However, if you are developing a Web site only for your department, then the root of your Web site may be a sub-directory under the main Web site directory.

Access the Site window with a couple of different commands. The command in the Launcher and Mini-Launcher is called Show Site. Under the Window menu the command is called Site Files. You can also select Site Map from the Window menu to open the Site window with the Site Map showing instead of files. We'll cover the Site Map in Hour 18.

When you define a Web site in the Site window, Dreamweaver considers that directory and all of the directories and files within it to be the entire "universe" that you will be working within. Dreamweaver will prompt you to save files into your root Web site if they are located outside of it. The Templates and Library directories are located in the root directory.

When you define a Web site in Dreamweaver, you define a local site that exactly *mirrors* a remote site. Mirroring means that the local site contains an exact copy of the files on the remote site. You work on the files in your local site and then upload them to the remote site using Dreamweaver's file transfer commands.

File and directory names containing spaces, punctuation, or special characters may cause problems on some Web servers. You can use underscores instead of spaces in names. In addition, file names are case-sensitive on some Web servers.

Set Your Local Site

Use an existing directory on your hard drive that already contains Web pages or create a new empty directory for your local site. You will create a local root directory for every Web site that you create.

I have a directory on my hard drive called Projects. The Projects directory contains a directory for each project. Within each project directory there is a directory called Web, set as the local root directory for the project. This directory structure enables me to put other directories and files in the clients folder without them being part of the Web site.

You may prefer to have one directory that contains all of your Web sites. Whatever works best for you. It is easier if you do not mix non-Web files into the root directory of your Web site. Since the remote site is a mirror image of your local site, you don't want to load files onto your Web site that do not belong there.

Put some thought into how your files will be organized in your Web site before you start a project. You will probably want to create a separate images folder to hold your images. If you have other types of assets, such as sound or video, you might want to create separate folders for those too.

If you have different sections of your Web site, do you want to create separate directories for the images in each section? It might be a good way to organize your site. Then again, if the same graphics are used across multiple sections, it might just make it hard to find. Make sure that your organizational logic isn't going to break down on your site in the future.

Luckily if you do have to rearrange assets that have already been used in Web pages Dreamweaver will update the links for you. When you move a file, Dreamweaver asks you if you want to search and update links to that file. It is still better to make wise design decisions at the beginning of a big project.

I also try to logically break up sections of Web sites into separate directories. If your Web site has obvious divisions (departments, lessons, products, and so on), you can create directories to hold the Web pages in each of the sections. You'll be surprised how even a small Web site becomes quickly unmanageable when all of the files are dumped into one directory.

You can create a directory structure right in the Dreamweaver Site window. The Site window enables you to create new directories and new files. If you prefer, you can create your directory structure somewhere else.

3

To create a new site in Dreamweaver

1. Select the New Site command under the Site directory. Or, select the Define Sites command from the Current sites drop-down menu shown in Figure 3.1.

FIGURE 3.1

Use the Current sites drop-down menu to select a site or to select the Define Sites command.

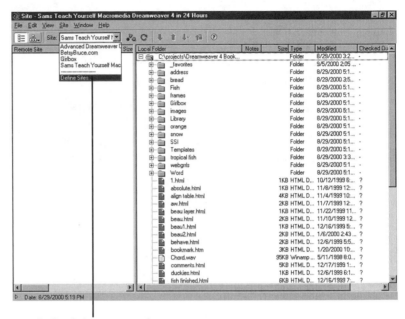

Defined sites command

2. If you already have one or more sites defined, the Define Sites dialog box appears as shown in Figure 3.2. Select the New button to open the Site Definition dialog box.

FIGURE 3.2

The Define Sites dialog box lists all of your defined sites. Use the New, Edit, Duplicate, and Remove buttons to manage your sites. Select the Done button to close the box.

Defined sites —

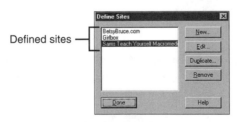

If you do not have any sites defined in Dreamweaver, the Site Definition dialog box (shown in Figure 3.3) automatically appears.

FIGURE 3.3

The Site Definition dialog box is where you enter all of the paths to your local and remote sites.

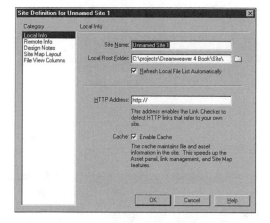

3. Make sure that the Local Info category is selected on the left side of the Site Definition dialog box. Enter a name for the Web site in the Site Name box.

4. Enter the path to the local folder that is the Web site root. You can use the folder button to browse to the folder and select it.

5. If you are working on an older computer, you may want to deselect Refresh Local File List Automatically to speed up performance in the Site window. This setting controls whether the local file list automatically refreshes every time a file is copied into the site. Most Dreamweaver users will want to keep this box checked.

6. Enter the URL that will eventually lead to the completed Web site. This helps Dreamweaver check absolute URLs in the site. If you don't know the URL, you can leave it blank and add it later.

7. Check the Cache box to create a record of the files in your site. Dreamweaver uses this record to automatically update links in your site if you rename or move a file.

8. Click the OK button. If you selected the Cache check box when setting up the site, Dreamweaver will tell you it is creating the cache, as shown in Figure 3.4.

> Creating a cache for your Web site is especially helpful for large sites. It will speed up Dreamweaver's automatic checking and updating of links.

The Define Sites dialog box shows your newly created site. When you select the Done button, the files in your site, if there are any, appear on the Local Folder side of the Site window. By default, the Local Folder site is located on the right side of the Site window. You can set which side of the screen the local and remote files appear on in the Site category in Dreamweaver preferences, as shown in Figure 3.5.

FIGURE 3.4

Dreamweaver tells you it is creating a cache for your site. This file speeds up updating links when you move or rename a file.

Site category   Configure the Site window

FIGURE 3.5

The Site category in Dreamweaver preferences enables you to configure which side of the Site window the local and remote sites appear on. You can also configure firewall and other settings here.

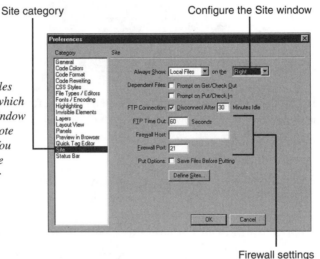

Firewall settings

The Site window's list of local files looks very similar to file management programs on your computer. You can move, rename, delete, copy, paste, and open files in the Site window. Notice that the file size and file type are displayed along with the date the file was last modified. You'll explore Checked Out By, the last column in the Local Site, in a few minutes when you examine Dreamweaver's Check In/Out functionality.

Drag the middle divider between the local and remote sites to make one side or the other wider. You can also drag the column dividers between the column headings in either the local or the remote sides of the Site window.

The Site window enables you to quickly locate and launch all of the files in your Web site. You may want to leave it open all the time and use it to open files. If you use the Site window to open files, you won't need to constantly select the Open command and navigate to files.

Add Your Remote Site

Define a remote site after you have defined a Web site in Dreamweaver by editing the Web site definition. A remote site can either be on a server that is on a Local Area Network (LAN) or a server that you access over the Internet. Either way, this server runs Web server software and makes your Web site available either over the Internet or a company intranet.

Edit a site to add remote site information by launching the Site Definition dialog box from either the Site menu or the Current sites drop-down menu. After you select your site to edit, the Site Definition dialog box contains five categories:

- Local Info
- Remote Info
- Design Notes
- Site Map Layout
- File View Columns

You just set up the local info—the name of the site, its local root folder, and other options. Now you can set up some additional characteristics of the site including the remote location information, design notes setup, and configuring how the file columns appear in the Site window. Select the categories listed above to set up these items. We'll cover Local Info and Remote Info later in this hour, and Design Notes, Site Map Layout, and File View Columns in Hour 18.

To define the Remote Info, select a site and click on the Edit button. The Remote Info category displays the Server Access drop-down menu. The menu has three selections: None, LAN, and FTP.

Set LAN Information

Select Local/Network access, shown in Figure 3.6, if the server is on a computer that you can connect to directly using a network.

If you can access the server just like you access your hard drive, moving files to and from it, then you have LAN access. You will need to know which directory your files should be located in to be accessible over the Web. Your Web administrator should be able to give you that information.

FIGURE 3.6

You select Local/
Network access when
the remote directory
resides within your
local area network.
Simply select
Local/Network as the
access method and
enter the path to the
directory as the remote
directory.

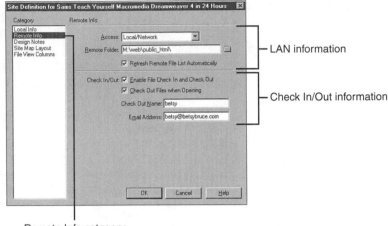

Remote Info category

Set up LAN access to the remote server by entering the path to the remote directory. Use the folder icon to browse to the directory or type in the path. Checking the Refresh Remote File List Automatically may slow down Dreamweaver's performance a bit, but you will always have an up-to-date reflection of the remote site.

It can be confusing to collaborate with someone and not know who has the most recent version of a file. Dreamweaver's Check In/Out capability helps you collaborate with others effectively by checking out a file to only one person at a time and placing that person's name beside the file. The name is visible to people connecting using Dreamweaver to the remote site, as shown in Figure 3.7.

You don't need to enable Check In/Out for all of your Web sites. If you are not collaborating with others, you may not need the functionality.

To turn on Dreamweaver's Check In/Out capability, check the box next to Enable File Check In and Check Out. You can select the Check Out Files When Opening check box if you want to automatically check out a file when you open it from the Site window. Enter a Check Out Name in the box. Others will see this name beside the file when you have a file checked out. You can also enter your email address so that others can automatically email you from Dreamweaver. Collaboration techniques will be further discussed in Hour 18.

FIGURE 3.7

When you are connected to a remote site, you see the names of people who have files checked out beside the file name.

Remote site files   Local site files

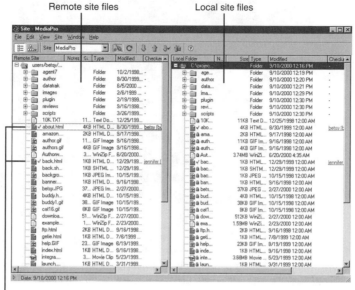

Checked out files

Set FTP Information

Select FTP access, shown in Figure 3.8, if you need to transfer files over the Web to a remote server. The server could be physically located in your same building, or it could be on the other side of the world. You need the name of the FTP server to enter into the FTP Host box. Often this is in the format: ftp.domain.com.

Do not enter the server name preceded with the protocol as you would in a browser (such as ftp://ftp.domain.com).

Enter the root directory of your Web site in the Host Directory box. You may need to get the path for this directory from your Web or network administrator. If the server runs on Windows NT, the directory path may look like a path on your local drive (such as users\web\). If the Web server runs on UNIX, the path won't contain a drive letter (such as users/web/).

FIGURE 3.8

You select FTP access when the remote directory resides on a server you need to access over the Internet.

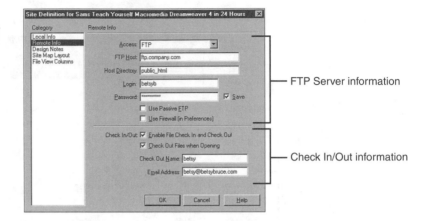

— FTP Server information

— Check In/Out information

If you are unsure what the root directory is on the remote site, try leaving the Host Directory box blank. The FTP server may put you directly in the correct directory because your account may be configured that way.

To access the remote directory with FTP you will need a login and password to the FTP server. The standard anonymous login, often used to download files over the Internet, will probably not work to upload files to a Web site. You need to log in as a user with access and permission to get and put files in the directories that will house your Web site. Dreamweaver saves your password by default. If other people have access to Dreamweaver on your computer and you don't want them to access your FTP account, deselect the Save check box.

If you are behind a firewall or using a proxy server you may have difficulties with FTP. Consult with the network administrator, or whoever administrates your local firewall, about which settings you will need to choose when setting up FTP. Select the Use Firewall check box if you go through a firewall to access the Internet. Configure the firewall port and host in Dreamweaver preferences (refer to Figure 3.5). Your firewall may also require you to select the Passive FTP setting.

If you have a slow connection to the Internet, the default FTP timeout may be too short, causing your FTP connection to timeout too often. You can increase this time in the Site preferences.

Set up Check In/Check Out as previously discussed for LAN access.

Set Source/Version Control Application Information

You can interface from Dreamweaver's Site window directly with source and version control applications. If you are not in a professional environment that uses source management software, you can skip this section or read it and file it away for later. The integration between Dreamweaver and source control software programs is an important new feature of Dreamweaver 4.

Dreamweaver supports direct integration with Microsoft Visual SourceSafe, a popular version control product. You can also exchange files with any source control program that supports the WebDAV protocol.

Set up a Visual SourceSafe database as your remote site by selecting the SourceSafe Database choice in Remote Info. Notice that you still have the Check Out Files When Opening option but cannot use Dreamweaver's internal Check In/Out functionality. You will use the checking in and out capability of Visual SourceSafe instead.

Set up the SourceSafe database by selecting the Info button. The Open SourceSafe Database appears as shown in Figure 3.9. Enter the Database Path, Project, Username, and Password in this dialog. You can get this information from the database administrator.

3

FIGURE 3.9

Enter the database, username, and password to connect to a SourceSafe database.

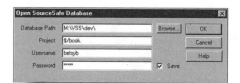

The standard WebDAV (sometimes just called DAV) version control information is set up similarly to a SourceSafe database. Select WebDAV from the drop-down menu and then select the Info button. The settings, shown in Figure 3.10, look different from the SourceSafe settings since you access this type of version control application over the Web.

FIGURE 3.10

Enter a URL, username, and password to connect to a source control application using the WebDAV protocol.

Import an Existing Web Site

When a Web site already exists at a remote site, you need to define the Web site in Dreamweaver, connect to the remote site, and download all of the files in the site to work on it. Remember, you can only edit files that are located on your own machine. You can download and edit an existing site even if it wasn't created with Dreamweaver.

The first time you download the site may take some time, depending on how you are accessing the site and what your network connection speed is. After you initially download all the files, however, you should only need to download any files that change.

To import an existing Web site, all you need to do is mirror the existing site on your local drive. There is no conversion process and the files will remain unchanged in Dreamweaver. To import an existing Web site

1. Set up both your local and remote info in the Site Definition dialog box.

2. Get all of the files on the remote site by selecting the top entry in the Remote Site of the Site window. Selecting the top entry, the root folder, selects the entire site. If you select a file, you will get only that file instead of the entire site.

3. Select the Get button, shown in Figure 3.11, to transfer all of the files on the remote site to your local site.

FIGURE 3.11

The Get button gets the entire remote site when you connect to the remote site and select the root folder.

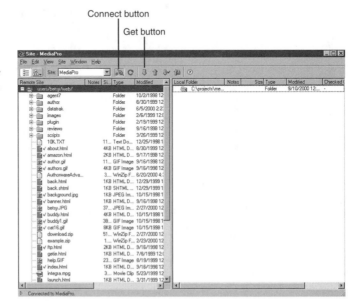

Summary

In this hour, you learned how to define a Web site and determine its root. You learned how to configure and access the files on the remote server. And you learned how to import an existing Web site into Dreamweaver.

Q&A

Q I'm importing a site into Dreamweaver that was originally hand coded. Any hints?

A You can automatically format the HTML in Web pages by selecting the Apply Source Formatting command in Dreamweaver's Command menu. You might also want to try the Clean Up HTML command on these imported pages to make sure there aren't open tags or incorrect nesting.

Q If I'm uploading my site to the Web server, won't people be able to see my site while it's still in progress?

A Yes, if they know the URL. It's better to create a "staging area" somewhere that isn't public on your server as your remote site until you are ready to launch your completed site. When you are finished, you can either upload the entire site to its final location or ask your Webmaster to direct the proper URL to your staging area.

Workshop

The Workshop contains quiz questions and activities to help reinforce what you've learned in this hour. If you get stuck, the answers to the quiz can be found following the questions.

Quiz

1. Why do you need to define a Web site?
2. What does the Dreamweaver cache do?
3. True or False: You must go through a conversion process to import an existing Web site into Dreamweaver.

Answers

1. You define a Web site so that Dreamweaver knows where the root of the site is. The directory that you connect to on the remote site is the mirror image of the root on the local site. Also, Dreamweaver places the Library and Templates directory at the site root.

2. Enabling the cache speeds up some Dreamweaver features such as updating hyperlinks.

3. False. No conversion process is necessary to import an existing Web site into Dreamweaver.

Exercises

1. If you aren't currently working on a LAN, simulate what LAN access would look like by pointing Dreamweaver to a local directory when setting up a Web site. You can simply browse to a local directory on your hard drive while in the Web Server Info category of the Site Definition dialog box.

2. If you have access to the Internet but do not have an FTP account anywhere, use `ftp.macromedia.com` as a test FTP Host. Enter your login as anonymous. Click the Connect button when you are connected to the Internet. You will see Macromedia's anonymous FTP area. Don't upload any files here. This exercise is just so you can experience connecting to an FTP server.

HOUR 4

Setting Lots o' Links: Hyperlinks, URLs, Anchors, and Mailto Links

A hyperlink allows the viewer to jump to another Web page, jump to another section of the current Web page, or launch an email application. A Web site is made up of a group of Web pages. Hyperlinks enable your Web page viewers to navigate from page to page. Hyperlinks, in the simplest form, are the familiar underlined and colored text that you click. Many Web sites take advantage of linked graphics, sometimes with mouse rollover effects, to implement hyperlinks.

Hyperlinks help make the Web a powerful source of information. If you've surfed the Web at all, I'm sure you've clicked many, many hyperlinks. But hyperlinks can also make the Web confusing. Sometimes it is difficult to remember the exact path you took to find information. That can make it difficult to get back to the information when you want to see it again.

Design your Web sites so viewers do not get confused. Don't link your viewers to dead-end pages within your site from which they have no way of returning.

A Web address is called a *Uniform Resource Locator* or *URL.* You can link many types of files over the Web but only a few file types will display in a browser. The browser displays supported image formats, HTML, plug-in applications, and a few other specialized types of files. If a link leads to a file that the browser can't display (a .zip file, for example), the browser will usually ask you if you'd like to save the file to your hard drive.

In this hour, you will learn

- When to use relative and absolute paths
- How to create a hyperlink to another page within your Web site and to a page outside of your Web site
- How to create hyperlinks within a page
- How to add a link that opens a pre-addressed email message

Explore Relative and Absolute Paths

Whenever you create a hyperlink or place an external file in your Web page, such as an image file, you need to enter its path. The two main types of paths are absolute paths and document relative paths.

An analogy for an *absolute path* is a house address. If I gave the address of my house to someone who lives in another town I would tell them, "I live at 123 Spruce, Seattle WA 98122." This is all of the information that anyone would need to get to my exact location or to send me a letter (this isn't my real address, so if you really want to send me a letter, send it in care of the publisher!). If I gave directions to my house to someone who lives on my street, I might tell them, "I live two doors south of you." The directions I give in this case are relative to my neighbor's location. The first example is analogous to an absolute path and the second example is analogous to a *document relative path*.

The link to the Macromedia Dreamweaver Support Center is an absolute path (see Figure 4.1). It contains the entire path to a file on the Internet. Because you have no control over this site, linking to it means that you need to check to see that the link remains valid. If the site moves in the future, you will need to update the link.

FIGURE 4.1

Entering an absolute path links to a specific Web page.

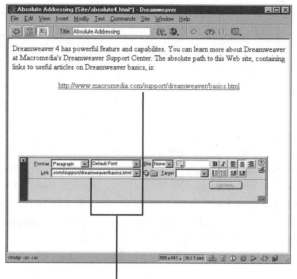

A hyperlink with an absolute address

URLs consist of up to five sections, as shown in Figure 4.2:

- The first part of the URL is the protocol. It will be http for Web pages. Sometimes you may want to link to a file on an ftp server, using ftp as the protocol instead of http.

- The second part of the address is the domain. This is the Web server where the Web page is located. A colon and two forward slashes (://) separate the protocol and the domain.

- An optional third part of a URL is the port. The default port for a Web server is port 80. When you enter http as the protocol, port 80 is inferred and doesn't usually need to be included. You may need to enter port information when entering addresses to specialized Web applications that listen on a different port than port 80.

- The fourth part of the address is the path and filename. The path includes all directories and the filename. Most Web pages end in .htm or .html.

- Other common file endings are .cgi, for *Common Gateway Interface*, .asp, for *Active Server Pages,* and .cfm, for *Cold Fusion Markup Language.* These file endings might be followed by an optional fifth part of a URL—a query string. A query string is added to a URL to send data to a script to be processed. We'll explore these files in Hour 17, "Sending and Reacting to Form Data."

4

FIGURE **4.2**

An absolute URL consists of multiple sections. All absolute URLs must contain a protocol, a domain name, and the complete path to a file.

You might see absolute URLs that do not have a filename referenced at the end, such as `http://www.macromedia.com/support/dreamweaver/`. This type of address works because the Web server knows the name of the default page for that directory. Most Web servers have a default page name that doesn't need to be explicitly entered. Usually the default page name is `default.htm`, `default.html`, `index.htm`, or `index.html`. On some servers, any of these names will work. This functionality is configurable in Web server software.

Default pages are often referred to as *home pages*. To create a home page for your Web site, ask your Webmaster or Web hosting service for the default page name of your Web server. If you don't have a default page on your Web site and a visitor doesn't enter a filename at the end of the URL, he may see all of the contents of your directories instead of a Web page.

You usually do not need to enter the protocol into the browser's address box to go to a Web page. Most browsers assume you want to use the `http` protocol. However, if you are surfing to an FTP file you will need to enter `ftp` as the protocol at the beginning of the URL. Even though browsers assume the `http` protocol, you still need to preface absolute links entered into Dreamweaver with `http://`. Use absolute paths to link to Web pages that are not within your own Web site.

Within your own Web site, you will use document relative paths so you can move your site anywhere and your links will still work. They are relative to each other and not their absolute location. While developing in Dreamweaver, you will create a Web site on your local hard drive and then move the site up to a Web server. Document relative paths will work the same in both locations.

It's important to use document relative paths instead of absolute paths in your Web site. If you have an absolute path to a file on your local drive, the link will look like the following:

```
file:///C|/My Documents/first_page.html
```

This file, `first_page.html`, is located on the C drive in a directory called `My Documents`. If you click on this link and look at it on your browser, it looks fine to you! So what's the problem? The reason it looks fine is that you have that page available on your hard drive, but other people will not have that file and will not be able to access the page.

Document relative paths don't require a complete URL. The path to the linked file is expressed relative to the current document. You use this type of path when inserting images into a Web page. You also use a document relative path when creating a hyperlink to a Web page within your Web site.

The following are some examples of document relative paths:

- Linking to a file that is in the same directory as your current file, you will enter only the filename as the path. For instance, if the file products.html in Figure 4.3 has a link to sales.html, the path would simply be the file name because both files are in the same directory.

FIGURE 4.3

The document relative paths depend on the relative position of the files in the directory structure.

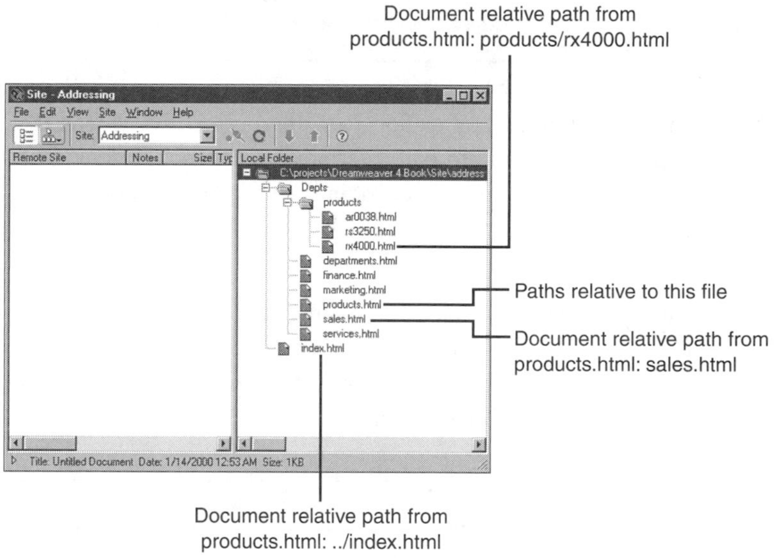

Document relative path from
products.html: products/rx4000.html

Paths relative to this file

Document relative path from
products.html: sales.html

Document relative path from
products.html: ../index.html

4

- To link to a file that is in a directory nested within the directory where the current file is located, enter the directory name and the filename as a path. For instance, if the file products.html in Figure 4.3 has a link to the file rx4000.html in the products directory, the path would be products/rx4000.html.

- Linking to a file in a directory above the current directory (called the *parent directory*), you enter ../ plus the filename as a path. The ../ means go up to the next parent directory. For instance, if the file products.html in Figure 4.3 has a link to the file index.html in the *site root*, the path would be ../index.html.

Prior to saving your Web page, Dreamweaver inserts all links as absolute links. It does this because it cannot calculate a relative link until the file is saved. After the file is saved, Dreamweaver can tell where your document is relative to all linked files and will change the links to document relative addresses. Accidentally using absolute paths is an easy mistake to make. Dreamweaver looks out for you, however, and attempts to correct these problems for you.

> Even though Dreamweaver is smart about changing absolute paths to document relative paths in hyperlinks and images, it doesn't change absolute paths entered in behaviors. You'll learn about Dreamweaver behaviors in Hour 13, "Inserting Scripted Functionality with Behaviors" and Hour 14, "Adding Advanced Behaviors: Drag Layer."

There is a third type of path, called *site root relative*. A link that contains a site root relative path means that the path is relative to the root of your entire Web site. The root of the Web site is defined as a certain directory of a Web site, usually where the site's home page is located. Site root relative linking is used in professional environments where the directory structure of the Web site is likely to change.

Site root relative paths may not be the best choice for beginning Web development work. The main difficulty is that you can only preview pages that have site relative links if they are loaded on a Web server. Therefore, you won't be able to preview your work in a browser without loading it onto the server.

> A site root relative path is preceded with a forward slash (/). An example of a site root relative path is
> `/depts/products.html`
> Be careful not to enter a path this way by accident when typing in an address.

Add a Hyperlink Within Your Web Site

If we create a new Web page and save it in the same directory with the Web page you created in the Hour 2, "Creating a Basic Web Page with Text," we will have the makings of a rudimentary Web site. We can use the two pages to practice linking using document relative paths.

It's generally bad form to explicitly reference a hyperlink by saying, "Click here to see our statistics." It's better to incorporate a hyperlink into a natural sentence, such as, "The 1999 statistics show that sales increased by 32%." Ideally, hyperlinks are meant to seamlessly blend into the text of the your documents.

Create a new page that links to an existing page:

1. Select the New command from the File menu to create a new document.
2. Save this document in the same directory with another HTML file.
3. Add some text to the document.
4. Select a word in the text that could logically be used to link to the other file. See Figure 4.4 as an example.

FIGURE 4.4

Select text in the Dreamweaver document window to become the hyperlink.

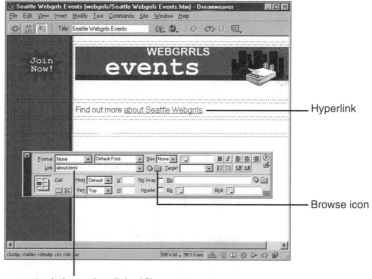

Document relative path to linked file

5. Select the browse (folder) icon next to the Link box. Navigate to the directory where the other page is located. Select the filename and click the Select button.

The selected text appears as an underlined blue hyperlink in the Dreamweaver document window.

Set the Link colors in Page Preferences, just as you set the default text color in Hour 2. Open your Page Preferences and add a Link color, Visited Link color, and Active Link color. When you apply the changes to your Web page, you should see all of your links as the Link color. When the viewer's browser has visited one of your links, the link will appear in the Visited Link color. The viewer sees the Active Link color while the mouse is actively clicking the link. The Link colors are defined for the entire page so all of your links will be the color you specify.

You can set an individual link color with Style Sheets. You can even turn off the hyperlink underline though many usability experts advise against it. You'll explore setting up and using Style Sheets in Hour 11, "Formatting Your Web Pages with Cascading Style Sheets and HTML Styles."

Organize a Long Page with Anchors

Have you ever visited a Web page where you click a link and it takes you to another part of the same Web page? That type of Web page is created with *named anchors*. Sometimes it's less confusing to jump within the same Web page than to jump to another Web page.

To create a long page with named anchors, first add a named anchor to the location on the page where the user will jump. Then create a hyperlink that is linked to the named anchor. We'll start creating a named anchor with a page that has multiple sections, such as the one shown in Figure 4.5.

FIGURE 4.5

A Web site can have multiple sections with a menu at the top of the page linking to the sections.

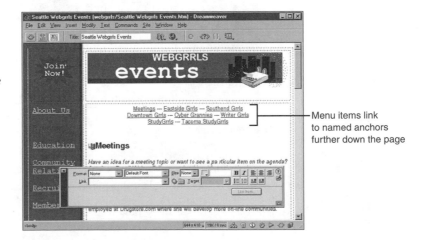

Menu items link to named anchors further down the page

1. Place the insertion point where the named anchor will be located.

2. Select the Named Anchor command from the Invisible Tags submenu of the Insert menu or from the Invisibles panel of the Object panel.

3. Name the anchor in the Insert Named Anchor dialog box shown in Figure 4.6. Click OK.

FIGURE 4.6

After selecting the Named Anchor command, you give the anchor a name in the Insert Named Anchor dialog box.

4. You may get a message saying that you will not see this element because it is invisible. Dreamweaver displays a number of messages that give you useful warnings like this one. You can always click the Don't Show Mc This Message Again check box if you don't want to receive the warning. If you receive this warning, select the Invisible Elements command from the Visual Aids submenu of the View menu to view Invisibles.

An Invisible with an anchor on it will appear at the location where you inserted the named anchor. This is the visual representation of a named anchor. With the named anchor symbol selected, you can change the name of your named anchor in the Property inspector.

To link to the new named anchor

1. Select the text that will link to the named anchor.

2. Enter the name of the named anchor preceded by a pound sign (#) in the Link box, as shown in Figure 4.7.

You can also link to a named anchor in another file. You simply append the name of the named anchor to the filename, as demonstrated in the following:

```
http://www.seattlewebgrrls.org/events/index.html#meetings
```

4

Figure 4.7
Enter the name of a named anchor, preceded by a pound sign, to create a link to it.

Named anchor

Link to named anchor

Use the Point-to-File Icon

There's a little tool that you might have noticed on the Property inspector that enables you to visually create links. *The point-to-file icon*, shown in Figure 4.8, can be dragged to a named anchor or a file located in a Web site defined in Dreamweaver.

Figure 4.8
Drag the point-to-file icon to a named anchor. While the icon is over the anchor, its name will appear in the Link box.

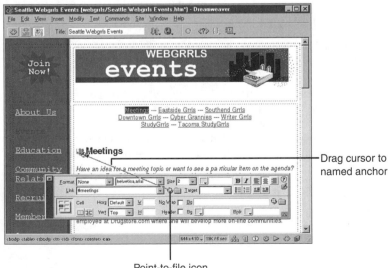

Drag cursor to named anchor

Point-to-file icon

When the point-to-file icon is dragged over the named anchor that you created previously, the name of the anchor will appear in the link box of the Property inspector. To select the named anchor, simply release the mouse button while the point-to-file icon is located over the named anchor. Using this icon is a nice way to link to objects or files without having to know or type in the filenames.

Add a Mailto Link

It's nice to put a link in your Web page that allows a viewer to send email. This type of link is called a *mailto link*. The Dreamweaver E-mail Link object helps you implement a mailto link. The user must have an email application set up to work with the browser for these links to work.

To create a mailto link, select some text to be the link. Click the E-mail Link object and the Insert E-mail Link dialog box appears (see Figure 4.9). Enter the email address and click OK. The text looks like a hyperlink, but instead of linking to another page, it opens a pre-addressed email message.

FIGURE **4.9**

Create a link that opens an email message with the E-mail Link object. The linked text is in the top box and the email address is in the bottom box of the Insert E-mail Link dialog box.

4

Spammers troll the Internet for mailto links. If you use mailto links in your Web pages, expect to get a lot of *spam,* or junk email, sent to the email address used in the mailto links.

Summary

In this hour, you learned the difference between absolute and relative addresses. You created links to external Web sites and relative links to pages within a Web site. You learned how to insert a named anchor and then link to it, and you created a mailto link to allow a viewer to launch an email message directly from a Web page.

Q&A

Q **The named anchor that I want to link to is much lower on the page and I can't see it on the screen. How can I use the point-to-file icon to reach it?**

A If you drag the point-to-file icon to either the top or the bottom of the document window, the window will scroll. Hold the icon near the edge of the window until it has scrolled to the point where the named anchor is visible on the screen.

Q **How will I know if an external Web page that I've linked to in my page has changed?**

A There are services on the Internet that will send you an email whenever a Web page changes. The Mind-it service, located at `http://www.netmind.com`, is one free example of this type of service.

Workshop

The Workshop contains quiz questions and activities to help reinforce what you've learned in this hour. If you get stuck, the answers to the quiz can be found after the questions.

Quiz

1. How can you view a named anchor if it isn't currently visible onscreen?
2. What is the difference between a document relative path and a site relative path?
3. When does a Web page viewer see the active link color?

Answers

1. Select the Invisibles command from the Visual Aids submenu of the View menu to see items that are invisible elements.
2. A document relative path begins with the directory (or directories), followed by a forward slash, followed by the filename. A site relative path begins with a forward slash and then the directories and filename.
3. While they are actively clicking a hyperlink.

Exercises

1. Surf the Web for ten to fifteen minutes with a new awareness for the different types of links. When you place the cursor over a link, you can usually see the address of the link in the status bar of the browser. Look for links to named anchors, too.
2. Create a favorite links page, including links to all your favorite Web sites. You can either use the URL of the link as the text that displays or create a hyperlink out of a descriptive word or phrase. Hint: The major browsers have methods of exporting all of your bookmarks or favorites. That will give you a huge head start on this exercise.

PART II

Adding Images and Multimedia

Hour

Hour 5

Displaying Images on a Page and Creating an Image Map

As Internet bandwidth increases, so does the opportunity to add images to your Web pages. However, much of the emphasis remains on optimizing image file sizes so that they are as small as possible. Images offer a powerful way to send a message. One drawing or photograph can communicate a huge amount of information.

In this hour, you will learn

- How to insert an image into a Web page and change its properties
- How to add a hyperlink to an image
- Which image formats can be used in a Web page
- How to create a rollover image and a navigation bar
- How to define an image map

Add an Image to a Page

Images are separate files that appear within a Web page. Because Dreamweaver is a WYSIWYG program, you will be able to see the images right in the Dreamweaver document window. Images are not actually part of the HTML, but remain separate files that are inserted by the browser when you view the Web page.

To insert a image into your Web page,

1. Place the cursor where you want to insert the image. You will see the insertion point blinking, as shown in Figure 5.1.

FIGURE 5.1

The insertion point signals where the image is to be inserted into the document.

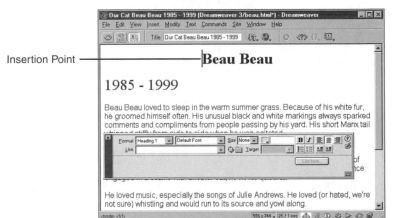

2. Select the Insert Image command from the Objects panel (or the Insert menu).
3. Click the browse icon (folder) in the Property inspector to navigate to the directory where the image file resides. The Select Image Source dialog box appears.
4. Select the image file (see Figure 5.2). A thumbnail image is visible on the right side of the dialog box if the Preview Images check box is selected. Notice the file size, dimensions of the image, and the download time located beneath the thumbnail.
5. When you locate the correct image, click the Select button.

If you have a Web site created in the Site window, Dreamweaver may ask you if you would like to copy the image to the current site. If you are working on an unrelated Web page, select No. It's always a good idea, however, to first define the Web site you are working in and have it selected in the Site window.

FIGURE 5.2

The Select Image Source dialog box enables you to preview the image before you select it.

Thumbnail

Image Statistics

Preview images check box

As shown in Figure 5.3, the image is now visible within the Web page. With the image selected, the Property inspector displays the properties of the image. The Src (Source) box displays the path to the image file. Notice that Dreamweaver automatically filled in the dimensions (width and height) of the image. Having the dimensions helps the browser load the image faster.

Height

Name   Width   Resize Handles

FIGURE 5.3

The Property inspector shows the width, height, and other image properties.

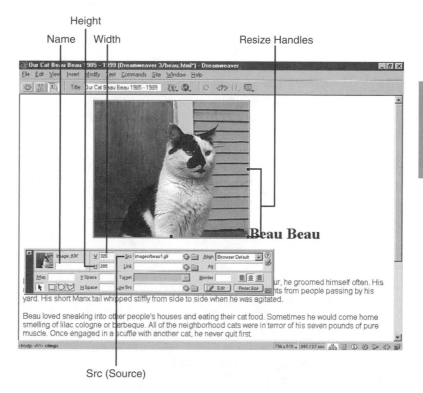

5

Src (Source)

To resize an image, drag the handle. To maintain the aspect ratio of the image (its width to height ratio), press Shift and drag a corner resize handle. You can also change the values of width and height in the Property inspector. The default measurement for width and height is in pixels. To return to the actual dimensions of the image, select the Refresh button on the Property inspector.

> It's usually not a good idea to resize images in Dreamweaver. If you make images smaller, be aware that the size of the image file size has not been reduced. The viewer will still have to download a file of the same size. If your image needs to be smaller, it's better to resize it in a graphics program, like Fireworks, so that the file will be smaller and will download more quickly.

Align an Image with Text

There are two different alignment commands for images. One command aligns the image on the Web page, similar to how you align text on the page. The second alignment command controls how objects that are located beside an image align with the image. To align an image in the center (or the left or the right) of the screen, select one of the alignment buttons on the expanded Property inspector. These buttons look exactly like the text alignment buttons.

The drop-down menu labeled Align in the upper half of the Property inspector sets how elements beside an image line up with the image. Figure 5.4 shows the browser default (usually the same as baseline alignment) Align option. The first line of text aligns with the bottom of the image in Figure 5.4. If there were more text, it would wrap underneath the image.

FIGURE 5.4

The Browser Default alignment is baseline. You can change the alignment in the Align drop-down menu in the Property inspector.

Alignment with other objects

Change the Align setting of the image so that all of the text appears to the right, beside the image. To do this, select Left from the Align options drop-down menu in the Property inspector. Why left? The image will be on the left. Remember that the Align options apply to the image but affect other elements within its vicinity. The different alignment choices are listed in Table 5.1.

TABLE 5.1 Image Alignment Options Available in the Property Inspector

Align Option	Description
Browser Default	Usually baseline, but depends on the browser.
Baseline	Aligns the bottom of the image with the bottom of the element.
Top	Aligns the image with the highest element. Additional lines of text wrap beneath the image.
Middle	Aligns the element in the middle of the image. Additional lines of text wrap beneath the image.
Bottom	Aligns the element at the bottom of the image, like Baseline.
TextTop	Aligns the image with the highest text (not the highest element like the Top option). Additional lines of text wrap beneath the image.
Absolute Bottom	Aligns the bottom of the highest element with the bottom of the image.
Left	Aligns the image to the left of other elements.
Right	Aligns the image to the right of other elements.

To increase the distance between the image and other page elements, set V Space and H Space. V stands for vertical and H stands for horizontal. To add space to the right of the image, put a value in H Space, as shown in Figure 5.5. H Space is added to both the right and the left of the image. V Space is added to both the top and the bottom of the image.

Add Alternate Text So That People Can Read a Description of the Image Before It Loads

Believe it or not, some people who may surf to your Web pages are still using text-only browsers, such as Lynx. Others are stuck behind a very slow modem or Internet connection and have the images turned off in their browsers. Others are visually impaired and have speech synthesizers that read the contents of Web pages. For all of these viewers you should add alternative text to your images.

Enter alternative text, or Alt text, into the Alt text box in the Property inspector, as shown in Figure 5.6. Make the text descriptive of the image that it represents. Don't enter something such as "A cute cat." A better choice would be "Black and white manx cat looking alert while protecting his territory." In some browsers, the Alt text also pops up like a tool tip when the viewer puts the cursor over an image.

You can run the Missing Alt Text report by selecting the Reports command from the Site menu. This report shows you all of the images that are missing the Alt text.

5

50 pixels of H Space

FIGURE 5.5
Put a value in H Space to increase the space to the right and the left of the image. Put a value in V Space to increase the space above and below the image.

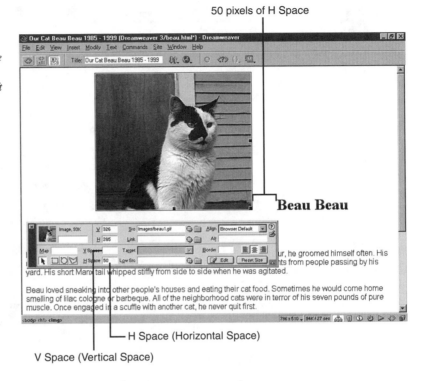

H Space (Horizontal Space)

V Space (Vertical Space)

Alt (Alternative) Text

FIGURE 5.6
Alt text is useful for viewers who don't have images in their browsers or are visually impaired.

Create a Linked Image

The link property appears in the Property inspector when you have text or an image selected. Linked images are common on the Web. With an image selected, you can add a hyperlink in a couple of ways:

- Type a URL into the Link box in the Property inspector.
- Browse for the linked page by selecting the folder icon beside the Link box.
- Select a link that has already been used in the page from the link drop-down menu in the Property inspector.

- Use the point-to-file icon to link to a file. The point-to-file icon requires that you also have the Site window open.

To enter a known URL as a hyperlink on an image, select an image on your Web page and make sure the Property inspector is open. Enter a URL in the Link box located underneath the Src (Source) box, as shown in Figure 5.7.

FIGURE 5.7

Set hyperlinks in the Property inspector in the Link box.

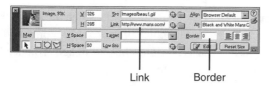

Link   Border

Notice the border property automatically changes to 0. This is so you do not have the hyperlink highlight as a border around your image. If you prefer to have a highlighted border, set the border to a value greater than 0. You can also set a border for an image that isn't linked to anything. The border will appear as a box around the image.

After you save the Web page, preview it in a browser. When you click the image with the hyperlink, your browser should go to the hyperlinked page.

Image Flavors: GIF, JPEG, and PNG

Most new browsers support the two standard image formats and one newer image format. The two standard image formats are called GIF (pronounced either "gif" or "jif") and JPEG (prounounced "J-peg"). The newer format is PNG (pronounced "ping").

- The GIF format is better for images that have blocks of continuous color, usually drawings.
- The JPEG format is better for photographic images and images that do not have blocks of continuous color—for example, images that contain a color gradient.
- The PNG format is a replacement for the GIF format. It supports alpha channels that are useful for transparency.

There are several image optimization software programs available that will help you decide which image format is the most efficient to use for that particular image. These programs also help you reduce the number of colors in an image and improve other factors that will reduce the file size and consequently the download time.

5

Under the Command menu, you can select the Optimize Image in Fireworks command when you have an image selected. This will open the image file in Fireworks if you have that program. Another image optimization program is Adobe ImageReady. Adobe Photoshop 5.5 or greater includes the optimization capabilities of ImageReady.

An Edit button appears in the Property inspector when an image is selected. This button will open the current image in a graphics program. Edit commands also appear in the context drop-down menu when you right-click an image. You need to set up an external image editor in Dreamweaver Preferences.

The File Types/Editors category of Preferences allows you to associate file extensions with different external programs, as shown in Figure 5.8. For example, you can associate .jpg, .gif, and .png file extensions with Fireworks. When an image is selected in Dreamweaver, you select the Edit button and the image file opens in Fireworks. You make your edits and save the file. To associate an editor with a file extension, select a file extension in the File Types/Editors category, click the plus button, and browse to the image editor program.

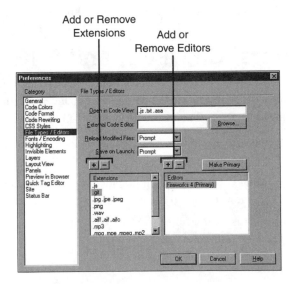

FIGURE 5.8

The File Types/Editors category in Dreamweaver Preferences configures other applications to edit linked files.

While in an external image editor, you might want to create a low-resolution version of the image to link to from the Low Src box in the Property inspector. This image will appear during the initial loading of the Web page and then will turn into the higher resolution version of the image. This functionality evolved to help speed up download times. Usually the low-resolution image is grayscale or a smaller version of a color image.

Add a Background Image

You set a background image for a Web page in Page Properties. Background images are tiled over the entire page. It's important to select a background image that complements your page design. Some images just don't look very good when tiled across an entire Web page.

> You can control the tiling of a background image through Cascading Style Sheets. A style sheet can be applied to a page enabling a background image to appear only once, tile only horizontally or only vertically, or tile a certain number of times. We'll cover style sheets in Hour 11, "Formatting Your Web Pages with Cascading Style Sheets and HTML Styles."

Create a Rollover

Dreamweaver makes it easy to implement rollover images by using the Rollover Image object. A rollover image is an image that swaps to another image when the viewer's cursor is over it. You'll need two image files with exactly the same dimensions to create a rollover.

To create a rollover image, do the following:

1. Place the insertion point where you want the rollover image to appear.
2. Select the Rollover Image object from the Object panel (or Rollover Image command from the Interactive Images submenu of the Insert menu).
3. The Insert Rollover Image dialog box appears. Name the image in the top box.
4. Select both the original image file and the rollover image file by clicking the Browse buttons.
5. Check the Preload Rollover Image check box if you'd like the rollover image downloaded into the viewer's browser cache. With a preloaded image, there is less chance that the viewer will place the cursor over the image and have to wait for the rollover image to download.
6. Add a link to the rollover image by clicking the Browse button, or type in the external URL or named anchor.
7. The Insert Rollover Image dialog box should look like Figure 5.9. Click the OK button.

5

FIGURE 5.9

A rollover image swaps one image for another when the viewer's cursor is over the image. Enter both image paths into the Insert Rollover Image dialog box.

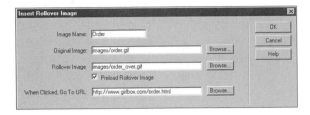

Add a Navigation Bar with Rollovers and Links

What if we want to create a bunch of rollover images as a navigation bar? And what if we wanted them to have a down button state too? We could create all these buttons individually, or we could use Dreamweaver Insert Navigation Bar object to create all the buttons at once.

To create a navigation bar, do the following:

1. Select the Navigation Bar object from the Object panel (or the Interactive Images submenu of the Insert menu).

2. An initial, unnamed button element is visible. Change the element name to the name of your first button. (If you simply go the next step, Dreamweaver will automatically give your button the same name as the name of the image file.)

3. Browse to load a button up image, a button over image, and a button down image. You can also enter an "over while down" image, a rollover image for the down state of a button. All these images must be the same size.

4. Enter a hyperlink in the When Clicked, Go To URL box. Type in a URL or browse to a Web page. The drop-down menu next to the URL box enables you to target a specific frame. We'll explore targeting and frames in Hour 12, "Understanding and Building Frames and Framesets."

5. Check the Preload Images check box if you want the images to be automatically preloaded. Check the Show "Down Image" Initially check box if you want the button to appear pressed in at first.

6. Add additional buttons by clicking the plus button and repeating steps 2 through 5. Rearrange the order of the buttons with the arrow buttons at the top of the Insert Navigation Bar dialog box. To delete a button, click the minus button.

7. At the bottom of the Insert Navigation Bar dialog box, you can choose to insert the navigation bar either horizontally or vertically into the Web page. Select the Use Tables check box if you'd like the navigation bar created in a table.

8. The Insert Navigation Bar dialog box should look like Figure 5.10 when you have added several elements. When you are finished adding buttons, click OK.

Reorder Elements

Add or Remove Elements

FIGURE 5.10

Each element in a navigation bar consists of multiple images linked to a URL. The navigation bar can be situated vertically or horizontally.

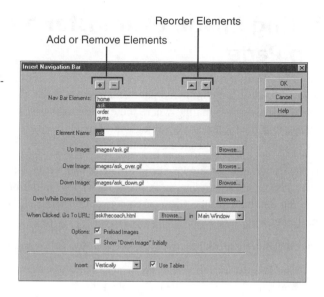

Save your file and preview it in the browser, as shown in Figure 5.11, to test the buttons. If you've made a mistake, don't fret! You can edit the navigation bar by selecting the Navigation Bar object again.

FIGURE 5.11

Testing a navigation bar in the browser to make sure the elements have the proper rollover and down states and link to the correct URL.

5

You can only have one navigation bar per Web page.

Rollover and button images require that the up, over, and down images are all the same size. Otherwise, the over and down images will stretch to the size of the original up image and will be distorted.

Use a Tracing Image to Transfer a Design to Your Web Page

The tracing image feature is useful when you are creating a page design and you have an image showing all of the completed page elements. You can use this image as a tracing image. Instead of estimating where the elements go onscreen, you can display a tracing image and lay the individual image and text elements over the tracing image perfectly. A tracing image makes it easy to align objects.

Load a tracing image into Dreamweaver in the Page Properties dialog box. The tracing image is only visible in Dreamweaver and is never visible in the browser. A tracing image covers up any background color or background image. The background color or background image will still be visible in the browser.

To load a tracing image into Dreamweaver, perform the following steps:

1. Open Page Properties and select the Browse button beside the Tracing Image box (at the bottom of the dialog box). Or, select the Tracing Image command from the View menu and choose Load.

2. Browse to the tracing image file. It needs to be a GIF, JPEG, or PNG.

3. Drag the Image Transparency slider to set how opaque (solid) or transparent the tracing image will be, as shown in Figure 5.12.

4. Click OK.

FIGURE 5.12

You can load a tracing image into the Page Properties dialog box. Set the transparency with the slider.

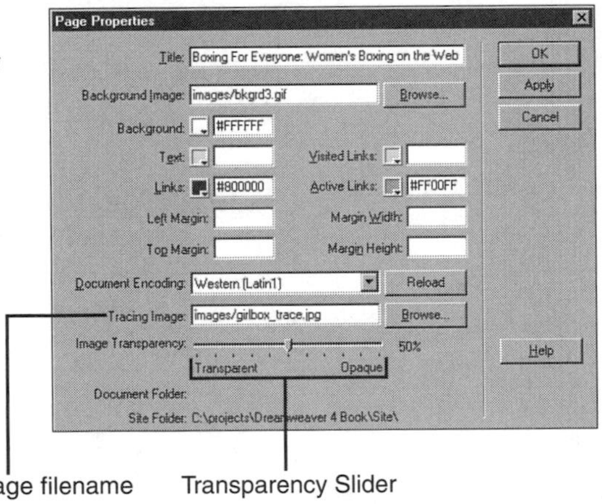

Tracing image filename   Transparency Slider

Add Links to a Graphic with Image Maps

An Image map is an image with regions defined as hyperlinks. These regions are called hotspots. When a viewer clicks a hotspot, it acts just like any other hyperlink. Instead of adding one hyperlink to an entire image, you can define a number of hotspots on different portions of an image. You can even create these hotspots in different shapes.

Image maps are useful for presenting graphical menus that the viewer can click to select regions of the single image. For instance, you could create an image out of a picture of North America. You could draw hotspots around the different countries in North America. When the viewer clicked the hotspot, he could jump to a Web page with information on that country.

Dreamweaver creates client-side image maps, meaning the Web page holds all of the defined coordinates and hyperlinks. The other type of image map, a server-side image map, depends on a program that runs on a Web server to interpret coordinates and hyperlinks. Client-side image maps react more quickly to user input because they don't have to contact the server for information. Older browsers, however, may not understand client-side image maps.

Netscape 2.0 and higher, all versions of Internet Explorer, and Mosaic 2.1 and 3.0 support client-side image maps. You can have both a server-side and a client-side image map defined for a single image. The client-side image map will take precedence if the browser supports client-side image maps.

5

Create an Image Map

With an image selected, you see four image map tools in the lower corner of the Property inspector (with the Property inspector expanded). These four tools are used to define image map hotspots. One tool draws rectangles, one draws circles, and one draws polygons. The fourth tool is an arrow tool used to select or move the hotspots.

To create an image map, you

1. Insert an image into your Web page. The image must be selected for the image map tools to appear in the Property inspector.
2. Give the map a name in the Map Name text box, as shown in Figure 5.13. The name needs to be unique from other map names in the page.

Map Name

FIGURE 5.13

Name the image map in the Map Name text box. The name needs to be unique within the Web page.

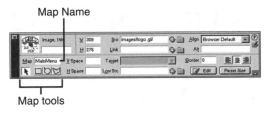

Map tools

3. Select one of the drawing tools described below to draw the hotspot.

4. With a newly drawn hotspot selected, type a URL in the link box, as shown in Figure 5.14, or click the folder icon to browse to a local Web page. You can also link a hotspot to a named anchor by entering a pound sign followed by the anchor name.

URL   Hotspot Alt text

FIGURE 5.14

Enter the URL to link a hotspot with another Web page or a named anchor within the current page.

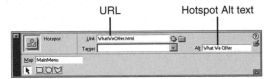

5. Enter alternative text for the hotspot in the Alt text box. As discussed with hyperlink Alt text, some browser's display this text as a tool tip.

6. Select a window target from the Target drop-down menu in the Property inspector. Target windows will be covered a little later in this hour when you will open a new browser window with the Target drop-down menu selections.

Set all of the image properties for an image map just like you would an ordinary image. You can set the V Space, H Space, Alt text, Border, and alignment. If you copy and paste the image map into another Web page, all of the map information comes along too.

Add a Rectangular Hotspot

To add a rectangular hotspot, first select the rectangle tool. Click and drag the crosshair cursor to make a rectangle the dimensions of the hotspot you want to create. When you release the mouse, a highlighted box over the image appears, like in Figure 5.15. With the hotspot selected, enter a URL into the link box of the Property inspector.

To move or adjust the size of the hotspot, you need to first select the arrow tool. You can't use the hotspot drawing tools to adjust the hotspot; you will end up creating another hotspot instead. Click the hotspot with the arrow tool and either move the hotspot to another location or resize the hotspot using the resize handles.

FIGURE 5.15

Create a rectangle and link it to a URL. Now it's a hotspot!

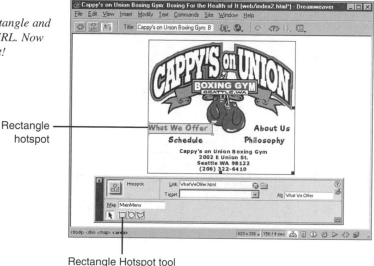

Rectangle hotspot

Rectangle Hotspot tool

In the Web page HTML, the rectangular hotspot is defined by two sets of x and y coordinates. The upper-left corner of the rectangle is captured into x1 and y1 and the lower right corner of the rectangle is captured into x2 and y2. The coordinates are in pixels and are relative to the image, not the Web page. The HTML code for a rectangular area looks like this:

```
<area shape="rect" coords="127,143,251,291" href="products.html">
```

In this example, the upper left corner of the rectangle is 127 pixels from the right of the image and 143 pixels from the top of the image. The bottom right corner of the rectangle is 251 pixels from the right of the image and 291 pixels from the top. It's nice to have a visual representation in Dreamweaver and not have to figure this out yourself, isn't it!

Add a Circular Hotspot

A circular area may better define some areas in your image map. You create a circular hotspot just like you created the rectangular one. Select the circle tool, then click and drag to create the hotspot as in Figure 5.16. Notice that the hotspot is always a perfect circle and not an ellipse. Reposition or resize the hotspot with the arrow tool.

You can understand why you can only have a circle and not an ellipse when you see how the circle hotspot coordinates are defined. A circle is defined by three values: The x and y values of the circle center and the circle's radius. The HTML code defining a circular area looks like this:

```
<area shape="circle" coords="138,186,77" href="marketing.html">
```

5

FIGURE 5.16

The circle tool creates hotspots that are perfectly circular.

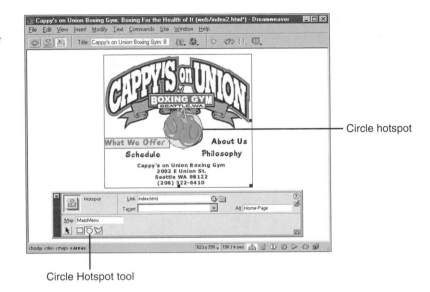

Circle hotspot

Circle Hotspot tool

Add an Irregular Hotspot

Sometimes the area you'd like to turn into a hotspot just isn't circular or rectangular. The polygon tool enables you to create any shape you want to define an irregular hotspot.

You use the polygon tool a little differently than the circle or rectangle tools. First, select the polygon tool from the Property inspector. Instead of clicking and dragging to create a shape, click once for every point in the polygon as shown in Figure 5.17. To close the polygon, select the arrow tool.

FIGURE 5.17

Create an irregular hotspot with the polygon hotspot tool. Click once for every point.

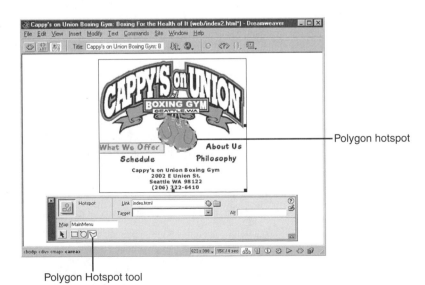

Polygon hotspot

Polygon Hotspot tool

A polygon is defined by an infinite number of x and y coordinates, each representing one of the corner points you create by clicking with the polygon tool. The HTML code for a polygon hotspot looks like this:

```
<area shape="poly" coords="85,14,32,33,29,116,130,99,137,130,140,70,156,66,
198,84,130,30,150,43" href="aboutus.html">
```

The polygon defined in the HTML is made up of ten points so there are ten pairs of x and y coordinates.

Align Hotspots

Dreamweaver has built-in alignment tools that you can use to align the hotspots in your image map. First, you need to select the hotspots you want to align. To select all of the hotspots in an image map, use the keyboard shortcut Ctrl+A. Or, you can Shift+click hotspots to add them to the selection. You can tell when hotspots are selected because you can see the resize handles.

Sometimes it is difficult to finely align hotspots with your mouse. You can use the arrow keys to move a hotspot or multiple hotspots one pixel at a time.

The Layers and Hotspots submenu under the Modify menu contains commands to align hotspots as shown in Figure 5.18. You can align multiple hotspots on the left, right, top, or bottom. You can make multiple hotspots the same height with the Make Same Height command or the same width with the Make Same Width command.

FIGURE 5.18

The Modify menu's Align submenu has commands to align hotspots.

5

Hotspots can overlap each other. Whichever hotspot is on top (usually the one created first) will be the link triggered by clicking on the overlapping area. You can change the stacking order of hotspots with the commands located in the Arrange submenu of the Modify menu. You might create overlapping hotspots on purpose as part of the design of your image map. For instance, you might use a circular hotspot over part of a rectangular hotspot to define a similar pattern in the image. Or, the overlapping might simply be a consequence of the limited shapes you have available to define the hotspots.

It's difficult to tell which hotspot is on top of another hotspot. If you've recently created the image map, you know which hotspot was created first and is therefore on top. You can manipulate the stacking order of the hotspots by selecting the Bring to Front or Send to Back commands from the Modify menu's Arrange submenu. If a hotspot overlaps another and needs to be on top, select the Bring to Front command.

Target a Link to Open in a New Browser Window

The Property inspector, when a hyperlink is selected, has a drop-down box called Target. Frames use the `target` attribute to load a page into a defined frame. Frames are covered in Hour 12. There are four reserved target names that you can use with any link.

Three of the four reserved target names are used mainly with frames. But the _blank reserved target name, as shown in Figure 5.19, is useful when you want to leave the current browser window open and have the link open a new browser window with the linked Web page in it. Select _blank from the Target drop-down menu when one of the hotspots is selected. Preview your Web page in the browser and select that link. Now both the original window containing your image map is open plus a new window with the linked file in it.

Opening up a new window is useful when you want to keep your original Web page open, but allow the user to jump to other Web pages. When they close the new window, the window containing your site will still be open. It's nice to warn the user about this so that they will not get confused.

FIGURE 5.19

The _blank reserved target name in the Target drop-down menu in the Property inspector opens the link in a new browser window. The original document remains open.

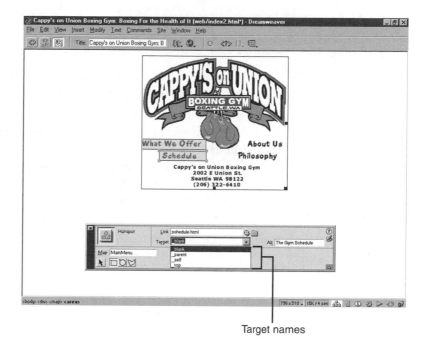

Target names

Summary

In this hour, you learned how to insert an image into a Web page and how to set a link, low-resolution source, V Space and H Space, and Alt text. You learned how to change the size of an image border and edit the image with an external editor. You learned how to align the image on the page and align it in relation to other elements beside it. Then you created a rollover image and a navigation bar. You also learned how to insert a tracing image into a Web page. You learned how to create a client-side image map.

Q&A

Q I created a Web page with some images in it. When I preview it in the browser the images don't show up. Why?

A Until you save your page, Dreamweaver doesn't know how to express the path to the image files. That's why the images don't show up. Save your page before you preview it and you should be all right.

Q I accidentally stretched an image. Help!

A It's easy to restore the original dimensions of an image by selecting the image and clicking the Refresh button.

Q Every time I use the polygon tool, I make a mess of it. I get extra points in the wrong section of the image map. What am I doing wrong?

A When you use the polygon tool to create a hotspot, remember to click, click, click around the edges of the hotspot border. After you have defined the border do not click the image again. Instead, immediately select the pointer hotspot tool to signal Dreamweaver that you are finished creating the polygon hotspot.

Workshop

The Workshop contains quiz questions and activities to help reinforce what you've learned in this hour. If you get stuck, the answers to the quiz can be found after the questions.

Quiz

1. What setting creates a box around an image?
2. What are the three widely supported image formats for Web pages?
3. What's the reserved target name that will open a new browser window?

Answers

1. Enter a value in Border to create a box, or border, around an image.
2. GIF, JPG (or JPEG), and PNG.
3. The blank reserved target name will open a new browser window.

Exercises

1. Insert an image into a new page. Resize it with the resize handles. Click the Refresh button. Resize the image by Shift+dragging the corner resize handle. Click the Refresh button. Change the width and height dimensions by entering different values into the W and H boxes in the Property inspector.

2. Add Alt text to an image. Open up your browser, select the Browser Preferences or Internet Options, and turn off viewing images. The command may be called Show Pictures or Automatically Load Images. Return to Dreamweaver and preview the Web page in that browser so you can see how the Alt text looks.

3. Create several hotspots. Align the hotspots using the alignment commands.

Hour 6

Using Fireworks to Create Images

Fireworks is an image creation and optimization tool that is an excellent addition to your Web development toolbox. You will need to create and optimize the images that you use in your Web sites, and Fireworks enables you to create images quickly with cool effects such as bevels and glows.

Dreamweaver and Fireworks are tightly integrated. You can open files created in Fireworks in Dreamweaver, make changes, and see those changes in the original Fireworks file. You can also export tables, rollovers, and HTML code created in Fireworks directly into Dreamweaver.

Fireworks is a professional image tool that could fill an entire 24-hour learning period on its own! In this hour, we will simply touch on some of the important elements and offer a few image manipulation techniques. There is so much more to learn about Fireworks.

In this hour, you will learn

- How to create an image in Fireworks
- How to add a stroke, fill, effect, and text to an image
- How to optimize images
- How to slice and export images

Acquaint Yourself with Fireworks 4

The Fireworks interface consists of a document window and panels just like Dreamweaver's interface. The Fireworks document window, shown in Figure 6.1, is tabbed with four different displays: Original, Preview, 2-Up, and 4-Up. You create and manipulate an image with the Original tab selected. The Preview tab shows you what the final image will look like.

FIGURE 6.1

The Fireworks document window has four different tabbed displays. Use the Original tab to create and manipulate an image.

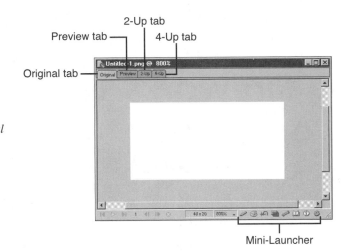

2-Up tab

Preview tab ——
4-Up tab

Original tab ——

Mini-Launcher

When you are ready to optimize the image for the Web, you can select either the 2-Up or the 4-Up tab. These tabs display the image either twice or four times. Why would you want to display the image multiple times? Because then you can optimize the image in different ways and compare how they look all at the same time. You'll optimize an image later this hour.

Fireworks displays the current image in either vector or bitmap mode. In vector mode, which is the default, you can draw objects onscreen that are easily sized and changed after they are created. If you open a GIF or JPEG image in Fireworks, the file is opened in bitmap mode because those image formats are bitmap formats. Switch to vector mode by selecting the Exit Bitmap Mode button, shown in Figure 6.2.

FIGURE 6.2
The Exit Bitmap Mode button enables you to add vector objects to an image.

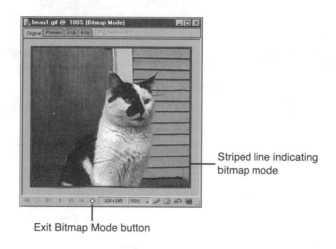

Striped line indicating bitmap mode

Exit Bitmap Mode button

 You can tell you are in bitmap mode when there is a striped border around the image. In vector mode there is just a thin blue line around the image.

Examine the Fireworks Tools

The Toolbox, shown in Figure 6.3, contains the tools you use to draw and select objects in the document window. Some of the tools are actually groups of tools. If the tool has a triangle in the lower-right corner of the tool button, it means that you can actually select from a tool group.

Some tools in the Toolbox function differently depending on whether you are in vector or bitmap mode. For instance, the Brush tool draws an editable path when in vector mode, but draws a line of pixels when in bitmap mode. You are probably going to do most of your work in Fireworks in vector mode and then export images to one of the bitmap formats popular for Web pages.

6

FIGURE **6.3**

The Toolbox has individual tools and groups of tools you can use to manipulate images.

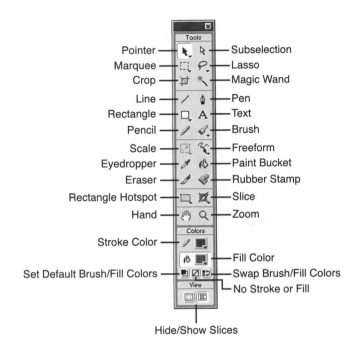

Hide/Show Slices

Examine Fireworks Panels

Just like Dreamweaver, Fireworks has tabbed floating panels, described in Table 6.1, that enable you to affect your image in various ways. Fireworks also has a Mini-Launcher like Dreamweaver at the bottom of the document window. You can launch or hide the Stroke, Color Mixer, Optimize, and Layers panels from the Mini-Launcher. Just like in Dreamweaver, all of the panels can be displayed by selecting them in the Window menu.

TABLE 6.1   Fireworks Panels and Their Functionality

Panel	Description
Stroke	This panel changes the stroke, which is either an individual line or a line that forms the border of an object. You can affect the amount of ink, tip size and shape, texture, edge effect, and aspect.
Fill	This panel changes the fill of an object. You can choose various fills, including gradients and patterns. You can add an edge effect and change the texture.
Effect	This panel enables you to add various effects to objects, such as glows and bevels. You can also add any Photoshop plug-in effects through this panel.

Panel	Description
Info	This panel provides information about the currently selected object or gives you size and coordinate information for a selection. It also displays the color of whatever the cursor is currently over.
Optimize	This panel contains all of the options to optimize images for the Web. You can select a palette, file format, number of colors, type of dither, and a transparent color.
Object	This panel enables you to affect how the stroke and fill of an object interact. You can round of the edges and select how the stroke and fill will blend together.
Behaviors	This panel adds behaviors, similar to Dreamweaver behaviors, to a hotspot or slice on your Fireworks image. You can create a rollover, an image swap, a navigation bar, and a pop-up menu, and you can set the text of the status bar.
Mixer	This panel gives you the power to set both the stroke and the fill colors either by sight with the color picker or with one of the available color models. The color models available are RGB, hexadecimal, HSB, CMY, and Grayscale. You select the color model from the Color Mixer Options drop-down menu.
Swatches	This panel displays color swatches. You can load different palettes from the Swatches Options drop-down menu.
Table	This panel displays the color table (palette) of the current image if it has been indexed (optimized).
Layers	This panel displays all of the layers in the current image. You can create and modify various layers and objects in Fireworks in this panel.
Frames	This panel organizes animations created in Fireworks into groups of animation frames.
History	This panel records all of the steps that you have completed in the current file and enables you to undo them.
Tool Options	This panel changes depending on which tool you have selected in the Toolbox. You can set the options for the selected tool.
Styles	This panel stores sets of pre-defined stroke, fill, and effects attributes that you can apply to objects. You can also create and save your own styles.
Library	This panel stores symbols, buttons, graphics, and animations that you can use over and over in Fireworks. Symbols are a Fireworks term for an object, text, or groups of objects that are re-used. The symbol is the original object. When it is updated all of its linked instances are updated.
URL	This panel stores URLs that you will apply to objects in Fireworks.

6

Create an Image

Now that you are familiar with the Fireworks interface, you can create a new image from scratch, such as a button graphic that you can use in your Web site. First you create a new file, and then add some color and text. Next, you apply an effect to make it look more realistic. To create a new file

1. Select the New command under the File menu.

2. The New Document dialog box appears, as shown in Figure 6.4. You set the width, height, and resolution of your new file in this dialog box. Enter 40 pixels for the width and 20 pixels for the height. The resolution should be 72 because that is the standard resolution for images that will be displayed on a computer screen.

FIGURE 6.4

Set the width, height, and resolution in the New Document dialog box. You also set the canvas or background color here.

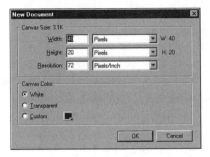

3. Select the radio button next to White for the Canvas Color. You can also select Transparent or a Custom color if you want.

4. Click OK.

5. Select 800% from the magnification drop-down menu at the bottom of the document window as shown in Figure 6.5. This will make it easier to see what you are working on.

You might have to make the document window larger to see the magnification drop-down menu.

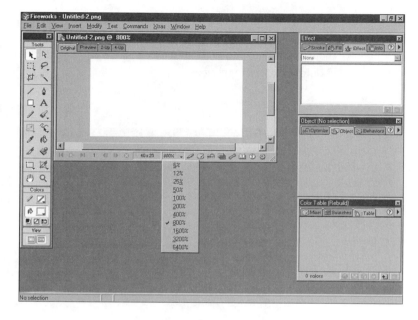

FIGURE 6.5

The document window can be magnified using the magnification drop-down menu. The magnification level is displayed at the bottom of the document window.

Add a Shape

You've created a new document and now you are ready to add the rectangular button shape. Fireworks has tools to draw any type of shape you might want. And, since the shapes are vector graphics, you can easily edit them later. After you create the rectangle, you can modify the stroke and the fill to make it more visually interesting. To create a rectangle:

1. Select the Rectangle tool from the Toolbox. The cursor becomes a crosshair for drawing.

2. Draw a rectangle by dragging in the upper-left corner. Drag the cursor to the lower-right corner, leaving a little room on the bottom and the right side of the canvas for a drop shadow that you will add later.

3. After you've drawn the rectangle, you may only see the four points that define the corners of the rectangle. You see these points because the rectangle is currently selected. You won't see the outline of the rectangle because you haven't yet added a stroke or fill color.

4. Make sure that the rectangle object that you just created is selected (in case you clicked your cursor somewhere else after step 3!). You will see the four points when it is. If the rectangle is not selected, select the Pointer tool from the Toolbox and click on the rectangle to select it.

6

5. Select the Stroke panel. Select Pencil in the Stroke category drop-down menu, select 1-Pixel Hard from the Stroke name drop-down menu, and select a color from the color picker. Just accept the defaults for the rest of the settings. The image should look like Figure 6.6.

Stroke panel

FIGURE 6.6

Set the stroke in the Stroke panel. You can set the stroke category, name, and color.

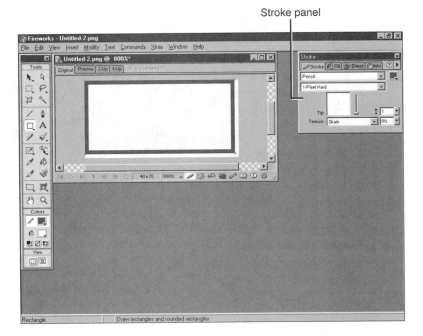

6. Select the Fill panel. Select Solid from the Fill category drop-down menu, select a color from the color picker, and select Dots as the texture (or choose another texture that you like). Select the slider beside Texture and set it to 50%. The image should look like Figure 6.7.

You might want to reduce the magnification to 100% so you can see what your button will look like in its final size.

Fill panel

FIGURE 6.7

Set the fill in the Fill panel. You can select a fill color and texture.

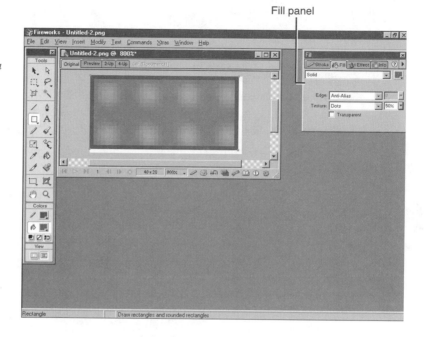

Add an Effect

Fireworks has a number of interesting effects that you can add easily to your images to make them look unique and beautiful. Even better, they are very easy to remove if they don't turn out quite the way you'd like. Each time you add an effect to an object, it is listed in the Effects panel with a check mark beside it. You simply uncheck the check box to turn the effect off for that object. In a few minutes you'll add a drop shadow effect. You can experiment with the bevel, emboss, glow, and other effects on your own.

If you have Photoshop, you can use Photoshop plugins in Fireworks. Point to the directory that contains the Photoshop plugins in the Folder category of Fireworks preferences (the Preferences command under the Edit menu). You'll need to restart Fireworks to load the Photoshop plugin commands. Fireworks displays the Photoshop plugin commands in the Effect Panel drop-down menu.

6

To add an effect to your image

1. Make sure you have the rectangle object selected. You'll apply the effect to this object.

2. Select the Effects panel.

3. Drop down the effects menu and select the Drop Shadow command from the Shadow and Glow submenu. You may see an hourglass cursor for a moment while Fireworks applies the effect.

4. Select the Info button beside the effect in the Effect panel as shown in Figure 6.8. The edit window enables you to change the attributes of the effect.

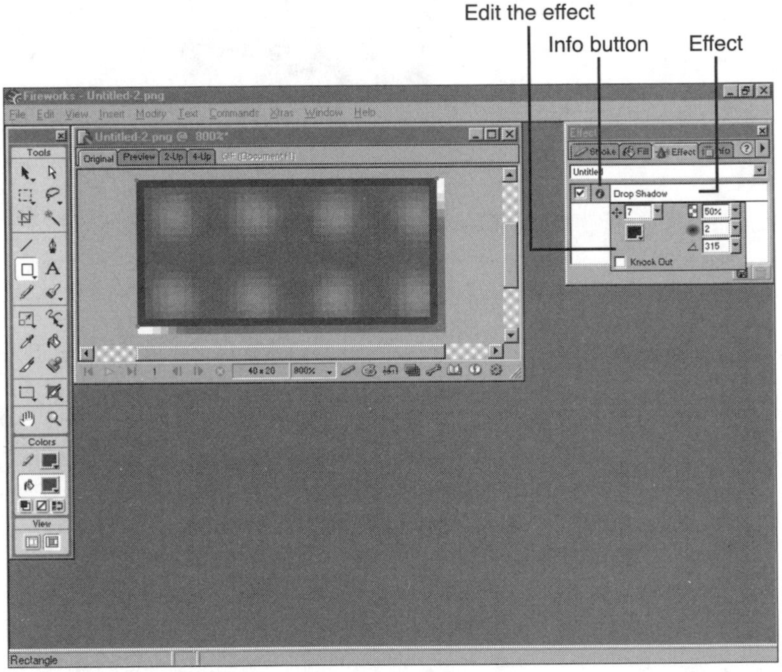

FIGURE 6.8

The Effects panel lists the effects applied to a certain object. You can set the attributes of the effect by selecting the info button.

5. Change the Opacity to 50% and the Softness to 2.

You can add bevels, glows, and blurs, and you can emboss images. You'll want to experiment with the different effects. Usually you can change the colors involved, too. For instance, you can make an object glow in yellow from its center or glow from the bottom of the image as if it were on fire. Fireworks effects enable you to get professional image results without having to know all the steps necessary to do the effects with the other tools in Fireworks.

Add Text

Now add some text to the button. Fireworks' Text tool enables you to place editable text into the document window. You will turn on guides so that you can judge whether you have the text centered in the button. You can use any font on your system and can apply anti-aliasing and other text effects.

To add text to your rectangle

1. Set guides in the middle of the image. Turn on the rulers by selecting the Rulers command under the View menu. The default setting for ruler units is pixels. Since the image is 40 pixels by 20 pixels, one guide will be 20 pixels from the left side and another guide will be 10 pixels from the top. With the rulers on, click within the ruler and drag a guide from the left and then the top. The guides should look like those in Figure 6.9.

FIGURE 6.9

Add guides to your image so you know where the middle of the image is.

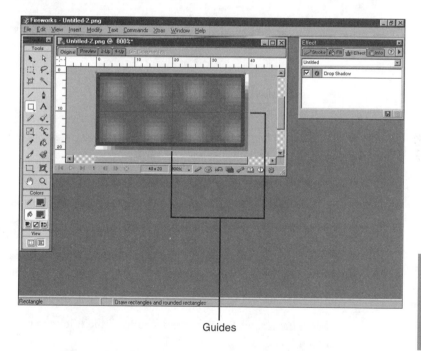

Guides

2. Select the Text tool from the Toolbox, and then click in the document window.
3. The Text Editor dialog box appears. Select a color for the text with the color picker. Make the font size 14. Enter some text for a button title.

6

4. Move the Text Editor to the side of the document window. Press the Apply button to see what the text is going to look like. If the Auto-apply check box is checked, the changes will be applied immediately.

5. Pick up and position the text object. The button should look like Figure 6.10.

FIGURE 6.10

Create a text object and set the font, font size, and font color in the Text Editor.

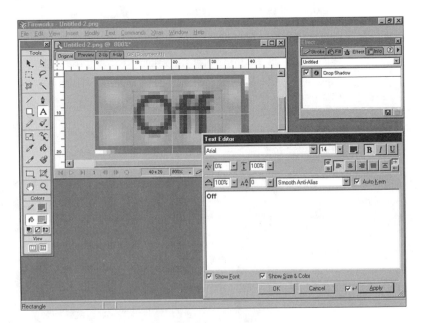

Optimize Images for Use in a Web Page

So now, you have created a button in Fireworks. You can save your file to your hard drive by selecting the Save command under the File menu. This saves your button in the PNG format, Fireworks native file format. Even though this format can be displayed on a Web page, there is a lot of extra information in the file that you really don't need. That's why you want to take advantage of Fireworks' optimization capabilities.

To optimize the image and save it for the Web:

1. Select the Export Preview command from the File menu. The Export Preview dialog box appears.

2. Select the 2 Preview Windows button. This splits the Preview window into two panes so that you can compare two different image formats, as shown in Figure 6.11.

Top pane

FIGURE 6.11

Split the Preview window into two panes so you can compare two different image formats.

GIF Options

Pointer   Zoom   Bottom pane

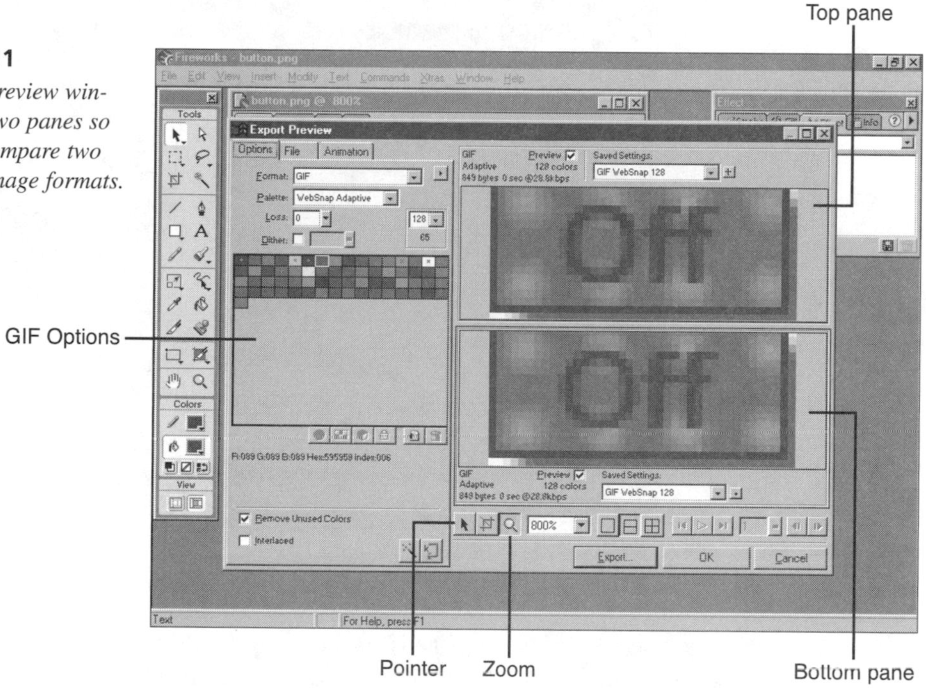

3. Select the Zoom In/Out tool and magnify the image in the Preview window by clicking on the image. You can Alt+Click with the Zoom tool to zoom out.

4. Select the Pointer tool and select the top pane. You can tell a pane is selected because it is highlighted with a box.

5. In the Saved Settings drop-down menu above the top pane, select GIF WebSnap 128. Make sure the check box next to the Preview option is checked so that you can preview what the final image will look like.

6. In the Saved Settings drop-down menu below the bottom pane, select JPEG-Better Quality. The Export Preview should look similar to Figure 6.12.

6

GIF file size

FIGURE 6.12

The Export Preview enables you to compare the file size and download time of different file formats.

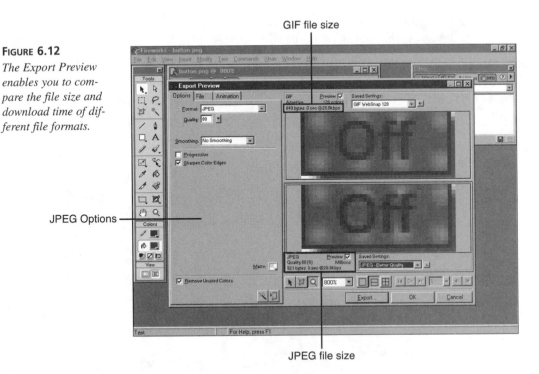

JPEG Options

JPEG file size

7. Notice that the GIF in the top pane is smaller than the JPEG in the bottom pane and takes less time to download. The file size and download time is displayed in each of the panes.

Explore the optimization settings in Fireworks further by reading the extensive help files that come with the program. You can change settings for GIF and JPEG in the left side of the Export Preview dialog box.

8. Select the GIF imagein the top pane, and click the Export button.
9. Enter a name for the file and select the Save button.

Slice an Image into Pieces

Fireworks enables you to slice an image into smaller pieces so that you can add interactivity to the individual pieces. You can draw slice objects over an image in Fireworks and then export the slices as individual graphic files.

To create a sliced image:

1. Open an image in Fireworks.
2. Make sure that the Show Slices button is selected in the Toolbox.
3. Select the Slice tool and draw a rectangle on top of the image, as shown in Figure 6.13.

FIGURE 6.13

Draw slices over the image to create individual image files held together by an HTML table.

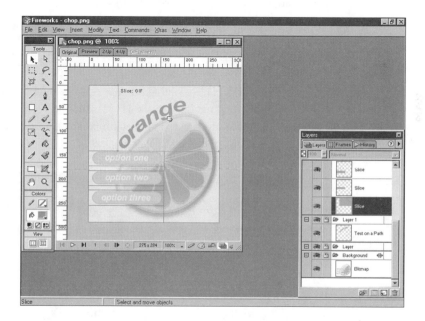

4. Slice up the entire image by repeating step 3.
5. Select the Export Preview command from the File menu. Split the pane and optimize the image as described above.
6. When you click the Export button, Fireworks enables you to export all of the slices as individual image files along with the HTML table that will display the images as if they were all one image. Make sure that Export HTML File is selected.
7. Select the Save button and save the HTML file and all of the sliced images into a directory.

If you open the HTML file that you just created, you'll see all of the slices pushed together as if they were a single image. You can open this file in Dreamweaver and edit it. In a minute, you will learn how to import the HTML into Dreamweaver.

6

Place a Fireworks File into Dreamweaver

Dreamweaver and Fireworks are tightly integrated so that you can efficiently use the two tools together. After you've imported HTML created in Fireworks into Dreamweaver, you can edit the HTML in Dreamweaver and update the original Fireworks files, too. Dreamweaver knows when you have inserted a Fireworks file into your Web page and keeps track of any edits that you make to the file.

To import the HTML and the sliced images that you created in Fireworks

1. In Dreamweaver, select the Fireworks HTML command from the Interactive Image submenu of the Insert menu.

2. The Insert Fireworks HTML dialog box appears, as shown in Figure 6.14. Select the Browse button and navigate to the HTML file that you saved in Fireworks. Select the Delete file after insertion check box if you would like the file to be deleted after it is inserted into the Web page.

FIGURE 6.14

Use the Insert Fireworks HTML dialog box to navigate to the HTML file that Fireworks created.

3. The HTML table and images are inserted into the Dreamweaver document window.

Now the HTML that Fireworks created is in the Web page. Dreamweaver knows that the HTML originally came from Fireworks. When you select the table or the images the Properties inspector shows that the table or image originated in Fireworks, as shown in Figure 6.15. There is also an Edit button that opens Fireworks to make any edits you'd like.

FIGURE 6.15

The Properties inspector shows that the object was originally created in Fireworks and can be edited in Fireworks.

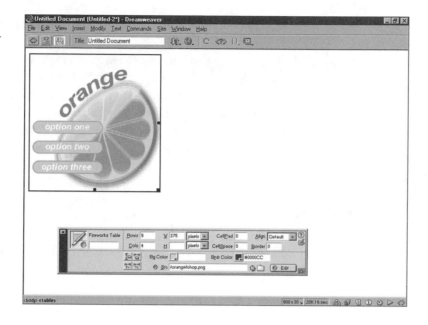

Summary

You learned how to create a button image in Fireworks using a stroke, fills, and effects. You learned how to add text to the button. You learned how to optimize the image to make it download quickly over the Internet. You learned how to slice a single image into multiple images, export those images and the HTML that holds them together, and import the HTML into Dreamweaver.

Q&A

Q How can I tell which file format makes the smallest file?

A That's what you use Fireworks optimization capabilities for. You don't need to know off the top of your head because you can experiment in Fireworks and find out what format creates the smallest file.

6

Q Why would I want to use Fireworks to add behaviors to images instead of Dreamweaver?

A Some people, mainly graphic designers, are more comfortable working in the program they know the best. If you know Fireworks then using Fireworks to add behaviors will be easier. Macromedia has given graphic designers the power to add HTML to their graphics with Fireworks. Since you are reading this book, you probably know (or wish to know) Dreamweaver. Therefore, it will probably be easier for you to apply behaviors using Dreamweaver. Dreamweaver has many more Web page coding capabilities than Fireworks.

Workshop

The Workshop contains quiz questions and activities to help reinforce what you've learned in this hour. If you get stuck, the answers to the quiz can be found following the questions.

Quiz

1. How do you create a guide in Fireworks?
2. What is Fireworks' native file format?
3. True or False: Edits made in Dreamweaver will update the Fireworks files when you import HTML from Fireworks.

Answers

1. Turn on the rulers, click within the rulers, and drag a guide into position.
2. Fireworks' native file format is PNG.
3. True. You don't need to make changes in two places!

Exercises

1. Try applying some of the various effects available in Fireworks to an image. What does glow do? What's the difference between drop shadow and inner shadow? Try using the bevel and emboss effects. What do they do? Try changing the color with the color picker.
2. Use the Fireworks Create Picture Frame command under the Creative submenu of the Commands menu.

HOUR 7

Adding Multimedia Files

You aren't limited to displaying text and graphics in your Web pages. Adding multimedia files, like sounds and movies, grows more popular as modems become faster and people browse the Web with more bandwidth.

Yes, that's right: Most multimedia files take up a lot of bandwidth. Bandwidth is the size of the Internet "pipe" you have when you connect to the Web. If you are on a T1 line, you have access to a higher Internet Bandwidth than someone connecting with a 56kbps modem.

Some formats, like RealMedia or Shockwave files, get around the large bandwidth requirements of sound and video files by streaming content to you. Streamed content begins to play immediately after a short buffer period; the content continues to download in the background while previously buffered content plays. Most multimedia delivered over the Web is also compressed using ever-improving techniques.

Dreamweaver comes with a number of multimedia objects on the Object panel. The Macromedia Web site has additional objects. Downloading and installing new objects makes adding different types of content to Dreamweaver easy. We'll explore how to install new objects in Hour 24, "Customizing Dreamweaver."

Some of the traditional multimedia formats such as WAV (audio), AVI (Windows movie), MOV (QuickTime movie), and AIFF (audio) are often too large to deliver over the Web. Some of these formats require that you download the entire file before it will play. To deliver this type of sound and video content you'll want to understand which technologies to choose; new compression and streaming tools appear all the time.

All multimedia files require a third-party program to play in a browser. Some of these programs, called *plugins* and *ActiveX controls*, are installed automatically with the browser or operating system software. Of course, you don't want to assume that a person viewing your Web page has the same browser plugins that you have installed. You always want to give the viewer information on how to obtain a necessary third-party program.

Dreamweaver has several features that improve your ability to successfully add multimedia files to a Web page. Dreamweaver gives you access to the properties that allow you to provide information on where to download a plugin. Dreamweaver enables you to add both Internet Explorer and Netscape specific plugin HTML code. There is a Dreamweaver *behavior* that will detect whether the viewer has a specific plugin.

In this hour, you will learn

- How to add multimedia files to a Web page
- How to add Flash and Shockwave movies
- How to add a URL to take the user to a plugin download page
- How to insert and configure a Java applet

Add a Sound File

Adding a sound file to a Web page can sometimes add to the experience. And, it's a good way for you to get familiar with adding multimedia files. You use the Plugin object from the Special panel of the Object panel (or the Plugin command from the Media submenu of the Insert menu) to insert a sound into a Web page.

Your operating system should have some sound files available for you to use. You want to search for a directory called media or sounds or multimedia. If you'd prefer to download sounds from the Internet, try http://www.comedy-central.com/download/southpark/sp_episode101.shtml to download sounds from South Park. Or, if you prefer the comedy of a more innocent time, try sounds from the Mary Tyler Moore show at http://www.nick-at-nite.com/tvretro/shows_nan/marytyler/ pics_index.tin.

To insert a Plugin object

1. Position the insertion point in the Dreamweaver document window where you would like the sound control to appear when the page is viewed in the browser.

2. Select the Plugin object from the Special panel of the Object panel. The Select File dialog box will appear. Navigate to a directory that contains a sound file and select a file as shown in Figure 7.1. Click the Select button after you've selected a file.

FIGURE 7.1

Select a sound file, in this case a WAV, in the Select File dialog.

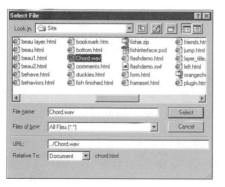

3. Save your changes and then preview your Web page in a browser to see what it looks and sounds like.

Notice the Property inspector for the Plugin object has some properties that are similar to ones you have seen while working with images (see Figure 7.2). Selecting a file fills in the Src box. There is an Align drop-down menu, similar to the one for images, which affects how other objects align with the Plugin object. Other familiar properties are W (width), H (height), V align (vertical), and H align (horizontal). You can also add a border to the Plugin object. Plg URL and the Parameters button are two additional properties that we will discuss later in this hour.

7

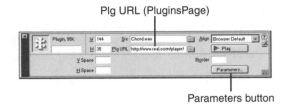

Plg URL (PluginsPage)

Parameters button

FIGURE 7.2
Some plugin properties are similar to image properties and some are not. Two additional properties appear when you insert a plugin in your page: parameters and Plg URL (PluginsPage).

It's a good idea to give your user control over whether a sound plays or not. Many plugins enable you to include controls when you embed a plugin object in a Web page. A Web page containing a sound that cannot be turned off can be an extreme annoyance.

When delivering multimedia, much depends on which browser and plugins the user has. Some plugins and some sound file formats are more popular than others are. The popularity of file formats is constantly evolving. As of this writing, the RealMedia and MP3 sound formats are popular and quite common on the Web. MIDI files are common, too. Table 7.1 lists some of the most popular sound file formats.

The last audio application that you installed on your computer probably set itself as the default application to play audio files. You may have different applications than what is depicted in this chapter.

TABLE 7.1 Common Web Sound Formats

Sound Format	Streaming?	Description
AIFF	No	A popular Macintosh sound format. Not ideal for longer sounds because of its large file size.
WAV	No	A popular Windows sound format. Not ideal for longer sounds because of its large file size.
u-Law (.au)	No	Originally, a popular Web sound format from Sun, but not as common now.

TABLE 7.1   continued

Sound Format	Streaming?	Description
QuickTime	Yes	Apple's movie format can also play sounds. File sizes can be large.
MIDI	No	Open standard sound format that uses defined MIDI sounds on the user's computer. Files are very compact.
RealMedia	Yes	Real-time streaming audio and video format.
Shockwave Audio	Yes	Real-time streaming audio format.
MP3 (MPEG 3)	Yes	Compact file size with excellent sound quality. This open standard sound format has become very popular.
Liquid Audio	Yes	Small file sizes with excellent sound quality.
Beatnik	No	Sound format combining MIDI and digital audio.

Resize the Control

The default size of the plugin object is 32×32 pixels. That's pretty small, but you can resize a plugin object by dragging one of the resize handles. You can also enter a width and a height in the Property inspector with the plugin object selected.

Predicting an appropriate size for a plugin can get tricky. If you have embedded a WAV file into your Web page, some viewers may use Netscape's default LiveAudio Java applet to play the sound. Others may have the QuickTime plugin registered to play WAVs in a Web page. Others may use the Windows Media Player.

Increasing the width and height attributes of a plugin can cause more controls to be visible. In Figure 7.3, giving the plugin a width of 144 pixels and a height of 35 pixels displays a portion of Netscape's LiveAudio plugin. In Figure 7.4 the plugin has a width of 144 pixels but a height of 60 pixels, making LiveAudio's volume control visible too.

FIGURE 7.3

Netscape's LiveAudio plugin with a width of 144 pixels and a height of 35 pixels displays only the portion of the plugin that contains the button controls.

7

FIGURE 7.4

Netscape's LiveAudio plugin with a height of 60 pixels displays the volume controls in addition to the button controls.

Figure 7.5 shows how the plugin object displays in Internet Explorer. Depending on what plugin or ActiveX control the browser has registered to play WAV files, yours may or may not look the same. This browser shows the Windows Media Player embedded in the page and controlling the sound.

Windows Media
Player plugin

FIGURE 7.5

Internet Explorer uses the Windows Media Player to play a sound.

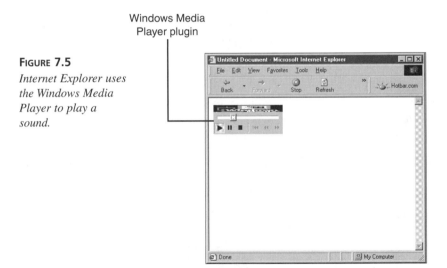

So far we have used an *inline* or *embedded* plugin, meaning the plugin controller appears within the flow of our Web page. When you add a hyperlink to a sound file, the user will launch the plugin controller in a separate window when they select the link. Figure 7.6 shows Netscape's LiveAudio controller in a separate window. Figure 7.7 shows Internet Explorer the Windows Media Player launching in a separate window to play the WAV file.

FIGURE 7.6

The Netscape LiveAudio controller plays a sound in a separate, small window.

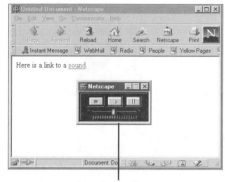

Live Audio Player

FIGURE 7.7

The Windows Media Player launches in a separate window to play a WAV file.

Add Looping to the Sound

Dreamweaver offers the flexibility to deal with advanced attributes of objects, and even attributes that haven't been created yet, through the Parameters dialog box. Selecting the Parameters buttons opens the Parameters dialog box as shown in Figure 7.8. Parameters consist of two parts: a parameter name and a value.

7

FIGURE **7.8**

The Parameter button in the Property inspector opens the Parameters dialog box, enabling you to enter additional parameters.

Table 7.2 lists some common sound parameters. Many plugins have optional or required parameters that you can set in the Parameters dialog box. The parameters available for sounds, such as `loop` and `autostart`, may or may not be available for other formats. Different plugins have different parameters available.

TABLE 7.2   Common Sound Parameters

Parameter	Values
loop	TRUE, FALSE, N (number of times playing)
autostart	TRUE, FALSE
hidden	TRUE, FALSE
volume	0–100
playcount	N (number of times playing-IE only)

After selecting the Parameters button, click the + button to add a parameter.

- To make the sound loop, type **loop** as the parameter name. Tab or click in the value column and type **TRUE**. The default is false so if you only want the sound to play once you do not need to enter the `loop` parameter. Netscape will recognize a number as the value of the `loop` parameter and will play the sound that many times.

- To create the same effect with Internet Explorer, add the `playcount` parameter in addition to `loop`.

You can enter multiple parameters in the Parameters dialog box. Figure 7.9 shows the Parameters dialog box with parameters entered. After you have finished adding parameters, click the OK button. To edit a parameter, select the Parameter button again and click in the parameter you want to change. To delete a parameter, click the – button. Use the arrow keys to rearrange the order of the parameters.

FIGURE 7.9
The Parameters dialog box can contain many parameters affecting the functionality of a plugin.

Allow for Plugin Download

If the viewer doesn't have the plugin to play your sound, it's good form to tell them where to get the plugin. You can, of course, place information in your Web page including a link to download the plugin.

You can enable the browser to automatically attempt a plugin download using the `pluginspace` attribute. To add the `pluginspace` attribute, enter the URL where the user can download the appropriate plugin in the Plg URL box in the Property Inspector. The RealMedia player is capable of playing most sound formats, including WAVs. Enter the URL to the RealPlayer download page, `www.real.com/player/index.html`, into the Plg URL box.

Learn About the Two Types of Plugins

Netscape Navigator and Internet Explorer deal with multimedia files in two different, but somewhat similar, ways. Netscape extends its capabilities with plugins. Netscape has a plugins folder where these programs are stored. You need to restart Netscape after installing a plugin for the plugin to be available.

Microsoft uses its ActiveX standard to launch and run multimedia content. *ActiveX controls* are similar to plugins and are installed on your machine to add the ability to play different file types. ActiveX controls work with Internet Explorer. Many third party browser extensions come as both a plugin and an ActiveX control. An ActiveX control usually installs itself in the background not requiring you to restart your browser.

Some users have either disabled their computer's capability to install ActiveX controls in their browsers, or are confused and possibly suspicious when a dialog box appears telling them they will be downloading and installing something. Make sure you tell users what to expect if you include content that requires them to download and install something on their computers.

7

Installing plugins and ActiveX controls registers the appropriate MIME type in the browser. MIME (Multipurpose Internet Mail Extensions) types enable your browser to recognize a extension. Your browser can then launch the correct plugin to play the file.

Add Flash Files

Macromedia Flash and Director have arguably become the standards for Web animation. Director, originally created for CD-ROM based interactive programs, has a streamed Web player called Shockwave. Flash is a more recent arrival, becoming extremely popular for creating small, interactive Web-based animation. The interactive functionality of Flash is limited when compared to Director, but Flash is popular because of its vector-based graphics—a graphical format that is small and scalable.

Another streamed interactive authoring tool available from Macromedia is the Authorware Web Player. Authorware is used to make highly interactive training applications. The Authorware Web Player object is not installed with Dreamweaver, but you can download the object from the Macromedia Web site.

You can get more information on the Authorware Web Player object on the Macromedia Web site at `www.macromedia.com/support/dreamweaverattain/how/experts/AWObject/AWObject.html`

You insert a Shockwave or Flash file just as you inserted the sound file. Select the Flash object to insert a Flash movie or the Shockwave object to insert a Shockwave movie. Figure 7.10 shows the Property inspector with a Flash movie selected.

You will find a sample Flash movie in the tutorial directory in Dreamweaver that you can use to experiment with in this hour. You can find some Shockwave movies to work with in the help\html\movies directory under Dreamweaver. Flash movies end with the .swf, .fla, or .swt file extensions. Shockwave movies end with a .dcr file extension. As previously discussed, you will need to have the Flash and Shockwave plugin installed to view these movies.

FIGURE **7.10**
FIGURE 7.10
The Property inspector shows the properties that you can set for a Flash movie. Some are standard properties while others are specific to Flash movies.

Unlike the sound that we embedded earlier in this hour, the Flash movie has a check box in the Property inspector for both the loop and the Autoplay parameters. Notice, however, that you still have the Parameters button in case you need to add an attribute to the movie that isn't shown in the Property inspector.

Use the `<object>` and `<embed>` Tags

When you inserted a sound earlier this hour, you used the Plugin object. The Plugin object inserts an `<embed>` tag, the standard Netscape plugin tag, into the HTML.

Dreamweaver automatically inserts both tags into your Web page. Using both tags enables the browser to handle the file in the optimum way. Netscape recognizes the `<embed>` tag and calls the Flash or Shockwave plugins. Internet Explorer recognizes the `<object>` tag and calls the Flash or Shockwave ActiveX controls. If Internet Explorer does not have the appropriate ActiveX control installed, it will alternately call the appropriate plugin.

Preview the Movie in the Dreamweaver Document Window

If you have the appropriate plugin installed on your machine, you can play the Flash movie in the Dreamweaver document window. When you install Dreamweaver, it automatically searches for plugins that you have installed in the plugins folders of the browsers you have installed on your computer. Dreamweaver can use plugins that are installed in your browser. If you do not have the plugins installed in your browser, you can also install plug-ins directly into the Dreamweaver plugins folder located in Configuration/Plugins.

To preview the Flash movie in the document window, select the green Play button in the Property inspector. While the movie is playing, the Play button turns into a red Stop button as shown in Figure 7.11. In fact, the Flash movie shown in Figure 7.11 is about Flash and shows the Flash user interface. Select the Stop button to stop the movie. You can also control plugin content by selecting the play and stop commands under the Plugins command in the View menu.

7

Stop button

FIGURE 7.11

*You can view a Flash
or Shockwave movie,
and other plugin-based
content, directly in the
document window.*

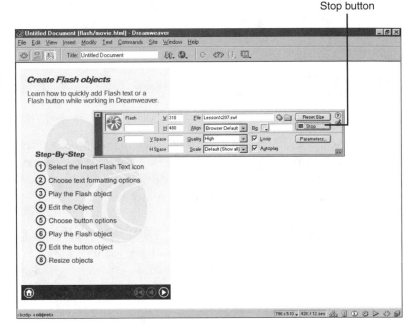

Create Flash Text

Dreamweaver 4 has added the capability to create Flash objects directly in Dreamweaver.
You do not need to have Flash installed on your computer to have this functionality. You
can now create Flash Text and Flash buttons right in Dreamweaver.

The Flash Text object enables you to create and insert a Flash movie consisting of text
into your Web page. Inserting Flash text has advantages over using simple HTML text:

- Flash text can be anti-aliased. Anti-aliasing blends text with the background so that
  the edges of the letters look smoother.

- You can use any font available on your computer. The viewer does not need to
  have the font installed on their computer.

- The text can be larger than HTML text.

To insert a Flash Text object into your Web page

1. First, save your Web page. Select the Flash Text object from the Object panel or
   the Interactive Images submenu of the Insert menu.

2. The Insert Flash Text dialog box appears (shown in Figure 7.12). Select the Font,
   Size, Style (Bold or Italic), and alignment. Select the Color, which is the initial
   color of the text, and Rollover Color, which is the color the user will see when
   they place their cursor over the text.

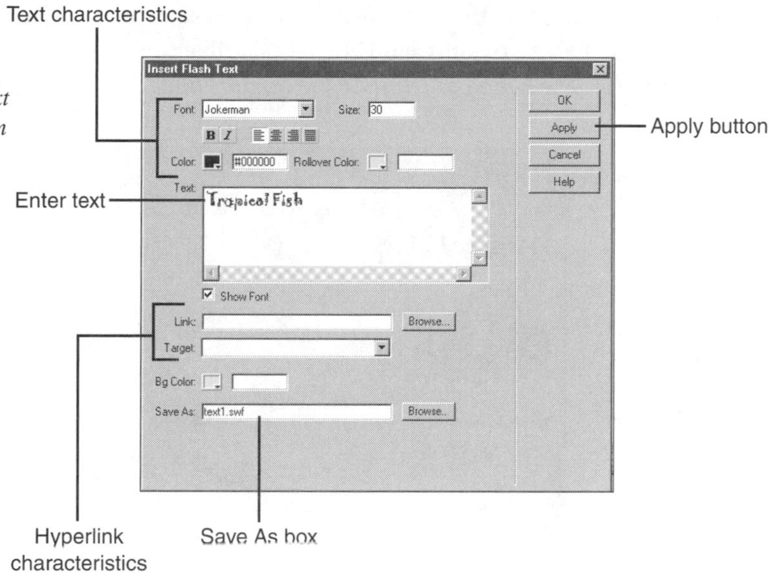

Text characteristics

FIGURE 7.12

Set up the Flash Text object with a custom font, rollover color, and hyperlink.

Enter text

Hyperlink characteristics

Save As box

Apply button

3. Type the text you want to appear in the Text box. Make sure the Show Font check box is selected beneath the box so you can see what the font you have selected looks like.

4. Enter a URL in the Link text box, or use the Browse button to browse to a Web page. It's a good idea to only link to local Web pages in the same directory where you save your Flash text movie. Document relative links do not work in some browsers if the files are not in the same directory.

5. Using the Target text box, you can target a window for the link just as you did in Hour 5, "Displaying Images on a Page and Creating an Image Map," when you launched a new blank window with the linked page. This capability will be used when you learn more about frames in Hour 12, "Understanding and Building Frames and Framesets."

6. Select a background color from the Bg Color drop-down list.

7. Dreamweaver creates a separate Flash movie for your Flash text. Enter a name for the Flash movie in the Save As box.

8. Click OK. You'll see the text appear in the Dreamweaver document window.

You can edit your Flash text movie after you have inserted it into a Web page by selecting the Edit button (shown in Figure 7.13) in the Properties inspector when the movie is selected in the document window. You can view the changes you make in the Insert Flash Text dialog box without closing the dialog box by selecting the Apply button.

7

In the document window, the Flash Text can be resized by either dragging the resize handles or entering new W (width) and H (height) attributes into the Property inspector. Select the Reset Size button to return to the original dimensions of the movie.

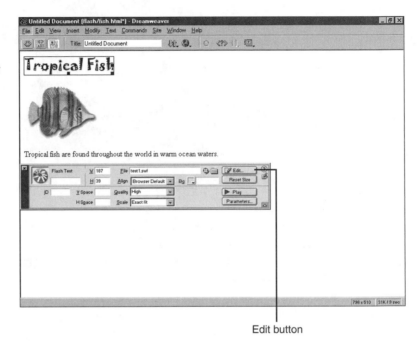

Edit button

Create a Flash Button

Dreamweaver comes with a number of templates (and you can download even more at the Macromedia Exchange; see Appendix B, "Internet Resources") for creating Flash buttons right in Dreamweaver. Like the Flash Text object you just created, Dreamweaver creates Flash button movies automatically. To insert a Flash button into your Web page

1. Save your Web page. Select the Insert Flash Button object from the Object panel or the Interactive Images submenu of the Insert menu.

2. The Insert Flash Button dialog box appears (shown in Figure 7.14).

3. Select a button style from the Style list. A preview of the button appears in the Sample window at the top of the dialog box. You can click on the preview to see what the down state of the button looks like and any animation effects that the button might have.

FIGURE 7.14

You select a Flash button and enter button text in the Insert Flash Button dialog box.

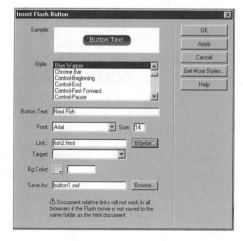

4. Add text to a button in the Button Text field. Only buttons that already have the default "Button Text" text in thc Sample window will display this text. You cannot add text to buttons that do not already display text.

You can create your own custom button templates in Flash to be used in Dreamweaver.

5. Set up font and font size for the button text in the Font and Font Size text boxes. You can choose from different fonts in the Font drop-down list.

6. Enter a URL for a hyperlink and a target, if necessary, in the Link and Target text boxes, respectively. As when you created Flash text, you need to be careful about document-relative addressing. It's best to save the Flash movie in the same directory as the linked Web page.

7. Add a background color from the Bg Color drop-down list. This color appears around the button, not within the button art.

8. Click OK. You'll see the button appear in the Dreamweaver document window.

You can edit the Flash button as you did the Flash text above. Both the button and the text movies are saved as Flash .swf files and can be edited in Flash. Some buttons can be used as groups. For instance, a number of e-commerce buttons are available to create a purchasing and checkout application.

7

Add a Link to a PDF File

The Adobe Acrobat Reader is a freely distributed plugin that has become the standard for viewing formatted text files over the Web. PDF (portable digital format) files enable a viewer to see a file exactly as it was meant to be seen—fonts, page layout, and graphics appear predictably. You create PDF files with an application called Adobe Acrobat Distiller and view them with the Acrobat Reader. An Acrobat Reader plugin is usually installed when the Reader application is installed.

To display a PDF file, you simply create a hyperlink with the URL to a PDF file. The file will open within the browser if the Acrobat plugin is present. If the plugin isn't installed but the Acrobat Reader is, the PDF file will open in the Acrobat Reader external to the browser. You can download the Acrobat Reader at
`www.adobe.com/products/acrobat/readstep2.html`.

Insert a Java Applet

Java is a programming language used to create self-contained programs called applets. Java applets run within the browser window just like the other multimedia objects you've been working with in this hour. You can put a Java applet into your page, add parameters, and add some interesting multimedia to your Web page.

> Java and JavaScript are not the same thing. Nor are they really related. JavaScript is a scripting language that is used in Web page development to set the properties of a Web page. Java is a compiled programming language that is used to develop applications.

To insert a Java applet into your Web page, you must have all of the appropriate files for the applet. The number and type of files may vary. You will need to read the documentation for the applet that you are using. The example here uses an applet downloaded from David Griffin's interesting (and free!) collection at `www.spigots.com`. David's "Snow Applet" simply requires the Java file that David has written, snow.class, and a Web image file to present an image that looks like snow is falling on it.

Some users may have Java turned off in their browser, so you should be careful about including information vital to the Web page in a Java applet.

Any Java applet that you intend on using in your Web page should come with instructions on how to set it up. Be sure to read the instructions carefully and enter all the parameters correctly, or the applet might not work. If you do not set up the applet correctly, users will simply see an empty gray box on the page.

To insert an applet into a Web page

1. Select the Applet object from the Special panel of the Object panel or from the Media submenu of the Insert menu. This opens the Select File dialog box.

2. Navigate to the directory containing the Java applet files in the Select File dialog box. Select the appropriate file stipulated in the applet documentation. For the Snow Applet, select the file snow.class. Dreamweaver fills in the Base property with the folder that the applet files reside in the Property inspector.

3. Enter all the parameters that are required by the applet documentation by first selecting the Parameters button to open the Parameters dialog box. The Snow Applet requires only one parameter: the address of the image file on which the snow will appear, as shown in Figure 7.15.

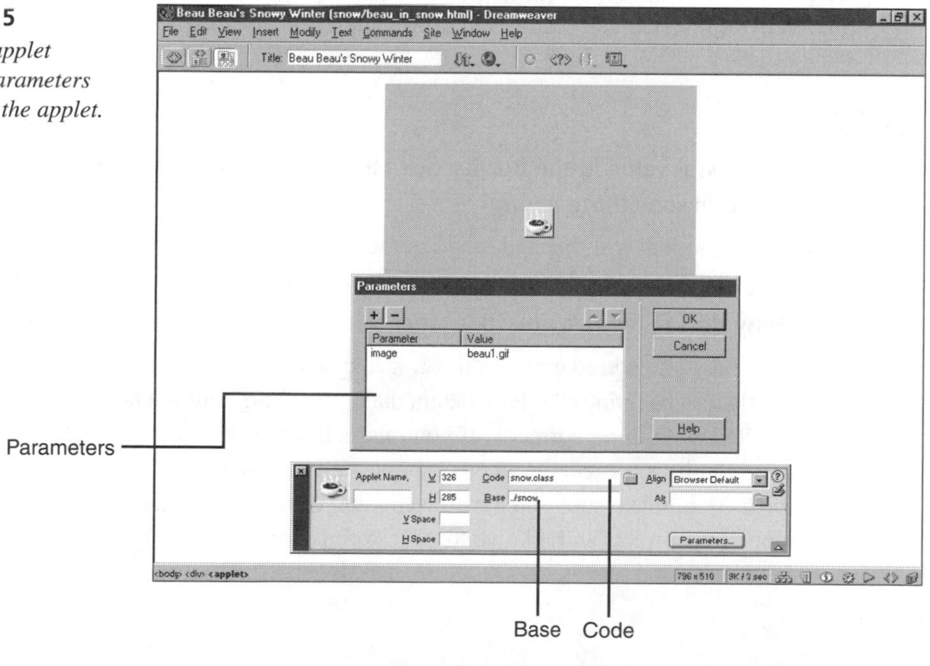

FIGURE 7.15
The Java applet requires parameters specific to the applet.

Parameters

Base   Code

7

4. Save your Web page and preview it in a Web browser to make sure that it looks the way you want it. The Snow Applet, viewed in the browser, is shown in Figure 7.16.

FIGURE 7.16

The Snow Applet, available from www.spigots.com, *viewed in the browser.*

Summary

In this hour, you learned how to add multimedia files to your Web page, including Flash and Shockwave movies. You added a URL that the browser can redirect the viewer to if they do not have the appropriate plugin to view your files. You added parameters to multimedia files to change properties that weren't specifically shown in the Property inspector. And you inserted and configured a Java applet.

Q&A

Q I placed a value in the Border box but no border appeared around the plugin. Did I do something wrong?

A Some plugins will respond to the border attribute and some plugins won't. The plugin that you tried to put a border around was not capable of adding a border.

Q Why do I only see a gray box when I insert a Java applet into my page?

A You haven't entered a required parameter or you have entered a parameter incorrectly. Go back into the Parameters dialog box and double-check that you have spelled everything correctly. If you misspell something or reference a file incorrectly you won't receive an error message; your applet will just appear as a gray box. Also, make sure you have saved your Web page so that the path to the Java applet is correct (and relative to your Web page).

Workshop

The Workshop contains quiz questions and activities to help reinforce what you've learned in this hour. If you get stuck, the answer to the quiz can be found following the questions.

Quiz

1. Which tag contains information for a plugin and which tag contains information for an ActiveX control?

2. True or False: Java and JavaScript are the same things.

3. What are the two components of a parameter?

Answers

1. The `<embed>` tag contains the information for a plugin and the `<object>` tag contains the information for an ActiveX control. Dreamweaver will configure both tags with the appropriate information automatically for Flash and Shockwave files.

2. False. Java is a programming language and JavaScript is unrelated. JavaScript is the language that Dreamweaver uses for Behaviors that we will explore in Hour 13, "Inserting Scripted Functionality with Behaviors."

3. A parameter consists of the parameter name and a value.

Exercises

1. Insert a sound or movie file into a Web page. Create a hyperlink to the same file. Explore how the two are different.

2. Insert a hyperlink to a PDF file into a Web page. The Internal Revenue Service (`www.irs.gov/forms_pubs/forms.html`) is a popular site to find PDF files. Don't get me wrong—I'm not saying the IRS is popular, just the PDF files! You can copy the URL to a file by right-clicking the link in the browser, and then selecting the Copy Shortcut command in Internet Explorer or selecting the Save Link As command in Netscape. Paste the link into Dreamweaver's property inspector as a hyperlink.

7

PART III

Layout, Design, and Dynamic HTML

Hour

HOUR 8

Displaying Data with Tables

Tables not only provide the ability to logically present data in columns and rows, but they also enable Web page designers to control where objects appear on the page. This hour will introduce you to creating tables. In the next hour you'll explore controlling page layout with tables.

Tables can be a powerful tool to display data in an organized way. You use tables in HTML just like you would use tables in a word processing application. Tables consist of rows, columns, and cells. Dreamweaver presents many ways to format tables the way you would like them to appear to your viewer.

In this hour, you will learn

- How to create and format a table
- How to add and sort data in a table
- How to import data to and export data from a table

Create a Table for Data

Begin exploring tables by adding a table to your Web page that will hold some data. Examples of this type of table are a phone list of people in your company or class at school, an ocean tide table with times and tide levels, or a recipe with amounts and ingredients. This type of table usually has a border around the cells, although it doesn't have to. Generally, tables used for page layout purposes, explored in Hour 9, "Designing Your Page Layout Using Tables," have the table borders turned off.

Add a Table to a Web Page

To insert a table into your Web page, do the following:

1. Place the insertion point in your Web page where you want the table inserted. Make sure that you are in Standard view and not Layout view.

2. Select the Table icon in the Object panel, or choose the Table command from the Insert menu. The Insert Table dialog box appears, as shown in Figure 8.1.

FIGURE 8.1

The Insert Table dialog box allows you set the initial values of the table. You can always edit these values in the Property inspector later.

3. Accept the default values or enter your own values into Rows and Columns. You can also select the width of the table and the border size in this dialog box. We'll talk about all of these parameters later in the hour.

4. Click OK.

Tables are made up of table rows containing table cells. There is no HTML tag for a table column. In the rest of this hour and the next hour you will modify the attributes of the table, table rows, and table cells.

Select Table Elements

You can select an entire table in a couple of ways. Position the cursor near one of the outside edges of the table until it turns into the crossed arrows cursor shown in Figure 8.2. You can select the table by clicking with this cursor.

Crossed arrows cursor

FIGURE 8.2

The crossed arrows cursor appears after positioning the cursor near the edge of a table. Select the entire table by clicking with this cursor.

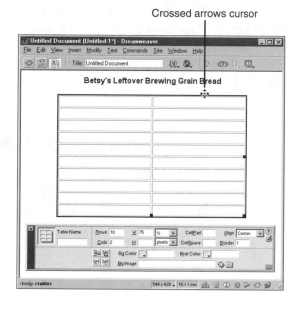

One of the easiest ways to select an entire table is to use the tag selector in Dreamweaver's status bar, as shown in Figure 8.3. Click inside one of the cells in your table. The status bar displays the tag hierarchy. Then simply click the table tag to select the entire table.

FIGURE 8.3

The tag selector makes it easy to select an entire table. Notice the tag hierarchy: the table (<table>) contains a row (<tr>) that contains a cell (<td>).

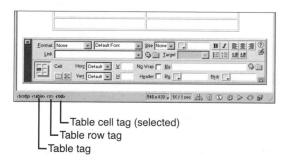

Table cell tag (selected)
Table row tag
Table tag

To select a cell, you can simply click inside of it. To select an entire row, position your cursor slightly to the left of the table row until the cursor turns into a solid black arrow, as shown in Figure 8.4. Click while the cursor is the solid black arrow to select the row. Do the same procedure to select an entire column except position your cursor slightly above the column.

Solid black arrow cursor

FIGURE 8.4

The cursor, positioned slightly to the left of a table row, turns into a solid black arrow. You select an entire row by clicking with this cursor.

When your table is empty it's easy to drag the cursor across the group of cells you want to select. Start dragging while your cursor is inside the first cell. When the cells are not empty, however, it's too easy to accidentally move objects from their cells with this procedure.

Another way to select a group of cells is to first select one cell and then Shift+click another cell. All the cells between the two cells will be selected. To select cells individually, Ctrl+click a cell to add it to the selection.

The Property inspector shows different attributes depending upon what you currently have selected. There are two basic ways that the Property inspector appears while working with tables:

• With the entire table selected, the Property inspector looks like Figure 8.5, displaying properties that affect the entire table.

Table properties

FIGURE 8.5

The Property inspector displays properties that apply to the entire table when the entire table is selected.

- With an individual cell, entire row, or entire column selected, the Property inspector looks like Figure 8.6, displaying properties that affect the selected cells.

FIGURE 8.6

The Property inspector displays properties of selected cells when an individual cell, entire row, or entire column is selected.

Add Header Cells to the Table

Contents of header cells appear bold and centered. To make a header row across the top of a table, select the first row in the table and check the check box beside Header in the Property inspector. Checking the Header check box turns the table cell tags, <td>, into table header cell tags, <th>.

I usually think of header cells as the top cells in table columns. But you can add header cells along the left edge of a table as headers for each row by applying the Header cell property to the first column of the table.

Add and Sort Data

To enter data, click in a table cell, type, and then Tab to the next cell. You can Shift+Tab to move backwards through the table cells. When you reach the rightmost cell in the bottom row, pressing Tab will create a new row. Continue to add data until you have enough data to make it interesting to sort.

> When you use Tab to create new table rows, Dreamweaver gives the new
> row the attributes of the previous row. This might be what you want. But if
> you Tab to create a new row from a header cell row, your row will be more
> header cells!

Dreamweaver makes it easy to sort the data in your table with the Sort Table command
under the Commands menu. To sort a table with the Sort Table command, do the following:

1. Select the table. Select the Sort Table command under the Commands menu. The
   Sort Table dialog box, shown in Figure 8.7, contains a number of drop-down
   menus to help you sort the table.

FIGURE 8.7

*The Sort Table dialog
box contains drop-
down menus with the
sorting options.*

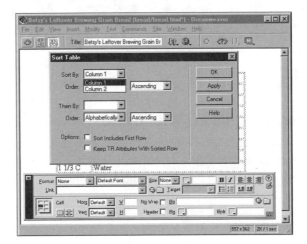

2. Select the column to sort in the Sort By drop-down menu.

3. Select whether you want to sort the column alphabetically or numerically in the
   Order drop-down menu.

4. Select whether you want to sort ascending or descending in the options directly to
   the right of the Order drop-down menu.

5. Below this first set of sorting options you can set up a second set of options.
   Dreamweaver will first sort by the primary column and will then sort on the
   secondary column.

6. If the first row of the table is a header row, leave the Sort Includes First Row box
   unchecked. If you don't have header cells, you want to include the first row in the
   sort. If you have header cells, you don't want to sort the first row.

7. The Keep TR Attributes With Sorted Row check box allows you to keep table row attributes with the row after the sort. If you have formatted your table in a certain way, you will want to check this box so your formatting isn't lost. The complete set of options is shown in Figure 8.8.

FIGURE 8.8

Sorting on column 2 alphabetically in ascending order and column 1 numerically in ascending order. The column 1 sort actually has no effect on this table.

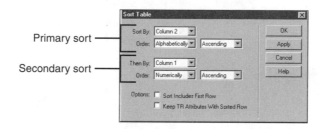

Primary sort

Secondary sort

8. Click OK to start the sort.

The resulting sorted table looks like Figure 8.9.

Sorted ingredients list

FIGURE 8.9

Data can be sorted alphabetically or numerically in either ascending or descending order by the Sort Table command.

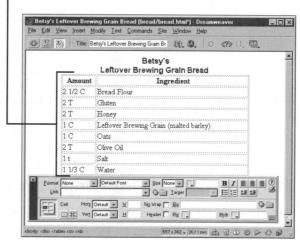

Add and Remove Rows and Columns

To add or remove a row or column, use the context menu that pops up when you right-click a table cell. Right-click a table cell and select the Table submenu; another menu appears with a number of commands to add and remove rows, columns, or both, as shown in Figure 8.10. Select one of these commands to make a change to the table.

FIGURE 8.10

The context menu has a Table submenu containing many commands to add, remove, or change the rows and columns of a table.

 When using the Insert commands, Dreamweaver inserts a new column to the left of the current column. It inserts a new row above the current row.

You can also add or remove rows and columns by editing Table Properties in the Property inspector. Adjust the number of rows and columns in the Property inspector with an entire table selected to add or remove groups of cells.

 When using the Property inspector, Dreamweaver inserts a new column to the far right of the table. It inserts a new row at the bottom of the table. If you remove columns or rows in the Property inspector, the columns will be removed from the right side and the rows will be removed from the bottom. You will lose any data that is in those columns or rows.

Change Column Width and Row Height

You can change column width and row height by dragging the cell borders or by entering values in the Property inspector. If you prefer to "eyeball" the size, position the cursor over a cell border until the cursor turns into the double-line cursor. Drag the double-line cursor to change the column width or row height.

Use the W (width) and H (height) boxes in the Property inspector to give exact values to widths and heights. Values are expressed in either pixel or percent values. Just like the horizontal rule we created earlier, a percent value will change your table size as the size of the browser window changes, while a pixel value will always display the table at a constant size.

Resize a Table and Change Border Colors

Just as you changed the size of cells, rows, and columns, you can change the size of the entire table. With the entire table selected, drag the resize handles to make the table a different size. If you have not given width and height values to cells, rows, and columns, the cells will distribute themselves proportionally when the entire table size is changed. Or, use the W and H boxes in the Property inspector, with the entire table selected, to give the table either pixel or percent size values.

To clear all of the width and height values from a table, select the Table submenu under the Modify menu. At the bottom of the menu are commands to clear the cell heights or clear the cell widths. Commands are also available to convert all the values to pixel values or to convert all the values to percent values. These commands are handy if you set table attributes to pixel values and want change them to percent values or vice versa. Buttons for these commands are available in the lower half of the Property inspector when the table is selected, as shown in Figure 8.11.

Clear buttons

FIGURE 8.11

The Property inspector with an entire table selected has buttons available to clear the row height and the column width. There are also buttons available to convert dimension values to pixels or percent.

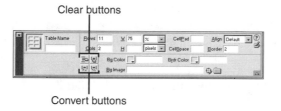

Convert buttons

Set Cell Padding and Cell Spacing

Cell padding sets the amount of space between an object contained in a cell and the border of the cell. *Cell spacing* sets the amount of space between two cells. Figure 8.12 illustrates these two values.

FIGURE 8.12

Cell padding is the amount of space around an object within a cell, while cell spacing is the amount of space between two cells.

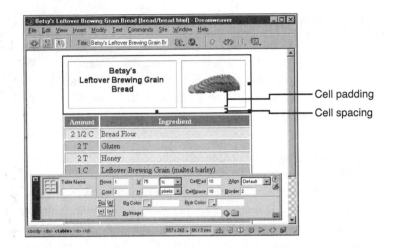

Use a Dreamweaver Pre-Set Table Format

Dreamweaver contains a number of pre-set table formats that you can apply to a table. The format affects the colors, alignment, and border size of the table. Instead of applying colors and alignment to each cell, row, or column, use the Format Table command to quickly format an entire table.

To apply one of the pre-set formats to a table, do the following:

1. Select the table.
2. Select the Format Table command from the Commands menu. The Format Table dialog box appears (see Figure 8.13).

FIGURE 8.13

The Format Table dialog box contains the commands to format all the cells, rows, and columns in a table.

8

3. Select a format from the scrolling menu in the upper-left corner of the dialog box. The little demonstration table in the dialog box shows a preview of the format appearance.

4. Click the Apply button to apply the format to your table. Change the format until you are satisfied, then click the OK button.

You can use the Format Table command even if you use a custom color scheme for your Web page. Select one of the formats available but enter custom hexadecimal numbers for specific colors into the boxes for the first and second row colors. You can also use a custom text color and add a background color for the header row.

The Options section at the bottom of the Format Table dialog box enables you to apply the formatting to table cells instead of table rows. Because there are usually more cells than rows, applying the formatting to all the cells results in more HTML code in your Web page. The HTML code applied to the cells, however, takes precedence over the code applied to rows.

Import Table Data

If you already have data in a spreadsheet or database, why retype it or paste it into Dreamweaver? You can import data exported from spreadsheet or database applications into Dreamweaver with the Import Tabular Data command. Most spreadsheets and database applications can export data into a text file so that Dreamweaver can import it.

You need to know what character is used in the data file as a *delimiter* before you can successfully import data into Dreamweaver. A delimiter is the character used between the individual data fields. Commonly used delimiters are tabs, spaces, commas, semicolons, or colons. When you are exporting your data file, you will need to pick a delimiter that does not appear in the data.

Microsoft Excel, a commonly used spreadsheet application, imports and exports files with the file extension .csv as comma-delimited and files with the file extension .prn as space-delimited.

Create your own data file to work with by opening a text editor, like NotePad, and enter some data. Create a single line of text with multiple fields separated by tabs. Create multiple records by repeating this process on subsequent lines in the text file. Save your file and import it into Dreamweaver as a tab-delimited data file.

To import table data to Dreamweaver, do the following:

1. Place the insertion point into the document window where you want the table located.

2. Select the Tabular Data object from the Object panels, the Import Tabular Data command under the Import submenu in the File menu, or the Tabular Data command under the Insert menu. The Insert Tabular Data dialog box appears, as shown in Figure 8.14.

FIGURE 8.14

Open the Insert Tabular Data dialog box from the File or Insert menus. Or, select the Tabular Data object in the Object panel.

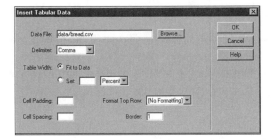

3. Select the Browse icon (folder) to browse to the table data file to import it into Dreamweaver.

4. Select the field delimiter from the Delimiter drop-down menu. If the delimiter isn't one of the four common delimiters listed, select Other and enter the delimiter in the box that appears to the right of the Delimiter drop-down menu.

5. Select whether the new table should fit to the data or be a certain pixel or percent value in the boxes beside Table Width.

6. Enter a value for cell padding and cell spacing, if necessary. Remember, you can always change these values by editing the table later.

7. Select a value from the drop-down menu for the format of the first (header) row. You'll need to know whether the data in the data file has column headings that will appear as header cells in your HTML table.

8. Enter a value for the table border size.

9. Click OK to import the table data.

Export Data from a Table

You can also export table data from an HTML table. The data can then be imported into a spreadsheet, database, or other application that has the capability to process delimited data.

To export table data from Dreamweaver, do the following:

1. Select a table or place your cursor in any cell of the table.
2. Select the Export submenu under the File menu, and then select the Export Table command. The Export Table dialog box appears, as shown in Figure 8.15.

FIGURE 8.15

Open the Export Table dialog box from the File menu, Export submenu. You can export delimited data that can be imported by other applications.

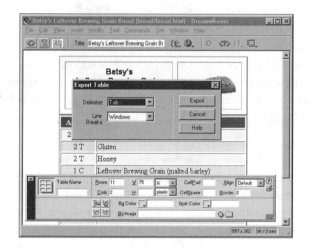

3. Select the data delimiter from the Delimiter drop-down menu.
4. Select the line break style from the Line Breaks drop-down menu. The line break style is dependent on the operating system, so select the operating system that will be running when the data file is imported. For example, if you are sending the data file to someone who will be running a spreadsheet on a Macintosh computer, select Macintosh.
5. Click the Export button and save the file.

Summary

In this hour, you learned how to add a table to a Web page. You also learned how to add or remove table cells and rows and how to set the column width and row height of a table. You entered data into a table and then sorted the data using the Sort Table command. You learned how to import data into a Dreamweaver table and how to export table data for an external application to use.

Q&A

Q **When I set a column width to a certain value, such as 50 pixels, why doesn't the column display at that value in the browser?**

A Have you set the width of the entire table to a value that is the sum of all the column values? If not, the table may be stretching the columns to make up for the extra width that the table has in its width property.

Some browsers will not make an empty table cell a given width. Web developers came up with the trick of stretching a one-pixel GIF to the desired width to force a table cell to be the correct width. If you use a transparent one-by-one pixel GIF, it will take up hardly any download time and will not be seen by the viewers.

Q **Are pixel values or percent values better to use with tables?**

A It depends. If you want your table to always appear the same size, use pixel values. However, if the browser window width is smaller than the width of the table, the viewer will have to scroll horizontally to view the entire table. Horizontal scrolling is not desirable. If you use percent values in your table, it's much harder to predict what the final table is going to look like in the viewer's browser. If you use tables with pixel values, you may need to mandate a certain screen resolution to view the table. Be aware that some people on the Web disapprove of this type of mandate.

Workshop

The Workshop contains quiz questions and activities to help reinforce what you've learned in this hour.

Quiz

1. What are the HTML tags, as displayed in the Dreamweaver tag selector, for a table, a table row, and a table cell? Extra credit: What's the tag for a table header?

2. What two ways can you sort a table automatically in Dreamweaver?

3. What's the name of the character that separates cell data held in a text file?

Answers

1. The tag for a table is `<table>`, the tag for a table row is `<tr>`, and the tag for a table cell is `<td>`. The tag for a table header is `<th>`.

2. There are two answers for this question. One answer would be sorting alphabetically or numerically. Another answer would be sorting by ascending or descending order.

3. A delimiter.

Exercises

1. Create a table with text in column one and numbers in column two. Try both ascending and descending sorts on both the alphabetic (text) data in column one and the numeric data in column two.

2. Create a table in Dreamweaver, enter some data, and export the table data using the Table Export command. Remember where you saved the file and then open it up with a text editor, such as Notepad. What does the file look like?

8

HOUR 9

Designing Your Page Layout Using Tables

In the last hour, we explored some of the properties of tables and table cells. You used tables in Web pages in the same way you might use tables in a spreadsheet or a word processing application—to present data in an organized way. In this hour, you will apply more properties and new commands, using tables to aid with Web page layout.

Page layout refers to designing the way the page will look when viewed in the browser. You position text, menus, and other page elements in an efficient and attractive way.

Tables give Web developers the ability to make page elements appear in a specific place on the screen. Dreamweaver enables you to work in Layout view so that you can draw table elements directly onto the document window. This makes it easy to create tables for page layout.

In this chapter, you will learn

- How to use Dreamweaver's Layout view
- How to merge and split table cells
- How to align the contents of table cells
- How to nest a table within a table cell
- How to turn a table into a group of layers

Use Layout View

Traditionally designing tables for page layout has been a complicated task. Making changes or creating the perfect number of cells required the Web developer to merge, split, and span various rows and columns to get the page to look the way they wanted it to. Dreamweaver 4 includes a Layout view, enabling you to easily draw, move, and edit table cells.

To turn on Layout view, select the Layout View button on the Object panel, shown in Figure 9.1. When you turn on Layout view, the two layout buttons on the Object panel become active. One of these buttons draws a layout table while the other button draws an individual layout cell.

FIGURE 9.1

Turn on Layout view in the Object panel. You can go back and forth between the Layout and Standard views.

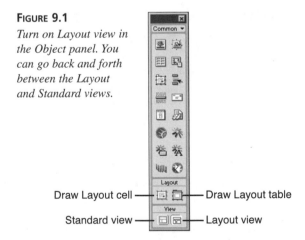

Draw Layout cell ——— ——— Draw Layout table
Standard view ——— ——— Layout view

Add a Layout Table and Layout Cells

Dreamweaver's Layout view enables you to draw your design in table cells directly onto the document window. Create areas for content, menus, and other elements of a Web page by selecting the Draw Layout Cell command and drawing cells for each page element.

Design for a specific screen resolution by first selecting a resolution from the Window Size drop-down menu in Dreamweaver status bar.

To create a page layout

1. Select the Layout Mode button in the Object panel.
2. Select the Draw Layout Cell button in the Object panel.
3. Draw cells in the document window for page elements, as shown in Figure 9.2. A layout table is automatically created to hold the layout cells.

Layout table

FIGURE 9.2

In Layout mode, you can draw table cells in the document window. The cells are contained within a layout table.

Layout cells

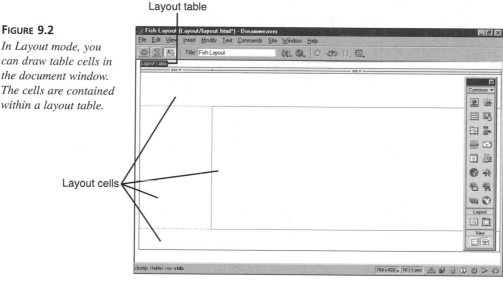

4. Move cells by selecting their edges, clicking, and then dragging them. The edges change from blue to red when you are near the area you can click to move the cells.
5. Resize cells by dragging the resize handles at the corners and sides of the cells.
6. Resize the table that contains the cells by dragging the resize handles at the corners and sides of the table.

To create multiple layout cells without having to click on the Draw Layout Cell button every time, hold down the Ctrl key.

Edit the properties of a layout cell by Ctrl-clicking on the cell to select it. The Property inspector, shown in Figure 9.3, presents the width, height, background color, horizontal and vertical alignment, and wrapping properties. These properties are exactly the same table cell properties that you learned about last hour. There's one additional property, Autostretch, which is unique to layout tables.

FIGURE 9.3

In Layout mode, the Property inspector displays layout cell properties.

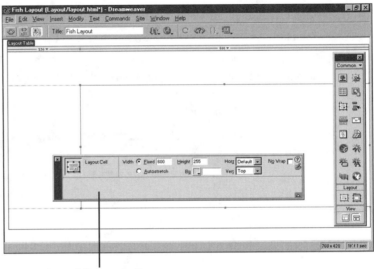

Layout Cell properties

Stretch Your Content to Fit the Page

Autostretch enables a column to stretch to fill all of the available space in the browser window. No matter what size the browser window is, the table will span the entire window. When you turn on Autostretch for a specific cell, all of the cells in that column will be stretched. This setting is particularly useful for cells that contain the main content of the page. The menus can stay the same width, but the content can stretch to take up all of the available space.

Dreamweaver will automatically add spacer images to your table cells to make sure that they remain the size that you intend in all browsers. The spacer image trick is an old trick used by Web developers to ensure that table cells don't collapse. A transparent one pixel GIF is stretched to a specific width. This image is not visible in the browser.

To turn on Autostretch

1. Select a cell by Ctrl-clicking it.
2. Select the Autostretch radio button in the Property inspector.
3. The Choose Spacer Image dialog box appears, as shown in Figure 9.4. You have three choices:

    - Create a spacer image file: Dreamweaver creates an invisible one pixel GIF image, adds it to the top cell of each column, and stretches it to the column width. When you select this option, Dreamweaver asks you where you'd like to store the spacer.gif image that Dreamweaver creates.

    - Use an existing spacer image file: If you've already created a spacer image, select this option. Dreamweaver asks you to navigate to where the image is stored.

    - Don't use spacer images for Autostretch tables: If you select this option, Dreamweaver warns you that your cells may collapse and not maintain the widths that you have set.

FIGURE 9.4

The Choose Spacer Image dialog box enables you to choose what spacer you use when you turn on Autostretch.

You can also apply the Autostretch command for an entire column by selecting the drop-down menu in the column heading, shown in Figure 9.5. Each column heading displays the width of the column in pixels. You can also simply add a spacer image to the column by selecting the Add Spacer Image command. When a column has a spacer image added, the line at the top of the column appears thicker.

You can set a spacer image for a site in Dreamweaver preferences. After you have set a spacer image for the site, Dreamweaver no longer prompts you to create or choose a spacer image; the image is simply added. Create or select a spacer image for an entire site by opening the Layout View category of Dreamweaver preferences, as shown in Figure 9.6. Note that you can also change the colors of how layout objects appear in Dreamweaver and whether or not spacer images are automatically inserted in this preferences category.

Figure 9.5

Use the drop-down menu at the top of a layout table column to turn on Autostretch for a table column.

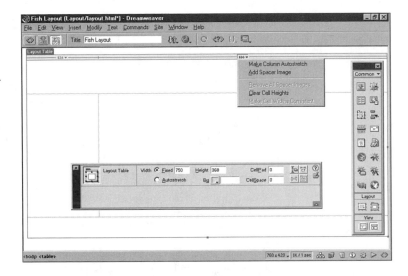

Figure 9.6

Set a spacer image for an entire site in the Layout Mode category of Dreamweaver preferences.

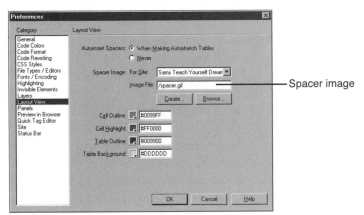

Spacer image

Edit a Table in Standard View

After you've designed your layout in Layout mode, return to Standard mode to add content. You can edit your layout table in Standard mode by changing the attributes of the table and its cells. You will also need to set the alignment of the contents of the cells.

Merge and Split Table Cells

You may want some rows or columns in your table to have fewer cells than other rows. For example, you may want the top row of a table to have a title that is centered over all the columns. How do you accomplish that?

You can increase or decrease the column span and row span by either splitting or merging cells. To merge an entire row so that it appears as one cell, select the row and click the Merge button, as shown in Figure 9.7. Now the content of the entire row can be positioned over all the columns. You can also right-click anywhere on the row and select the Merge Cells command from the Table submenu of the context menu.

FIGURE 9.7

The Merge button appears in the Property inspector when an entire row is selected. This button causes all of the selected cells to appear as one cell.

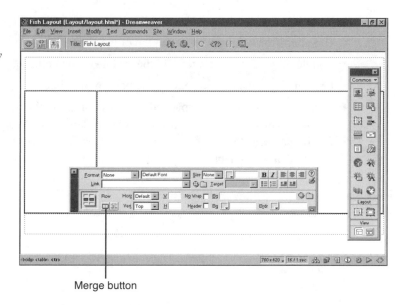

Merge button

Use the Split Cell command to add additional rows or columns to a cell. The Split button is located beside the Merge button in the Property inspector. Select the Split button and the Split Cell dialog box appears, as shown in Figure 9.8. Enter the number of rows or columns you would like the cell to be split into and click OK. Now a single cell is split into multiple cells. You can also right-click in the cell and select the Split Cell command from the Table submenu of the context menu.

FIGURE 9.8

The Split Cell dialog box enables you to split a single cell into multiple columns or rows.

Align Table Cell Contents

The vertical alignment drop-down menu (see Figure 9.9) sets the alignment for the contents of an individual cell or a group of cells. Align the contents of a cell or a group of cells vertically—from top to bottom. When setting the vertical alignment, you have the following options:

- Default is usually the same as middle alignment of the cell contents.
- Top aligns the cell contents at the top of the cell.
- Middle aligns the cell contents in the middle of the cell.
- Bottom aligns the cell contents at the bottom of the cell.
- Baseline is applied to multiple cells in a row, aligning the bottom of the objects across all cells. For instance, if you have very large text in the first cell and small text in the second cell, the bottom of both lines of text will be aligned with baseline vertical alignment.

FIGURE 9.9

The vertical alignment drop-down menu aligns cell contents vertically from the top and the bottom of the cell.

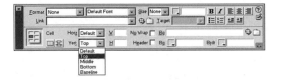

Align the contents of a cell or a group of cells horizontally—from left to right—with the Horizontal Alignment drop-down menu shown in Figure 9.10. When setting the horizontal alignment, you have the following options:

- Default usually is the same as left for cell content and center for header cell content.
- Left aligns the cell contents on the left of the cell.
- Center aligns the cell contents in the center of the cell.
- Right aligns the cell contents on the right of the cell.

FIGURE 9.10

The Horizontal Alignment drop-down menu aligns cell contents horizontally from the left and the right sides of the cell.

Nest a Table Within a Table

Placing a table within a table cell creates a *nested* table. To nest a table, place the insertion point inside a table cell and insert a new table. The dimensions of the table cell limit the nested table's width and height.

You can also nest an existing table within another table. Select the table and drag it to a table cell. Apply horizontal and vertical alignment to the table cell to align the nested table. Figure 9.11 shows a table nested within another table. Instead of splitting the single cell into six cells, a table with a single column and six rows is nested in the cell. Each cell contains a single graphic. Because the borders, cellspacing, and cellpadding are all set to 0, the contents of the cells appear to be one graphic. Also note that the bottom row was merged together to make everything line up properly.

9

FIGURE 9.11

You can nest a table within another table by either creating it within the parent table or dragging it into a table cell.

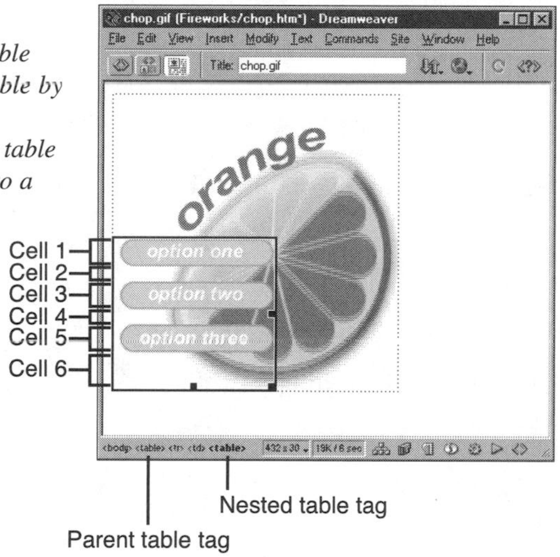

Cell 1
Cell 2
Cell 3
Cell 4
Cell 5
Cell 6

Nested table tag

Parent table tag

It's fine to nest tables within tables within tables. But if you nest too much, the browser may display the tables slowly. If the browser software has to labor to render your table, it may be better to format the information in a different way.

It may be easier to nest tables in Layout mode. Drawing a layout table using the Draw Layout Table tool enables you to draw a table over an existing cell, as shown in Figure 9.12. The nested table will snap to the size of the cell it is drawn over.

Nested table

FIGURE 9.12

A nested table in Layout mode snaps to the size of the cell that it's drawn over.

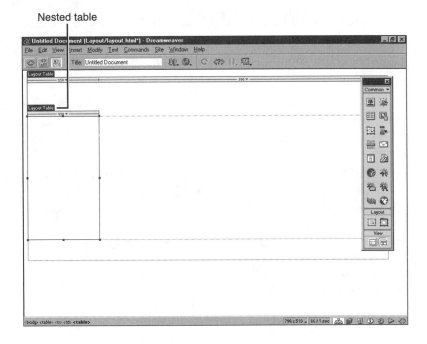

Add Color to Your Table

There are several places you can add color to your table:

- A background color for a table cell or group of cells
- A background color for the entire table
- A border color for a table cell or group of cells
- A border color for the entire table

Figure 9.13 shows where the different borders are located. Cell properties always have priority over the same properties in the table. For instance, if you applied a blue color as the table background color and then applied a red color to an individual cell, the one cell would be red while all the other cells would be blue. Set the table background and table border in the Property inspector. The Brdr Color sets the border color of the entire table.

You can add a background image to a table cell or an entire table. Enter the URL for a background image in the box labeled Bg in the Property inspector.

Table border

FIGURE 9.13

Adding colors in the Property inspector controls the table border and table background color attributes.

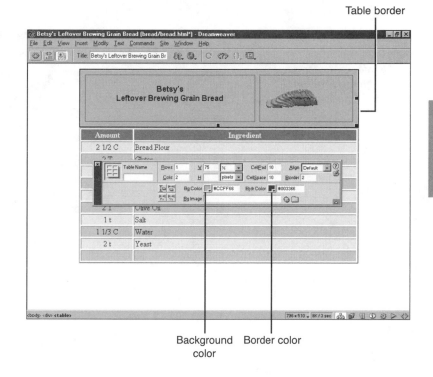

9

Background   Border color
color

 You need to enter a pixel value in the Border size property to see a border. If you are applying colors and don't see the border, you may have the border size set to zero.

Set the cell background and cell border colors in the Property inspector with a cell or group of cells selected, as shown in Figure 9.14.

 Did you notice the small representation of the table in the lower-left corner of the Property inspector? This little table shows what cells you have selected: a single cell, a row, or a column. The words *cell*, *row*, and *column* appear to the right of this little table. This little table can also be used like an Apply button; click it to apply the changes you make in the Property inspector.

Cell border

FIGURE 9.14

Set the background and border colors for a cell or group of cells in the Property inspector.

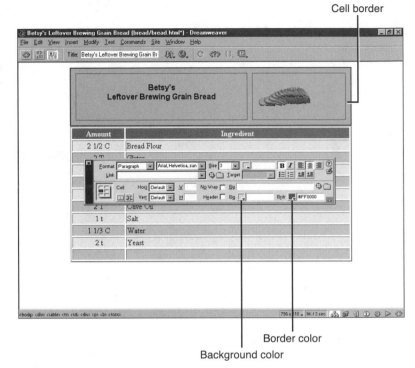

Border color

Background color

Turn Your Table into Layers

During Hour 10, "Using Dynamic HTML and Layers," you will use *layers* to position objects on a Web page. Layers allow absolute placement of objects on the page but require a recent browser version, such as Internet Explorer 4.0 or later or Netscape 4.0 or later. Dreamweaver converts a table into a group of layers. To convert a table into layers, do the following:

1. Select the table.
2. Select the Convert Tables to Layers command from the Convert submenu under the Modify menu. The keyboard shortcut for this command is Ctrl+F6. (Did you notice that there's also a command to convert layers to a table?)
3. The Convert Tables to Layers dialog box appears, as shown in Figure 9.15.
4. You'll explore the properties controlled by the check boxes in the Convert Tables to Layers dialog box in the next hour. For now, accept the defaults and click OK.

The Layer panel, shown in Figure 9.16, lists all of the layers that Dreamweaver created from the table.

FIGURE 9.15

The Convert Tables to Layers dialog box creates a layer for every table cell.

9

A layer   Layer Invisibles

FIGURE 9.16

The Layers panel lists the layers that were created from a table.

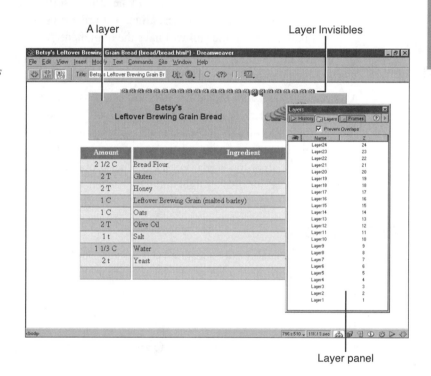

Layer panel

Summary

In this hour, you learned how to use Layout mode to draw cells and tables to create a page layout. You used the column and row spanning properties to merge and split individual cells and groups of cells. You also learned how to align the contents of cells both vertically and horizontally. You learned how to apply colors to an entire table, table cells, and table borders, and you learned how to convert a table into a group of layers.

Q&A

Q Why shouldn't I center objects in a table cell with the text alignment buttons?

A You can use the text alignment buttons to center an object. That command will add an additional tag around the selected object and then apply the center property. Everything in the table cell may not be centered however. Only the objects within the added tags will be centered. If later you add an object to the cell, it may or may not be centered, depending on exactly where the insertion point was when you inserted the new object. Using the alignment properties of a cell is the way to make certain all objects in the cell will have the alignment you want.

Q When I add a dark and light border color, the original color that I applied to the border doesn't show. What am I doing wrong?

A You can't have both the border property (the Brdr box in the Property inspector) and light and dark borders showing in Internet Explorer. Setting the border property applies a color to the entire table border. The light border property replaces a portion of that border, and the dark border replaces the rest of the border. You will want to set all of the border colors for dual-browser compatibility because Netscape doesn't display light and dark borders.

Workshop

The Workshop contains quiz questions and activities to help reinforce what you've learned in this hour. If you get stuck, the answers to the quiz can be found following the questions.

Quiz

1. If you apply a background color to an entire table and you apply a background color to a cell, which color shows up in the cell?

2. What's the easiest way to add a row at the bottom of a table?

3. How do you horizontally align all of the objects in a cell in the center?

Answers

1. The cell attributes take precedence here, so the color you applied to the cell will show up.

2. Put the insertion point in the last cell, the one in the lower right, and press the Tab key. Or, add to the number of rows in the Property inspector with your table selected. It's your choice.

3. Put the insertion point in the cell and select Center from the horizontal alignment drop-down menu in the Property inspector.

Exercises

1. Surf the Web looking for Web page layouts that have used tables. You may be surprised how many Web sites use tables heavily. If you are not sure whether a site uses tables or not, select the View Source command in your browser and look for table tags in the HTML code.

2. Insert a table and experiment merging and splitting cells. Insert a new, nested table into one of the cells.

9

HOUR **10**

Using Dynamic HTML and Layers

Dynamic HTML (DHTML) provides you flexibility to lay out your Web pages and make them interactive. Dreamweaver's layers provide a way to control where objects are placed on the page. You can place items precisely where you want without having to create elaborate tables. If you want to deliver your Web page to older browsers that cannot render Dynamic HTML elements, Dreamweaver can create a table with the format you've created with layers.

In this hour you will learn the following:

- What layers are, how they work, and how they are used
- How to add a layer and position it on the page
- How to set the stacking order, background color, and visibility of a layer
- How to convert layers to a table

What Is Dynamic HTML, or DHTML?

Dynamic HTML is an extension of HTML that enables greater control over page layout and positioning. DHTML also allows greater interactivity without depending on interaction with a server. When we talk about DHTML, we usually mean the combination of HTML 4—as defined by the W3C Web standards organization—and cascading style sheets (CSS). These elements work together through a scripting language, usually JavaScript.

> Internet Explorer and Netscape have defined DHTML differently through different DOMs (Document Object Models). For more information on the various flavors of DHTML, try Microsoft's site: `http://msdn.microsoft.com/workshop/author/default.asp`, Netscape's site: `http://developer.netscape.com/docs/manuals/communicator/dynhtml/`, and (for an "official" answer) the W3C site: `www.w3c.org/DOM/`.
>
> Despite the two browser DOMs, Dreamweaver generates HTML code that works with both browsers.

Dreamweaver uses the term *layer* to implement part of the CSS standards' defining layout. Layers are containers that enable you to position items on the screen wherever you want. Layers can also be animated in Dreamweaver; we'll use layers to create a timeline animation in Hour 15, "Animating with Timelines."

Add a Layer

You can create a layer in Dreamweaver in two different ways:

- The simplest is selecting the layer drawing tool from the Object panel and dragging the crosshair cursor on your page to approximately your desired layer size, as shown in Figure 10.1.
- Select the Layer command under the Insert menu to insert a layer with whatever width and height values are currently set in your layer preferences.

> If the Layer object is grayed out in the Object panel, you are currently in Layout view. Select the Standard View button at the bottom of the Object panel to have access to the Layer object.

FIGURE **10.1**

Selecting the Layer object from the Object panel enables you to draw a layer by dragging the crosshair cursor.

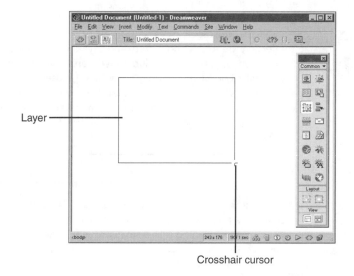

Layer

Crosshair cursor

The Layers category in Dreamweaver Preferences, as shown in Figure 10.2, is where you set the default layer values. You can set the default tag, visibility, width, height, background color, and background image. You can also enable nesting by checking the Nesting check box. Check the Netscape 4 Compatibility check box to have Dreamweaver automatically insert the Netscape Layer Fix whenever you insert a layer into a Web page. If you have a standard layer size that you use often, you might want to set that size as the default in Preferences.

FIGURE **10.2**

The Layers category in the Preferences dialog box is where you set the default values of layer attributes.

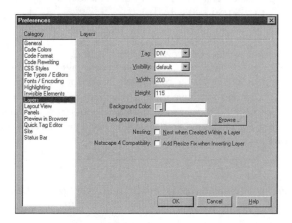

Insert the Netscape Layer Fix either by setting it in Layer preferences or by selecting the Add/Remove Netscape Layer Fix command in the Command menu, on any page that includes layers and will be viewed in Netscape. This fix resolves problems that happen when the user resizes a page that contains layers in Netscape. You can let Dreamweaver insert the fix automatically (in Preferences), or you can set it manually (from the Command menu) on a page-by-page basis. Dreamweaver inserts JavaScript into the page that solves the problem.

Don't insert the Netscape Layer Fix unless it is absolutely necessary. The fix causes the page to reload and might be distracting to Netscape users. Test your page by opening it in a small browser window and then maximize the window. Do your layers stay small? If so, then you need to apply the Netscape Layer Fix.

You'll notice the resize handles on each border of your layer. You can drag these handles to make your layer bigger or smaller. You can also set the width and height of the layer in the Property inspector. The W and H properties in the Property inspector are the width and height of the layer. The default measurement unit is pixels.

It's a good idea to get in the habit of naming your layers. Once you start adding behaviors or animating your layers, names will help you identify specific layers. You can specify a name in the Layer ID box in the Property inspector, as shown in Figure 10.3

Don't use spaces or punctuation in your layer names. If you later apply a behavior to the layer, sometimes JavaScript isn't happy with the spaces or punctuation you have used. If you want to name your layer with multiple words, you can use capitalization or underscores to make the name readable. For instance, `CestLaVieBakery` and `GreenGrocer` are possible layer names.

You can also name Dreamweaver layers in the Layers panel. Double-click on the name in the Layers panel Name column until it becomes editable, and then type in a new name as shown in Figure 10.4. Notice that when you select a layer in the Layers panel, the layer is selected in the document window also.

FIGURE 10.3

Change the layer name in the Layer ID box of the Property inspector. It's important to name layers with meaningful names.

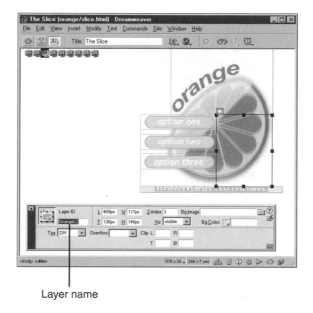

Layer name

FIGURE 10.4

You can edit the name of a layer in the Layers panel by double-clicking the name and changing it.

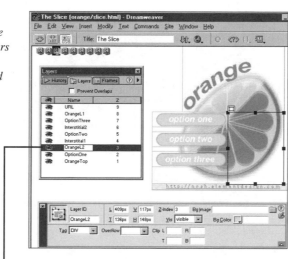

Editing name

Set Layer Positioning

Layers have a selection handle in the upper-left corner. You can reposition your layer by picking it up and moving it with this handle. To select multiple layers, hold down the Shift key while clicking on layers to add them to the selection.

Get in the habit of moving layers by picking up the selection handle. It's very easy to accidentally move items contained in the layer instead of the layer itself. If you get in the habit of using the handle, you won't make that mistake.

If you can't use the layer selection handle because the layer is at the very top of the document window, select it in the Layers panel and use the arrow keys to move the layer. Or, enter positioning values in the Property inspector.

You can also use the Layers panel to select one or many layers. The Layers panel, as shown in Figure 10.5, enables you not only to select layers, but also to see and set some layer characteristics. We'll talk about the two characteristics that you can set—the z-index and the visibility—in a few minutes. Notice you can select a check box at the top of the Layers panel to prevent layers from overlapping.

FIGURE 10.5

The Layers panel displays all of the layers in a Web page. The name, visibility, and z-index are easily accessible in this panel.

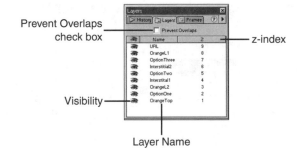

Why set the Prevent Overlaps check box? Because if you intend to eventually convert a layer design to a table so that it is viewable on all browsers, you cannot have overlapping layers. If you do not intend to do this, then you do not need to check Prevent Overlaps.

If you don't see layer properties in the Property inspector, it's because you don't have a layer selected. You might have accidentally selected the contents of the layer instead of the layer.

The Property inspector also enables you to set the exact positioning of a layer. The L and T properties stand for the left and top position of the layer. These positions are relative to the entire browser window. You can move a layer by dragging it (by its selection handle), or position it exactly by entering values in the L and T boxes, as shown in Figure 10.6.

FIGURE 10.6

Position a layer exactly by entering values in the L (left) and T (top) boxes of the Property inspector.

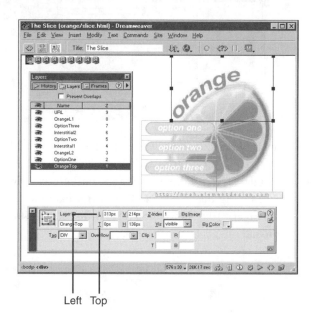

Left Top

Add a Background Color and Background Image

Layers can also have a background color, as shown in Figure 10.7. You can either use the color picker or type in a color in the standard HTML hexadecimal format proceeded by a #. Make sure you leave this option blank if you want your layer to be transparent.

FIGURE **10.7**

A layer can have a background color just like a table cell. Enter a background color in the Property inspector.

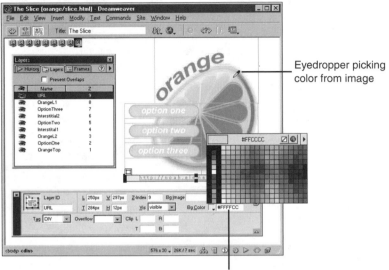

Eyedropper picking color from image

Layer background color

You can also place a background image in a layer. The image will repeat multiple times (called *tiling*) within the layer if the layer is larger than the image. Any objects or text that you put within the layer will be on top of the background image. Select the browse icon (folder) beside the Bg Image box in the Property inspector and navigate to the background image file. Figure 10.8 shows the Property inspector with a layer selected that contains a background image.

FIGURE **10.8**

A background image will tile within a layer if the image is smaller than the layer.

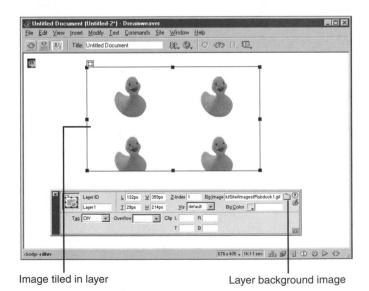

Image tiled in layer   Layer background image

Explore Layer Stacking Order

Not only can you position layers in exact places on the page, but you can also allow layers to overlap each other. So which layer is on top? The stacking order decides which layer is on top of other layers. The z-index value is what determines the stacking order. The z-index can be either a negative or a positive number.

The layer with the highest z-index is the one on the top. The term *z-index* comes from the coordinate system that you used back in algebra class—remember x and y coordinates? Well, the z-index is the third coordinate that is necessary to describe three-dimensional space. Imagine an arrow coming out of the paper or screen towards you and another going back into the screen or paper. That is the z-index.

Dreamweaver prefers to give each of your layers its own z-index value. In HTML, you legally can have multiple layers that have the same z-index. Remember, though: If you reorder the layers, Dreamweaver will renumber them with a unique z-index again.

You can set the z-index in the Z-Index box in the Property Inspector, as shown in Figure 10.9. The Layers panel also displays the z-index to the right of the layer name. The Layers panel displays the layers by z-index value, the top being the highest z-index and the bottom being the lowest. You can easily rearrange the stacking order by selecting the layer name in the Layers panel and then dragging and dropping it somewhere else.

10

FIGURE 10.9

The z-index value represents the stacking order of layers. You can set the z-index (as either a positive or negative value) in the Property inspector.

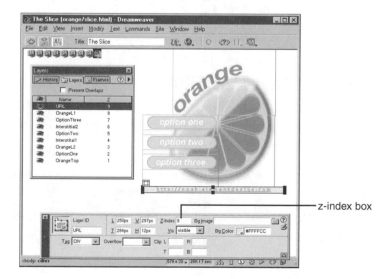

Align Your Layers and Use the Grid

The Dreamweaver Grid commands are found in the Grid submenu of the View menu. You can show the grid, snap to the grid, and adjust the grid settings. After you show the grid by selecting the Show Grid command, you'll see the grid lines in the design window. You can turn off the grid by deselecting this same command. You can also turn the grid on and off from the View Options menu in the Dreamweaver toolbar.

The grid is especially useful if you have elements in your site that must be lined up and are similar in size. You can require layers to snap to the grid by selecting the Snap To command. You can also configure the gap between the grid lines.

Open the Grid Settings dialog box, as shown in Figure 10.10, by selecting the Edit Grid command under the Grid submenu of the View menu. If you need the grid to have larger or smaller increments, you can adjust its value in the Spacing box. You can also change the snapping increment. The grid can be displayed with either solid lines or dots. The dots are nice because they are lighter and less invasive on your page design. You can also select a grid color with the color picker.

FIGURE 10.10

The grid settings enable you to change the appearance of the grid (the color and the line type) and set the snapping increment.

Change Layer Visibility

Layers have a visibility attribute that can be set to either visible, hidden, inherit or default. The Vis drop-down menu, as shown in Figure 10.11, is in the middle of the Property inspector when a layer is selected.

FIGURE 10.11

The Vis drop-down menu enables you to set the visibility attribute for a layer.

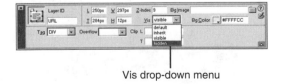

Vis drop-down menu

It's obvious why you might want layers to be visible, but why might you want them to be hidden? So you can display them later after something has happened, that's why! We'll discuss using the Show-Hide Layers behavior in Hour 13, "Inserting Scripted Functionality with Behaviors."

The Layers panel represents visibility with a picture of an eye. The eye beside a layer is open when the layer is set to visible. It's closed when the layer is hidden. The inherit setting does not have an eye representation. The eye is a toggle that moves through the default, visible, and hidden settings, and then goes back to default.

You can set the visibility characteristics of all of the layers by selecting the eye icon in the header of the Layers panel.

> Be careful when clicking on the eye-icon column setting for your top layer. It's easy to accidentally click on the header instead and set all of the eyes in the column.

10

The visibility settings are

- A layer set to visible will appear on the Web page upon loading.
- A layer set to hidden will not appear on the Web page. The layer can be made visible later by using the Show-Hide Layer behavior.
- A layer set to inherit will have the same visibility as its parent. You'll learn more about nesting and parent layers in a few minutes. If the parent is set to hidden and a layer is nested within that parent and set to inherit, it will also be hidden.
- Default visibility actually means inherit visibility in most browsers.

Explore Overflow and Clip

The layer's Overflow setting, shown in Figure 10.12, determines what happens if the content of a layer is bigger than the layer. An example of a layer with Overflow set to scroll is shown in Figure 10.13.

There are four Overflow settings:

- The visible setting expands the layer, down and to the right, so that everything in the layer is visible.
- The hidden setting keeps the current size of the layer so that content might not appear if it is larger than the layer size.

- If you want the layer to scroll no matter if the content is larger than the layer, then choose the scroll setting.

- Auto allows the layer to scroll only if the content overflows the size of the layer.

FIGURE 10.12

The Overflow setting determines what happens if the layer content is bigger than the layer size. Overflow can be set to visible, hidden, scroll, or auto.

FIGURE 10.13

In Internet Explorer the layer content is scrollable, but in Netscape the layer content is simply clipped.

Netscape does not recognize some of the Overflow and Clip coordinates settings when your layers are contained in `<div>` tags. Remember to always preview your Web pages in both browsers to make sure what you are trying works in each of them.

The Clip coordinates define what the size of the visible area will be. This setting allows you to show only a portion of what the layer actually contains. You can set four values under the Clip settings in the Property inspector that can define a box around the layer content. These settings are T for top, L for left, R for right, and B for bottom. The values that you type into each box define the distance from the edge of the layer, not the page.

This is a bit confusing, but follow me: The L value determines the pixels from the left edge of the layer, while the R value is also pixels from the left edge of the layer. The difference between these two values is the size of the content that will be showing. The same goes for the T value and the B value; they are both pixels from the top of the layer. An example is shown in Figure 10.14.

FIGURE 10.14

The L (left), R (right), T (top), and B (bottom) Clip values make up the area of the layer that is visible.

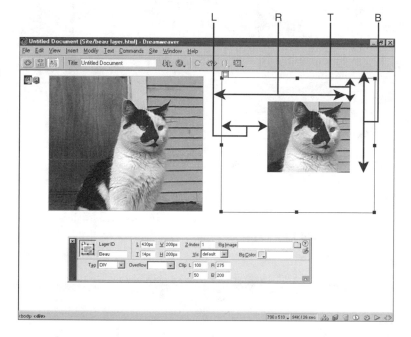

10

Nested Layers

You can create a layer within another layer; the new layer is nested within its parent layer. When you move the parent layer, the new child layer moves with it. The child layer also inherits its parent's visibility attributes.

To create a nested layer, place the cursor inside of the parent layer and choose the Layer command from the Insert menu. Draw a nested layer by using the Draw Layer object to draw inside an existing layer while holding down the Ctrl key. Also, you can place an existing layer within another layer by picking it up in the Layers panel, holding down the Ctrl key, and dropping it on another layer. The nested layer will appear indented in the Layers panel, as shown in Figure 10.15.

Nested layers

FIGURE 10.15

A layer nested within another layer appears indented in the Layers panel.

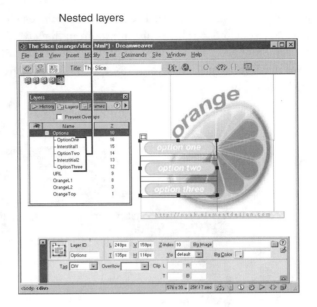

The easiest way to un-nest a layer if you make a mistake or change your mind is to pick it up in the Layers panel and drop it somewhere else in the list of layers, as shown in Figure 10.16.

FIGURE 10.16

Pick up the nested layer and move it to another position within the Layers panel to un-nest it.

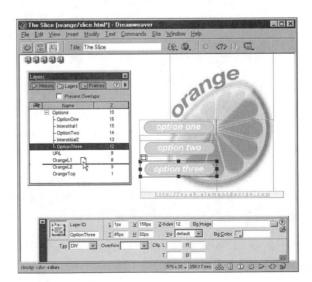

If Dreamweaver doesn't seem to be allowing you to nest layers, you probably have the option turned off in your preferences. To turn it on, select the Preference command under the Edit menu, select the Layers category, and make sure the Nesting box is checked.

Did your layer disappear from the screen when you un-nested it? When a layer is nested, its position is relative to its parent. When you un-nest the layer, its position is now relative to the page. The layer coordinates might cause the layer to be off the screen. To fix this problem, select the layer in the Layers panel and give it Left and Top attributes that will place it back on the screen.

10

Explore Layer Tags

Set the default tag for layers in the layer preferences. However, you can change the tag in the Property inspector by selecting another tag from the Tag drop-down menu, as shown in Figure 10.17. Different tags allow different functionality in different browsers. The <div> tag is the most common tag to use in cross-browser development. <span> and <div> tags create what are called Cascading Style Sheet, or CSS, layers. These tags implement the W3C standards for laycrs.

FIGURE 10.17

You can select which tag is used to implement a layer in the tag drop-down menu in the Property inspector. Most layers will use the cross-browser <div> tag.

Even though either the <div> or the <span> tag will work to define a layer, the <div> tag is the more logical choice and is more in keeping with what the W3C standard intended. The <div> tag is used to logically divide a Web page into sections. The <span> tag is usually used to apply a style to a span of text within a paragraph.

The `<layer>` tag is Netscape Navigator specific and will not work in Internet Explorer. The `<div>` tags work in both browsers but Internet Explorer 4.0 and higher supports more properties of the tags. Netscape Navigator 6.0 and greater will no longer support the `<layer>` tag.

Use Layers to Design a Table

In the last hour, you used Dreamweaver's Layout mode to design tables. If you have a complicated design in mind, you can also use layers to position your design, and then deliver the design in a table. Use the Convert Layer To Table command under the Layout Mode submenu of the Modify menu. This conversion might be necessary if some of your audience is using older browsers that won't display layers.

Since table cells cannot overlap, you need to make sure that the layers in your design also do not overlap. You do this by checking the Prevent Overlaps box at the top of the Layers panel.

After you have placed all of your layers on the page, it's time for the conversion. Select the Layers to Table command from the Convert submenu of the Modify menu. A dialog box appears. This dialog box has a Table Layout section and a Layout Tools section. The Layout Tools section turns on the grid (and is another place you can turn on the Prevent Overlaps option). The Table Layout section helps you set up the way your table will eventually look.

- The Most Accurate setting forces Dreamweaver to convert every layer into a table cell so that the table reflects the layers as accurately as possible.

- The Smallest: Collapse Empty Cells setting forces Dreamweaver to remove empty rows or columns if they are within a set number of pixels from an existing row or column.

- The Use Transparent GIFs setting fills in the table's last row with transparent GIFs. This is an old trick to make sure that the table columns do not shrink in certain browsers if they are empty. Dreamweaver inserts a transparent GIF into the cell and gives it the same width as the cell.

- The Center on Page setting will, as the title suggests, center the table on your HTML page.

Summary

In this hour, you learned how to insert a layer into your Web page. You learned how to change its size, position, background color, and name. You also explored setting the stacking order, or z-index, of layers and setting layer visibility. You used layers to design a table and became familiar with the different tags that can be used to implement layers.

Q&A

Q The `<div>` and `<span>` tags are described as implementing CSS layers. I thought that CSS, or cascading style sheets, had to do with text. Am I right?

A The CSS standard does define many attributes for manipulating text. But it also defines "box elements," which are what layers are. This might make more sense to you after you have completed the next hour on cascading style sheets. You'll see the different attributes of box elements, or layers, that we will be able to set up in a style and how powerful that capability is.

Q Is there any way I can design my site with layers that are cross-browser compatible, yet still take advantage of some of the extra attributes that the `<layer>` tag gives me in Netscape Navigator and the `<div>` tag gives me in Internet Explorer?

A The only way to use both tags in the same page is to create your page twice, once with the `<layer>` tag and once with the `<div>` tag, and use the Check Browser behavior to send your viewers to one page or the other. Trying to create and maintain a Web site that uses both tags in layers will be a lot of work.

Workshop

The Workshop contains quiz questions and activities to help reinforce what you've learned in this hour. If you get stuck, the answers to the quiz can be found following the questions.

Quiz

1. How do you select multiple layers on the Web page?
2. What is the most common cross-browser tag used to implement layers?
3. True or False: The layer with the lowest z-index is the one on the top.

Answers

1. Hold down the Shift key while either clicking on the edges of the layers on the screen or clicking on their names in the Layers panel.

2. The `<div>` tag is the most logical choice. It is meant to logically divide sections of the page, and it works in most version 4.0 and higher browsers.

3. False. The layer with the highest z-index is the one on top.

Exercises

1. Create a Web page with multiple layers. Experiment inserting images and text into the layers. Change the background color of one of the layers. Be sure to make a few of the layers overlap so you can see how the z-index attribute works.

2. Create a banner and a navigation bar for a site by placing a layer across the top for the banner. Place individual layers with the text Home, Previous, and Next in them. You can make these hyperlinks if you want. Then convert these layers into a table.

HOUR 11

Formatting Your Web Pages with Cascading Style Sheets and HTML Styles

Cascading Style Sheets (CSS) enable you to apply a property or group of properties to an object by applying a style to that object. You define and apply styles in Dreamweaver's CSS Styles panel. When thinking about styles, you usually think of creating and applying styles to text, which certainly is possible. However, styles can be used for positioning objects, creating borders, and lots more.

One of the benefits of using styles is the ability to update every object that has a certain style at once. If you create a default style, such as a style defined as Arial 12-point text, you can later change the font to Times Roman and all the objects with that style will instantly appear in the new font.

Cascading Style Sheets are part of dynamic HTML. Your viewers will need to have 4.0 or later to view styles. Dreamweaver displays most styles in the Document window. The styles that Dreamweaver can't display are noted with an asterisk when you are defining the style.

There are three different style types, and you will create a style with all three this hour. You will create a custom style (probably the most common type of style), you'll redefine an existing HTML tag, and you will use a CSS Selector style to create a hyperlink rollover effect.

In this chapter, you will learn

- How to create each of the three style types: a custom style, a redefined HTML tag, and a CSS Selector style
- How to apply styles to objects
- How to create an external style sheet for your entire Web site
- How to convert a Web page containing styles so that older browsers can display the text formatting
- How to create an HTML style

Create and Apply a Custom Style

The CSS Styles panel, as shown in Figure 11.1, lists custom styles that have been defined and are ready to apply to objects on your Web page. You define custom styles by creating a new style and defining it in Dreamweaver. The Dreamweaver Style Definition dialog box has panels listing numerous style settings.

FIGURE 11.1

The CSS Styles panel lists all the styles in your Web page.

Create a custom style to apply to text. You'll define the font, font size, and font color. To create a custom style

1. Select the New Style button or the New Style menu command from the CSS Styles panel. Both are shown in Figure 11.2.
2. The New Style dialog box appears as shown in Figure 11.3. Select the radio button beside Make Custom Style (class).

3. Enter a name for the style in the Name box at the top of the New Style dialog box. Custom style names always begin with a period; Dreamweaver will enter the period for you if you forget to enter it.

FIGURE 11.2

The CSS Styles panel has two ways to quickly create a new style: the New Style button, in the lower-right corner, and the New Style command in the panel drop-down menu in the upper-right corner.

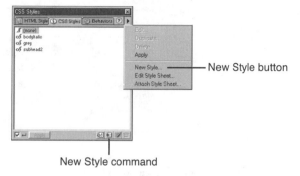

New Style button

New Style command

FIGURE 11.3

You select which of the three types of styles you are defining in the New Style dialog box.

Style types

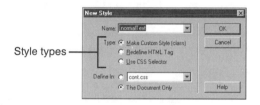

It's usually a good idea not to use spaces or punctuation in style names.

4. Select the radio button beside This Document Only in the Define In section. This places the style definition at the top of the current Web page. If you forget this step, Dreamweaver will prompt you to save the style as an external style sheet. We'll discuss external style sheets later this hour.

5. The Style definition dialog box appears as shown in Figure 11.4. The box opens with the Type category selected. In the Type category, select a font and font size from the appropriate drop-down menus. Also, select a font color with the color picker.

6. Select OK to save the style. The CSS Styles panel lists the new custom style.

Apply the custom style to objects by first selecting the object and then clicking on the style in the CSS Styles panel. You select a block of text by dragging the cursor across it. You can also select a layer, table cell, or other objects in the Web page and apply the style. All the text in the layer, table cell, or other object will then appear as defined by the style.

Font size   Font

Figure 11.4

The Style definition dialog box is where you set up the attributes of the style.

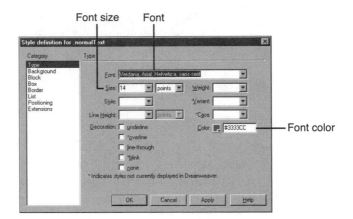

Font color

Apply the custom style that you just created to some text in the Dreamweaver document window. First, select the text, and then click on the style name in the CSS Styles panel to apply the style.

Some style attributes will only work when applied to certain tags. For instance, a style called bigcell with the cell padding values set to 100 will not have any effect on text because padding is not an attribute of text. Applying this style to an appropriate object, like a table cell, will have an effect.

If you accidentally apply a style to an object, you can remove it by selecting (none) in the CSS Styles panel.

Explore Style Settings

The Style definition dialog box has eight panels with numerous settings you can use in defining a style. As you are defining a style, you select the panels to gain access to the settings for that category. Any settings that you do not need to set should be left alone. The following categories are available:

- The Type panel defines type attributes such as font and font size. These style settings can be applied to text or objects that contain text.

- The Background panel defines background attributes such as color or image. These style settings can be applied to objects such as layers and tables where you can set a background.

- The Block panel defines type attributes for paragraphs.

- The Box panel defines attributes such as margin size that are applied to an object.
- The Border panel defines attributes that are applied to objects that have borders such as layers and tables.
- The List panel defines list attributes such as bullet type.
- The Positioning panel defines layer attributes such as visibility and z-index.
- The Extensions panel defines miscellaneous attributes that are either future enhancements or for Internet Explorer only.

Table 11.1 lists the style settings available in the various categories of the Style definition dialog box.

TABLE 11.1   Style Settings in the Style Definition Dialog Box

Setting	Description
Type Panel	
Font	Sets the font family.
Size	Sets the font size and unit of measurement.
Style	Specifies the font as normal, italic, or oblique.
Line Height	Sets the height of the line of text and the unit of measurement. This setting is traditionally called *leading*. It is added before the line.
Decoration	Adds an underline, overline, or line through the text.
Weight	Adds an amount of boldface to text. Regular bold is equal to 700.
Variant	Sets the small caps variant on text.
Case	Capitalizes the first letter of each word or sets the text to all lowercase or uppercase.
Color	Sets the text color.
Background Panel	
Background Color	Sets the background color for an object.
Background Image	Sets a background image for an object.
Repeat	Controls how the background image gets repeated. No Repeat displays the image only once, Repeat tiles the image horizontally and vertically, Repeat-x tiles the image only horizontally, and Repeat-y tiles the image only vertically.
Attachment	Sets whether the background image scrolls with the content or is fixed in its original position.
Horizontal Position	The initial horizontal position of the background image.
Vertical Position	The initial vertical position of the background image.

11

TABLE 11.1 continued

Setting	Description
Block Panel	
Word Spacing	Adds space around words. Use negative values to reduce the space between words.
Letter Spacing	Adds space between letters. Use negative values to reduce space between letters.
Vertical Alignment	Alignment of the object relative to objects around it. Like the Alignment settings discussed in the section on images.
Text Align	Aligns text within an object. Choices are left, right, center, and justify.
Text Indent	Sets how far the first line is indented. Use negative values to set an outdent.
Whitespace	Sets how whitespace will appear in an object. Normal collapses whitespace, pre displays all the whitespace, and nowrap sets the text to wrap only when a tag is encountered.
Box Panel	
Width	Sets the width of an object.
Height	Sets the height of an object.
Float	Sets which side other objects (such as text) will float around the object.
Clear	Clears the floating so that objects (such as text) do not float around another object.
Padding	Sets the amount of space between the object and its border (or margin).
Margin	Sets the amount of space between the border of an object and other objects.
Border Panel	
Width	Sets the border thickness. You can set the widths of the top, right, bottom, and left borders separately.
Color	Sets the border color. You can set the colors of the top, right, bottom, and left borders separately.
Style	Sets the style appearance of the borders. The choices are dotted, dashed, solid, double, groove, ridge, inset, and outset.
List Panel	
Type	Sets the appearance of the bullets. The choices are disc, circle, square, decimal, lower-roman, upper-roman, lower-alpha, and upper-alpha.
Bullet Image	Sets a custom image for bullets.
Position	Sets whether the list content wraps to the indent (outside) or to the margin (inside).

TABLE 11.1   continued

Setting	Description
Positioning Panel	
Type	Sets how the layer is positioned. The choices are relative (at the coordinates relative to its position), absolute (at the exact coordinates), and static (at its place in the document flow).
Visibility	Sets the layer's visibility. The choices are inherit, visible, and hidden.
Z-Index	Sets the layer's z-index (stacking order).
Overflow	Sets what happens when the layer's contents exceed its size. The choices are visible, hidden, scroll, and auto.
Placement	Sets the left, top, width, and height attributes for a layer.
Clip	Sets the top, bottom, left, and right clipping attributes for a layer.
Extensions Panel	
Pagebreak	Forces a page break during printing either before or after the object. This style is not widely supported but may be in the future.
Cursor	Changes the cursor when it is placed over the object. Only supported in Internet Explorer 4.0 or better.
Filter	Applies special effects including page transitions, opacity, and blurs to objects. Only supported in Internet Explorer 4.0 or better. See http://msdn.microsoft.com/workshop/Author/filter/filters.asp for more information.

11

Redefine the Heading 1 <h1> Tag

Text formatted with the <h1> tag by default looks like Figure 11.5. You can redefine HTML tags with CSS styles. Redefined HTML tags do not appear in the styles list in the CSS Styles panel. You apply the HTML tags as you normally would. For instance, you apply the <h1> tag by selecting Heading 1 from the format drop-down menu in the Property inspector. After you redefine the <h1> tag, any text with that tag will immediately appear with the new style formatting.

Type some text in the Dreamweaver document window and apply Heading 1, the <h1> tag, to it. Do this so that you can see what the text looks like before you redefine the <h1> tag. Create a new style by either selecting the New button or the New command from the CSS Styles panel drop-down menu. The New Style dialog box appears. Select the radio button beside Redefine HTML Tag and then select h1 from the New Style drop-down menu as shown in Figure 11.6.

FIGURE 11.5

The Heading 1 format's default appearance is bold with size 6 text and is left justified. You can redefine the appearance with CSS styles.

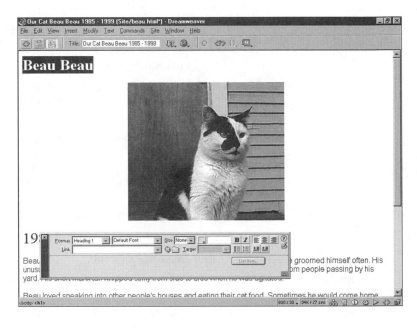

HTML Tag drop-down menu

FIGURE 11.6

The Redefine HTML Tag drop-down menu contains a list of all of the HTML tags that you can change with CSS styles.

By default, the <h1> tag makes objects left justified. To center align all object with the <h1> tag applied, redefining it with styles, select the Block category. Select Center from the Text Align drop-down menu, as shown in Figure 11.7, and click the OK button. Immediately after you click OK, the h1 text in your Web page should jump to center alignment.

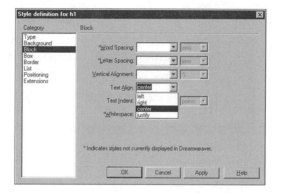

FIGURE 11.7

The Block properties apply to blocks of text. You can change the default alignment of the text block in the Text Align drop-down menu.

Styles are defined in the <head> section of the Web page. Dreamweaver automatically records the styles you create in the CSS Styles panel into the <head> of the document. The code for the h1 style looks like this:

```
<style type="text/css">
<!--
h1 {  text-align: center}
-->
</style>
```

Paired style tags surround the redefined <h1> tag style definition. Nested within the style tags are paired comment tags (the <!-- and the closing -->). The comment tags are added so that older browsers simply ignore the styles and don't cause an error. The style definition has the tag name, h1, followed by paired curly brackets containing the property name and the property value. Notice that a colon separates the property name and property value. We only have one property defined in this style, the text-align property, but you can have a list of many.

CSS styles are supported by Internet Explorer and Netscape Navigator 4.0 or better browser versions. If your viewer's browser doesn't support styles, he simply won't see what the styles would have defined. If you have redefined the <h1> tag as centered, for example, the viewer's browser will continue to see any objects with that tag applied as left-justified.

11

Position a Layer with a Style

So far, you've applied styles to text. When dealing with layers, it's useful to position objects on the page with styles. If you need to position layers in a consistent place on the screen, then it's an excellent idea to define a style for those layers. To define a positioning style for a layer

1. Create and name a new custom style as you did earlier in this hour.
2. Select the Positioning category in the Style definition dialog box. Notice the properties in this category are properties that you used in the last hour creating layers.
3. Select Absolute in the Type category at the top of the dialog box. Set the Left, Top, Width, and Height properties as shown in Figure 11.8.

FIGURE 11.8

To create a positioning style, set the Left, Top, Width, and Height properties in the Positioning category of the Style definition dialog box.

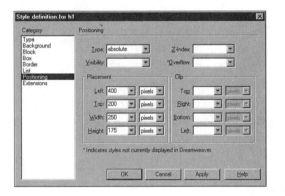

4. Select the OK button to save your style.

Create a layer in your Web page and position it in another area of the screen from the area you just defined. Delete the L (left), T (top), W (width), and H (height) layer properties and apply the style to the layer. It should hop to the position you defined in the style. You need to remove the properties that are within the <div> tag of the layer for the layer to take on the properties defined in the style. You can tell that this layer has a style applied to it because the style name is highlighted in the CSS Styles panel when you select the layer.

> If you accidentally move the layer, you will override the style's Top, Left, Width, and Height attributes. To return the layer to its style-defined position, select the layer and remove the values in the Top, Left, Width, and Height boxes in the Property inspector. The layer should return to the location and size you defined in the style.

Instead of creating a layer first, you can simply apply the style you just created to an object in your Web page. The style will create a layer around the object.

Create a Hyperlink Rollover

The third type of style is a CSS Selector. This type of style redefines a group of HTML tags instead of just one. For instance, you could define what a specific heading tag looks like only within a table cell by entering the table cell tag, td, and then the heading 1 tag, h1. To do this, you enter all of the tag names in the Selector box, as shown in Figure 11.9, and then define the style.

FIGURE 11.9

You can define attributes for multiple HTML tags with CSS Selector styles in the New Style dialog box.

Creating hyperlink rollovers is a common and fun use of CSS Selector styles. These CSS Selector styles redefine the anchor (<a>) tag, the tag that is used in hyperlinks. Define an anchor style that makes the link color change when the user has his cursor positioned over a hyperlink. To create a hyperlink rollover

1. Create a new style and select the radio button beside Use CSS Selector.

2. The Selector drop-down menu displays the four link styles, shown in Figure 11.10. Select the a:hover selector to add a rollover to all of the hyperlinks in your Web page. Click OK.

FIGURE 11.10

The four link styles appear in the drop-down menu when you select the Use CSS Selector radio button.

3. The Style definition dialog box appears. In the Type category, select a color and then press OK.

To see the selector, create a hyperlink in your Web page. Save the page and preview it in Internet Explorer. When your cursor is over the hyperlink, it changes color! This effect only works in Internet Explorer; the hyperlink appears as usual, without the rollover effect, in Netscape.

Create an External Style Sheet

Adding styles to a single Web page is nice, but wouldn't it be great to apply the same styles to a number of Web pages? External style sheets allow you to do this. Instead of defining styles in the head of a Web page, all of the styles are defined in one text file. External style sheets end with the .css file extension. When you update a style in a external style sheet, the changes apply to every page that is linked to that style sheet.

To create a external style sheet

1. Create a new style, and then select the top radio button beside the Define In section of the New Style Dialog Box. Select (New Style Sheet File) from the drop-down menu beside the radio button as shown in Figure 11.11. Select the OK button.

FIGURE 11.11

Select the (New Style Sheet File) to define a new external style sheet.

Create New Style Sheet File

2. The Save Style Sheet File As dialog box opens. Browse to the directory where you want to save your external style sheet. Enter a filename, as shown in Figure 11.12, followed by the .css file extension. Click OK.

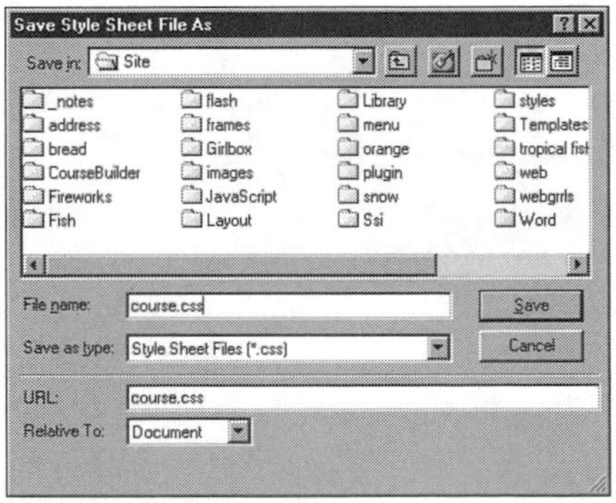

FIGURE 11.12

Create a external style sheet by browsing to the correct folder and saving a file with the file extension .css.

3. The Style Definition dialog box opens. Notice that the title bar says that you are defining this style in the external style sheet name that you just created. Create and save your style as you did earlier this hour.

When you create an external style sheet, Dreamweaver creates a new file and places the style definitions in it. Dreamweaver also references the external style sheet in the head of your Web page. To add additional styles to the external style sheet, select the name of the external style sheet from the Define In drop-down menu when you are defining a new style, as shown in Figure 11.13.

FIGURE 11.13

Select an external style sheet from the Define In drop-down menu to create a new style in the external style sheet.

Edit Style Sheets

After you create styles you may need to edit them. You can edit styles that are both internal to a Web page and contained in an external style sheet. To edit a style

1. Select the Edit Style Sheet button from the CSS Style dialog box as shown in Figure 11.14.

2. The Edit Style Sheet dialog box lists the external style sheet along with any styles that are local to the Web page as shown in Figure 11.14.

FIGURE 11.14

The Edit Style Sheet dialog box lists the external style sheet, followed by the word link in parentheses, along with styles that are defined locally in the Web page.

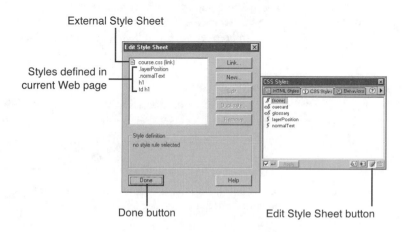

11

3. Edit an external style sheet by selecting its name in the Edit Style Sheet dialog box. Another Edit Style Sheet dialog box opens with the name of the external style sheet in its title bar. This box lists the styles that are contained in the external style sheet, as shown in Figure 11.15.

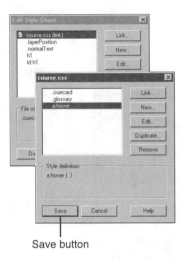

Save button

4. Edit styles by double-clicking them in the Edit Style Sheet dialog box. The Style Definition dialog box appears where you can make and save your changes to the style.

You can also easily edit styles by double-clicking them in the CSS Styles dialog box when you have nothing selected on the Web page. Be sure you have nothing selected. If you do have something selected you will simply apply the style to the object you have selected.

5. Select the Save button to save the edits to your external style sheet. Select the Done button to return to the CSS Styles panel. All of your styles, in both the local Web page and the external style sheet, will appear in the CSS Styles panel.

You can tell that a style is in an external style sheet because it has a Link icon, represented by a piece of chain, beside it in the CSS Styles panel.

If you've already created some styles in a Web page before you decide to use an external style sheet, then use the Export CSS Styles command under the Export submenu in the File menu. Link to this file instead of creating a new file.

View Head Content

Dreamweaver places styles in the head of the document. Each HTML page has two main sections, and the majority of content goes in the body section of the Web page. Some objects are always located in the head of the Web page, like the title, CSS style definitions, references to external styles sheets, and JavaScript.

You can access the objects in the head section of your Web page without looking at the HTML. Select the Head Content command from the View menu and Dreamweaver displays the objects contained in the head of your Web page as shown in Figure 11.16. When you click on the icon representations of the objects, information about the object appears in the Properties inspector. Turn off displaying the head content by deselecting the Head Content command.

FIGURE 11.16

When you view the head content, Dreamweaver displays icons representing elements in the head section of the Web page.

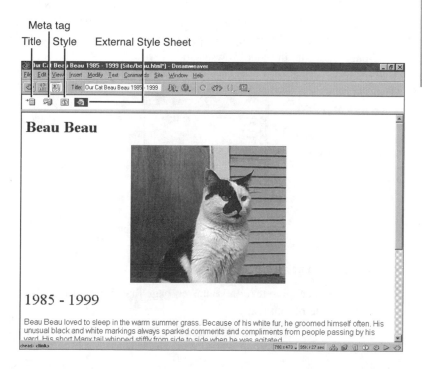

11

Convert Styles to HTML Markup (`<font>` Tags)

If you need to deliver your Web pages to viewers with older browsers, you can still take advantage of the ease and speed that style sheets afford. It's quicker to apply styles to format text than it is to configure all of the font attributes in the Property inspector. Dreamweaver will convert your Web page from CSS Styles to `<font>` tags with the CSS Styles to HTML Markup command.

First, save your Web page because Dreamweaver actually opens another Web page with the converted Web page. Select the CSS Styles to HTML Markup command from the Convert submenu in the File menu. Select the radio button beside the command and click OK. The new Web page contains HTML markup instead of CSS styles. Anything that can't be expressed in HTML markup, such as our positioning style we created earlier, will be discarded.

Save HTML Markup as an HTML Style

Use the HTML Styles panel, shown in Figure 11.17, to apply HTML styles to text in your Web page. Dreamweaver comes with a number of HTML styles already defined. These HTML styles do not require newer browser versions (Internet Explorer or Netscape 4.0 or later) to work so they are great to use when formatting text for a Web page viewable in older browsers.

FIGURE 11.17

The HTML Styles panel enables you to apply styles that work with older browser versions.

New Style button

To create a new HTML style

1. Select some text on your Web page first, if you'd like Dreamweaver to pick up the style of that text.

2. Select the New Style button (see Figure 11.17).

3. The Define HTML Style dialog box appears as shown in Figure 11.18. If you selected text this dialog box should display the attributes of that text.

FIGURE **11.18**
Set up HTML Style attributes in the Define HTML Style dialog box.

Apply to attributes ———

Font attributes ———

Paragraph attributes ———

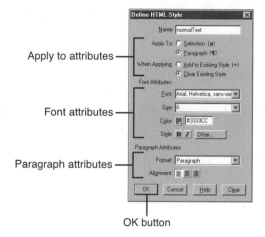

OK button

4. Select whether the style is applied to the selected text or an entire paragraph. Select the font and all other attributes that you want the HTML style to have.

5. Apply the HTML style by selecting text on the Web page and then selecting the HTML style in the HTML Styles panel.

11

 You can edit the HTML styles that are available in the HTML Styles panel by double-clicking the name of the HTML style while nothing is selected in the Web page.

Summary

In this hour, you learned how to create and apply the three types of CSS styles: a custom style, a redefined HTML tag, and a CSS selector. You also made an external style sheet that allows the same styles to be used throughout an entire Web site. Then you were kind to those with older browsers, converting your style sheet formatting into HTML markup. You also created an HTML style.

Q&A

Q Can I link more than one style sheet to a Web page?

A You can link as many different style sheets as you'd like to a Web page.

Q How can I remove the underline from hyperlinks with CSS styles?

A Some people may advise against doing that, but if you feel your design demands it, it's your call. To remove the underline from hyperlinks, redefine the <a> (anchor) tag in CSS Styles. Set Decoration (in the Text category of the Style Definition dialog box) to none. All of the hyperlinks on the page will be without an underline.

Workshop

The Workshop contains quiz questions and activities to help reinforce what you've learned in this hour. If you get stuck, the answer to the quiz can be found below the questions.

Quiz

1. What are the three different types of CSS styles?

2. What should you create to use the same styles for all the Web pages in a Web site?

3. What is another name for custom CSS styles?

Answers

1. The three types of CSS styles are custom, redefined HTML tags, and CSS selectors.

2. Create an external style sheet and link it to each page in your Web site.

3. Custom CSS styles are also called *class styles* because the class attribute is added to tags.

Exercises

1. Create a page and create a custom style that modifies text. Explore applying this style to text in the page, table cells, layers, and other objects in the page.

2. Create different definitions for the four hover styles: a:active, a:hover, a:link, and a:visited. Write down the four colors and figure out when they appear.

Hour 12

Understanding and Building Frames and Framesets

Love 'em or hate 'em, many people seem to have strong opinions about frames. Frames can be an excellent way to present information on your Web site, but they can also be a navigational nightmare to your users. Take care and make sure that your frames are carefully created so that the user can navigate to links that you provide in your site without being perpetually caught in your frames.

Certain types of Web sites are excellent candidates for a frame structure. A good example is a site with a table of contents constantly available so the user can make multiple selections. Why make the user continually navigate back to a table of contents page? You can load the table of contents page into a frame and load the requested content into another frame so both are present on the screen. The Dreamweaver 4 Help pages are an excellent example of this type of frame configuration.

There may also be navigational issues that you can address with frames. If one part of the page never changes, for instance the main navigational buttons at the top of the screen, then why continually reload them? You can put the navigational elements in a frame at the top of the page and allow the user to load new parts of your Web site into the bottom frame of the page.

In this hour, you will learn

- The difference between frames and framesets
- How to target content to load in a specific frame
- How to set frame attributes such as scrolling and borders
- How to use behaviors to load content into more than one frame at a time

Create a Frameset

Frames consist of individual Web pages—one for each frame, held together by a Web page that contains the frameset. The frameset defines the size and position of the individual frames. You can either load an existing Web page into a frame or create a new Web page.

When you are working with frames, using the Save command becomes more complicated. Are you saving the frame or the frameset? While you are working with frames, Dreamweaver activates the Save Frameset and the Save Frameset As commands in the File menu. You can also use the Save All command to save all of the frame content and the frameset, too. There also is an additional Open command, the Open in Frame command, which appears in the File menu when you are working with frames. You can open an existing Web page in a frame with this command.

There are three different methods of creating frames:

- View the frame borders and then drag the borders to create new frames.
- Use the commands under the Frameset sub-menu in Dreamweaver's Modify menu. You may need to use the menu commands when the frame configuration you want to create is not possible by dragging borders.
- Use the pre-built frame configurations available in the Object panel.

View Frame Borders

You need to view the frame borders before you can drag them to create frames. Select the Frame Borders command from the Visual Aids submenu of the View menu. You see a set of borders surrounding the page as shown in Figure 12.1.

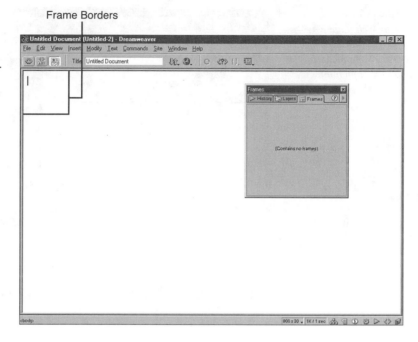

FIGURE 12.1

When you view the frame borders, another set of borders appears surrounding the Web page.

Split a Page into Frames

To create frames drag the frame borders while holding down the Alt key. Create two frames, top and bottom, in an empty Web page by Alt-dragging the top frame border. You now have three HTML files: the top frame, the bottom frame, and the Web page with the frameset. When viewers enter the URL of the frameset page, the browser automatically loads the individual pages that belong in each frame.

If you change your mind about a frame, just drag the border off the edge of the page and it will be deleted.

Name Your Frames

Naming and keeping track of frames can be confusing. Type the word "top" into the top frame. With the cursor in the top frame, save the frame as top.html by selecting the Save command from the File menu. When you are first working with frames, it's less confusing to save each frame individually. Repeat this procedure with the bottom frame: type the word "bottom" in the frame and save it as bottom.html. Your frames will look like Figure 12.2.

12

FIGURE 12.2

This Web page was divided into two frames, named top.html and bottom.html.

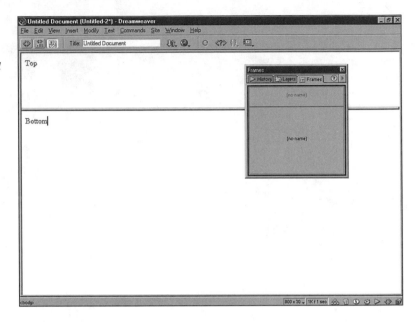

Note that in Figure 12.2, the Frame panel displays (no name) in both of the frames even though we just saved them. You named the files that are contained in the frames but you did not yet name the frames themselves. You will do that in a few minutes.

When the Frame Borders command is not checked under the Visual Aids submenu of the View menu, the Web page appears as it will in the browser. Later in this hour, we will change the border sizes and other attributes of frames. It will be helpful to turn the frame borders off to approximate how the frames will look in the browser. Turn off the frame borders in the Visual Aids submenu of the View menu to see what your Web page looks like without them and then turn the borders back on again.

Now you will divide the bottom frame into two frames. If you drag the left frame border, you will end up with four frames—two on the top and two on the bottom. Instead, split the bottom frame into two frames with the commands in the Frameset submenu under the Modify menu.

To split the bottom frame

1. With the cursor in the bottom frame select the Split Frame Right command from the Frameset submenu in Dreamweaver's Modify menu as shown in Figure 12.3. This command places the existing frame on the right and adds a new frame on the left.

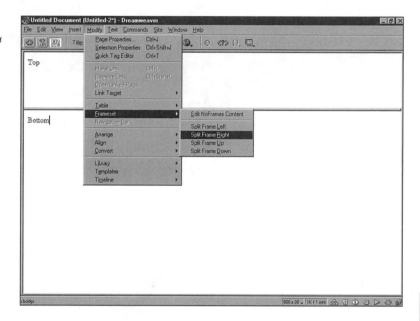

2. Replace the word "bottom" with the word "right" and add the word "left" to the new frame.

3. Save the Web page contained in the new frame (with the word "left" in it). Remember to place your cursor in the frame and then select the Save command from the File menu. You can name this Web page left.html.

You have created three frames and saved the Web pages that they contain. Save the frameset Web page holding the three frames by selecting the Save Frameset command from the File menu. It might be a good reminder to put "frameset" or "f" in the file name to remind you that this is the frameset page. You can call this Web page frameset.html.

If you haven't already saved the Web pages in the frames and the frameset Web page, Dreamweaver will prompt you to save before you preview in the browser. The first time you save, it's less confusing to individually save the Web pages contained in each frame and the frameset Web page rather than saving all the files at once when Dreamweaver prompts you. Dreamweaver will prompt you to save the files every time you preview the frames.

12

Use the Frames Panel

The Frames panel, shown in Figure 12.4, enables you to select individual frames and set frame attributes. Notice that the Frames panel visually represents the frames that are in your Web page. Select a frame by clicking on the frame's representation in the Frames panel. You can also select a frame by Alt-clicking (Shift-clicking for the Macintosh) inside the frame in the document window.

FIGURE 12.4

You select Frames in the Frames panel. This inspector visually represents the frame configuration in the current Web page.

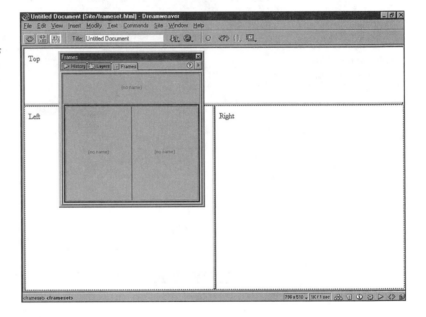

When you click on the representation of a frame in the Frames panel, the properties for that frame are available in the Property inspector as shown in Figure 12.5. You can change the name of the frame in the Frame Name box and change the URL that loads into the frame in the Src box. This is also where you set up the frame scrolling and border attributes that you will explore in a few minutes.

Each frame needs a name. The frame name is used to target a hyperlink to load into the frame. Click on each frame in the Frames panel and type a name in the Frame Name box in the Property inspector. You can name the top frame "topFrame", the left frame "toc" (for table of contents), and the right frame "main".

FIGURE 12.5

The Property inspector presents frame attributes, like frame name, when an individual frame is selected.

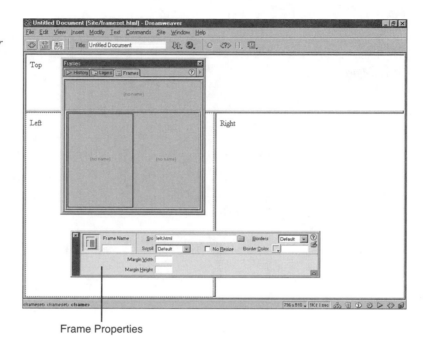

Frame Properties

 Frame names should not contain punctuation such as periods, hyphens, or spaces. You can use underscores in frame names. Also, you should not use the reserved words top, parent, self, or blank.

12

Nested Frames

You can nest one frameset inside another frameset to have *nested frames*. Actually, that is what you just did! When you split the bottom frame into two frames, Dreamweaver created another frameset defining the bottom two frames. The original frameset now consists of a frame on top of another frameset.

Click on one of the lower frames in the Frames panel and look at the tag selector. You will see a frame inside of a frameset inside of another frameset as shown in Figure 12.6. Click on the top frame in the Frames panel. The tag selector shows the frame is in one frameset. The bottom two frames are in a nested frameset.

FIGURE 12.6

The tag selector shows that the currently selected frame is contained in a frameset nested within another frameset.

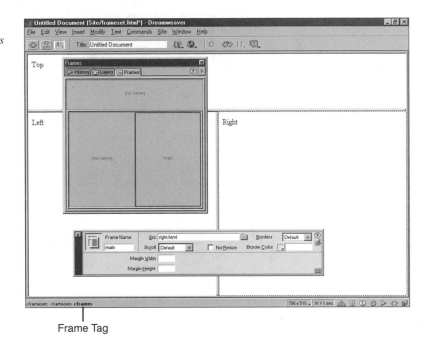

Frame Tag

Dreamweaver creates an additional frameset because framesets can contain either rows or columns but not both. The first frameset you created has two rows. The second frameset you created has two columns.

Use Existing Web Pages with Frames

So far, you have created new Web pages in all of your frames. You might want to load a Web page that you have created prior to setting up your frameset into a frame. To load an existing Web page into a frame:

1. Open the Frames panel and click on the frame that will contain an existing Web page.

2. Select the folder icon to browse to an existing Web page or type a URL into the Src box in the Property inspector.

3. You will see the Web page displayed if it is on a local drive. If you have referenced an absolute URL to a Web page on the Internet, Dreamweaver will display a message, shown in Figure 12.7, saying that the frame contains a remote file and lists the URL.

FIGURE 12.7

If a frame references an external URL, it will contain a message displaying the URL.

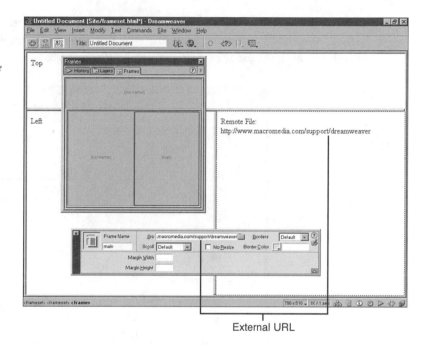

External URL

 You can open an existing Web page in the frame where the cursor is located using the Open in Frame command.

 Be careful of loading another Web page that contains a frameset into a frame. The frames may appear way too small at some monitor resolutions to show the Web site properly.

12

Set the Scrolling and Resize Attributes

It's important to consider whether you want the user to be able to scroll the material in a frame. Scrollbars can appear either horizontally or vertically in the browser window. Horizontal scrollbars are not common and are not generally desirable. Vertical scrollbars are very common and appear when the material in the Web page is longer than what is visible in the browser window.

Each frame has its own scrolling attributes displayed in the Property inspector when a frame is selected in the Frame panel. There are four different settings in the scroll drop-down menu of the Property inspector, shown in Figure 12.8.

FIGURE 12.8

The Property inspector lists scroll choices when a frame is selected.

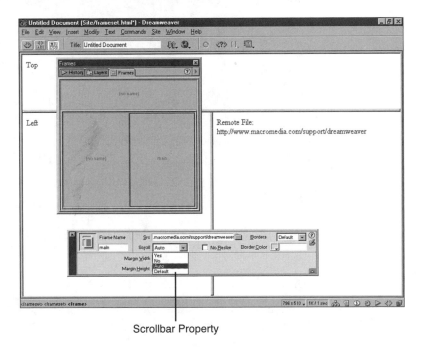

Scrollbar Property

- The Yes setting turns scrollbars on whether the content requires them or not. Both vertical and horizontal scrollbars may appear depending on the browser.
- The No setting turns scrollbars off whether the content requires them or not. If the viewer cannot see all the content in the frame they have no way to scroll to see it.
- The Auto setting turns the scrollbars on if the content of the frame is larger than what is visible in the browser window. If all the content is visible, the scrollbars are off. This setting only turns on the necessary scrollbars, horizontal or vertical, and is usually a better choice than the Yes setting.
- The Default setting for most browsers is the same as Auto.

Select the No Resize check box if you do not want the user to be able to resize your frames. If you do not check this check box, the user can drag the borders to any size they want. Allowing users to resize the borders can sometimes help the user maintain the readability of your Web page, but it also may ruin your design. If a frame-based Web page is well designed, taking into account how the page will look at various monitor resolutions, the user shouldn't have to resize the frames.

Set Borders

The default look for frame borders is a gray shaded border between the frames. You may not want your frame-based Web page to be so obviously "framed." Identifying some frame-based Web sites is difficult because they have turned off the frame borders or colored them to blend with the site design.

You can turn borders on and off, set the border color, and change the border width. Border attributes are a little tricky because some border attributes are set in the frame, some are set in the frameset, and some can be set in both places. Setting properties in a frame overrides the same property set in the frameset.

If you set attributes for frames but they don't seem to work, check to make sure you have set the attributes in all of the framesets. Frames in nested framesets may need to have the attributes set in all of the framesets.

Set the border width in the frameset. The easiest way to select the frameset, displaying the frameset attributes in the Property inspector, is to select the `<frameset>` tag in the tag selector. The tag selector displays the `<frameset>` tag when a frame within the frameset is selected. Remember that nested frames may be in more than one frameset.

You can select the frameset in the Frames panel by clicking on the edges around the frames. I think this is quite a bit harder than selecting the `<frameset>` tag in the tag selector.

Select a frame in the Frames panel and click on the `<frameset>` tag farthest to the left. The `<frameset>` properties, shown in Figure 12.9, enable you to change border width and color. Give the border a width value and select a color from the color box. You should see these changes immediately in the Dreamweaver document window.

If you want finer control over the size of a frame, you can set frame sizes in the Property inspector while the frameset is selected. Note that the last frame is defined as "relative," which means "the rest of the space." You can select the rows or columns in the frameset by clicking on the small representation in the Property inspector.

12

FIGURE **12.9**

The Property inspector enables you to set frameset properties, such as border width and border color.

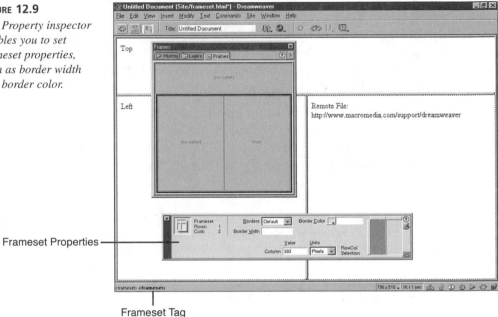

Frameset Properties

Frameset Tag

If you set frame widths to exact pixel values, don't expect Netscape to follow those values. Netscape translates all pixel values for frame definitions to percent so it is very difficult to have frames render cross-browser at exact values.

To turn off the frame borders, select No from the Borders drop-down menu, shown in Figure 12.10, with the frameset selected. You will need to turn the border off in all the framesets in the page. If the borders in the individual frames are set to yes they will override the frameset settings and borders will be visible. To turn off a border, all the adjacent frames must have borders turned off too. If you do not want borders to appear, you should also make sure they don't have a border color assigned.

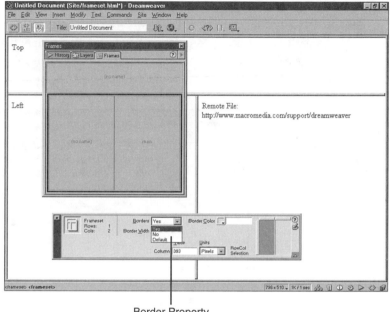

FIGURE 12.10

You can turn the borders off by selecting No in the border drop-down menu of the Property inspector.

Border Property

Add a Title

The title that you see in the browser's title bar is the title in the frameset page. To set the title, select Page Properties while the parent frameset is selected. Type a title into the title box.

Create an Alternative to Frames

Not many people are using browsers that do not support frames anymore. Just in case you get that stray viewer who is attached to their Netscape 1.0 or is using a text-based browser, you should enter some *NoFrames Content*.

One reason some people do not like frames is because of usability issues. Some people with disabilities, such as the visually impaired, may use software that does not easily interpret content in frames.

12

Select the Edit NoFrames Content command from the Frameset submenu of the Modify menu. Note that there is a gray bar across the top of the document window that says NoFrames Content as shown in Figure 12.11. You can simply type in a disclaimer or you can recreate the content of your frames-based Web site here. Turn off the NoFrames Content by de-selecting the same command.

FIGURE **12.11**

The NoFrames Content appears to viewers who have older or text-based browsers.

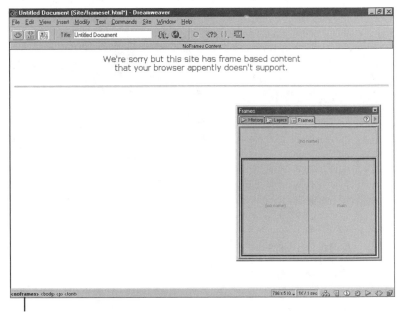

NoFrames Content bar

I don't know of any way to preview the NoFrames Content in a browser other than installing an old browser version on your computer. You will probably have to trust the WYSIWYG Dreamweaver display to be a true representation of what the Web page will look like to those with very old browsers. When you preview the Web page with a modern browser, you will see the frame content.

Use Frame Objects

The quickest way to create frames in Dreamweaver is to use the pre-build frame objects available in the frames panel of the Object panel. The Object panel, shown in Figure 12.12, has several common frame configurations that can get you going quickly with a set of frames.

FIGURE 12.12

The frames panel of the Object panel contains templates of common frame configurations to help you set up frames quickly.

If one of these configurations fits the way you want your frames to look, you'll have a head start by using the frame objects. You can fine-tune the frame settings with the same methods you've used earlier in this hour.

With a new Web page open, add a frame object by either clicking or dragging the icon in the Object panel. The frameset in these frame templates all have the borders turned off. The frames are already named, but you will need to save each file as we did earlier in the hour.

Target Linked Pages to Open in a Specific Frame

The frameset is the parent, and the frames or framesets it contains are its children. Understanding these concepts helps in understanding *targeting*. You can load a Web page into a frame or window by targeting it. You add the target attribute to a hyperlink to send the linked content into a specific window or frame.

There are four reserved target names:

- _top opens a linked Web page in the entire browser window.
- _self opens a linked Web page in the same window or frame that contains the link. This is the default setting.
- _parent opens a linked Web page in the parent frameset. If the parent frameset is not nested, the linked page will fill the entire browser window.
- _blank opens a linked Web page in a new browser window.

The target drop-down menu in the Property inspector lists all the reserved target names plus the names of any named frames showing in the Dreamweaver document window as

12

shown in Figure 12.13. Creating a hyperlink and selecting a frame name from the target drop-down menu will cause the linked page to load in that window. If no target is entered the linked page will load in itself.

FIGURE 12.13

The Target drop-down menu lists the reserved target names plus all the frame names in the current Web page.

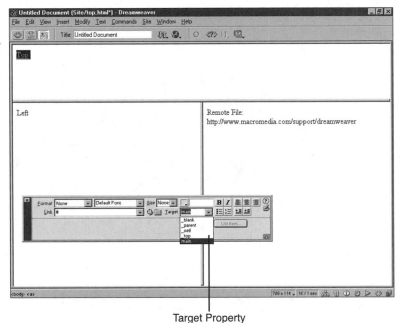

Target Property

Use the original group of frames that you created at the beginning of this hour to target a hyperlink:

1. Create a hyperlink in the frame named toc.
2. Select main from the Target drop-down menu.
3. Save All.
4. Preview the frames in the browser. Click on the link and the Web page should load in the targeted frame (named main).

Use the Go To URL Behavior to Load Frames

The Go To URL behavior has the capability to target frames and is a good way to get content to load into two frames at once. For instance, you might want to change both the topFrame and the main content when the user clicks on a hyperlink in the frame called toc. They might have selected a different section of the content that has a different title in the topFrame. Since a hyperlink can only change the contents in one frame you have to use the Go To URL behavior. To use the Go To URL behavior:

1. Select an object in the frame called topFrame to hyperlink.
2. Place `javascript:` into the Link box in the Property inspector to create a null link.
3. Select the + button in the Behavior panel and select Go To URL.
4. The Go To URL dialog box opens. Select the frame named `toc` as shown in Figure 12.14. Enter a URL in the URL box, and then click OK.

FIGURE 12.14
The Go To URL dialog box enables you to select the target frame for the URL.

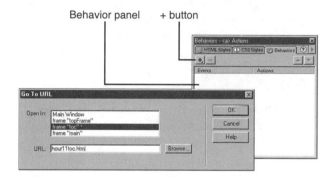

5. Select the Go To URL action by double-clicking it in the Behavior panel.
6. Notice that there is an asterisk by the frame named toc. That means that there is a URL entered for this frame (you entered it in step 4 above). Add another URL to a different frame by first selecting the frame named "main". Enter a URL in the box below, and click OK.
7. Save the frames and preview the page in a browser. Click on the link in the top frame and both lower frames should have the new URLs load.

Summary

In this hour, you learned how to create, name, and save frames and framesets. You learned how to change the border, scrollbar, and resize attributes. You learned how to target content to a specific frame or browser window and you learned how to load two frames at once using behaviors.

Q&A

Q **What's the difference between the reserved target name _top and the reserved target name _parent?**

A The _top target name targets the entire window where the _parent target name targets the parent of the frame where the link resides. Sometimes these are the same.

Q **Why do my frames look different in Internet Explorer and Netscape?**

A Internet Explorer can display frames with sizes defined in either pixel values or percent. Netscape translates pixel values to percent values, causing some rounding to occur. You are more likely to get similar results in both browsers by actually using percent values to define the frames.

Workshop

The Workshop contains quiz questions and activities to help reinforce what you've learned in this hour. If you get stuck, the answers to the quiz can be found after the questions.

Quiz

1. How many files are needed for a Web page with three frames in it?

2. Can a single frameset contain rows and columns?

3. Where would linked content targeted with the reserved target name _self load?

Answers

1. The Web page would contain four files. Three files would be loaded into frames and the fourth file would hold the frameset.

2. No. A frameset can only contain rows or columns but not both.

3. Linked content targeted with the _self reserved target name would load in the same frame with the original link.

Exercises

1. Surf the Web, looking for whether some of your favorites Web sites use frames. The Macromedia site uses frames, for example. How can you tell?

2. Use one of the pre-built frames from the Frames panel of the Object panel. Explore all the attributes of both the individual frames and the framesets.

PART IV

Getting Interactive with Dreamweaver's Behaviors and Timelines

Hour

HOUR 13

Inserting Scripted Functionality with Behaviors

Dreamweaver behaviors enable you to add interactivity to your Web pages. Interactivity usually requires coding in JavaScript, but Dreamweaver adds all the JavaScript for you so you don't have to understand scripting to use behaviors. Behaviors enable you to make something happen when the viewer clicks the mouse, loads a Web page, or moves the cursor.

Because some JavaScript doesn't work with older browsers, Dreamweaver enables you to choose browser versions. When you target 4.0 or later versions of Internet Explorer or Netscape, you have access to many more behaviors than if you target 3.0 browsers. Dreamweaver also enables you to select Netscape and Internet Explorer since these browsers sometimes capture different event triggers. Dreamweaver behaviors are written to work in both Internet Explorer and Netscape.

In this hour, you will learn

- What a Dreamweaver behavior is
- How to apply a behavior to an object in your Web page
- How to use behaviors to add interactivity to a Web page
- How to select events to trigger behaviors

What Is a Dreamweaver Behavior?

Dreamweaver adds behaviors to a Web page to capture input from the user or the Web page. After the input is captured, it causes something to happen. A behavior is an *action* triggered by an *event*, or you could look at it this way:

event + action = behavior

- Events are triggers captured by the browser. Table 13.1 lists examples of common browser events. Different browsers may capture different events. Also, different objects capture different events.
- Actions are JavaScript code. The JavaScript is inserted into your Web page by Dreamweaver.

TABLE 13.1   Common Browser Events with Descriptions

Event	Description
onMouseOver	Triggered when the viewer places the cursor over an object
onMouseDown	Triggered when the viewer presses the mouse button
onMouseUp	Triggered when the viewer releases the mouse button
onClick	Triggered when the viewer presses and releases, or clicks, the mouse button
onLoad	Triggered when the object or Web page finishes loading
onBlur	Triggered when an object loses focus
onFocus	Triggered when an object receives focus

Dreamweaver comes with many powerful behaviors. You can also download third-party behaviors; we'll discuss how to install new behaviors into Dreamweaver in Hour 24, "Customizing Dreamweaver." Table 13.2 lists the behaviors that install with Dreamweaver.

TABLE 13.2   Dreamweaver Behaviors

Behavior	Description
Call JavaScript	Specifies custom JavaScript code
Change Property	Changes an object's properties
Check Browser	Determines the viewer's browser
Check Plugin	Determines whether the viewer has a particular plug-in installed
Control Shockwave or Flash	Controls Shockwave or Flash movies: play, stop, rewind, or go to frame
Drag Layer	Makes a layer draggable and defines a target to drag it to
Go To URL	Loads a URL into the browser
Jump Menu	Edits a jump menu
Jump Menu Go	Adds a custom jump menu go button
Open Browser Window	Opens a new browser window
Play Sound	Plays a sound
Popup Message	Pops up an alert box with text
Preload Images	Preloads images into the browser cache in the background
Set Nav Bar Image	Changes the image in a Nav Bar
Set Text of Frame	Puts text into a frame
Set Text of Layer	Puts text into a layer
Set Text of Status Bar	Puts text into the browser status bar
Set Text of Text Field	Puts text into a text field in a form
Show-Hide Layer	Shows or hides a layer or group of layers
Swap Image	Swaps the image source for another image source
Swap Image Restore	Restores a previous image swap
Go To Timeline Frame	Goes to a specific frame in a timeline
Play Timeline	Plays a timeline
Stop Timeline	Stops a timeline
Validate Form	Validates the data in a form

13

You attach behaviors to objects in your Web page. When you attach a behavior, Dreamweaver opens up the appropriate behavior dialog box. After you've set up the behavior characteristics in the dialog box, you select the event to trigger the behavior. Dreamweaver inserts the necessary JavaScript into the head section of your Web page. Code is also added to the object's tag capturing the event and calling the JavaScript.

You need to attach behaviors to appropriate objects. Dreamweaver won't let you attach behaviors that aren't appropriate for the object selected; the inappropriate behaviors will be grayed out. You can tell which object you currently have selected because it is displayed in the title bar of the Behaviors panel as shown in Figure 13.1.

Current tag

FIGURE 13.1

The tag of the object that is currently selected is displayed in the title bar of the Behaviors panel.

You can attach multiple behaviors to an object. One event can trigger several actions. In Figure 13.2, the onClick event triggers a number of actions. The actions happen in the order they are listed. You can change the order that the actions occur in by moving the actions with the up and down arrow buttons on the Behaviors panel.

Events　　Actions

FIGURE 13.2

One event, for example the onClick *event shown here, can trigger multiple actions. The actions occur in order. The order can be changed with the up and down arrow buttons.*

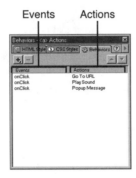

Various browser versions recognize events differently and older browsers aren't able to process the JavaScript for DHTML. The Show Events For drop-down menu, shown in Figure 13.3, enables you to target a specific browser or browser version. Depending on the selection in this menu, different actions and events will be available.

You will have access to the largest number of events by choosing IE 5.0 and the fewest number of events choosing 3.0 and later. The IE 4.0 and Netscape 4.0 events should also work in newer versions of these browsers.

If you select an event that does not work in a certain browser, viewers using that browser will either have nothing happen or will receive a JavaScript error.

FIGURE 13.3
The Show Events For submenu enables you to choose browsers and browser versions. Only the actions and events that work with the browser and version you choose will be available.

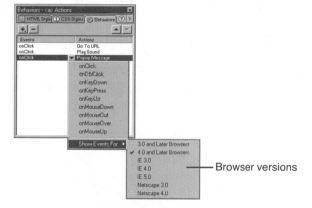

Browser versions

Show and Hide Layers

Let's add your first behavior. The Show-Hide Layers behavior has a name that pretty much says it all. You can show or hide a layer on the Web page. You need to have an event that triggers the action.

Select the Behavior

You will now use the Show-Hide Layers behavior, so create a layer that our behavior will affect. The Show-Hide Layers behavior will be grayed out if there aren't any layers in your Web page. It's important to name your layers when using the Show-Hide Layers behavior. The Show-Hide Layers dialog box displays all the layers on the page by name, so it helps to have a meaningful name. Type some text in the layer, insert an image into it, or give it a background color.

13

To add a Show-Hide Layers behavior to a hyperlink:

1. Hide the layer you just created by changing the visibility attribute to hidden.

2. Create text somewhere on the Web page that says, "Show the layer!". Clicking on this text will trigger the Show-Hide Layers behavior. Add a null hyperlink to the text by first selecting all the text. Type # in the link box of the Property inspector to create the null link.

> Placing a # in the link box in the Property inspector creates a link but it doesn't go to another Web page. This is a common way to create a null hyperlink to apply a behavior to an object. You could also enter **javascript:** to create the same effect.

3. Open the Behaviors panel and click somewhere within your newly created hyperlink. Make sure that <a> Actions is in the title bar of the Behaviors panel, as shown in Figure 13.4. This means that we are applying the behavior to the anchor tag, the tag that implements hyperlinks.

FIGURE 13.4

The title bar of the Behaviors panel shows the tag that the behavior is applied to.

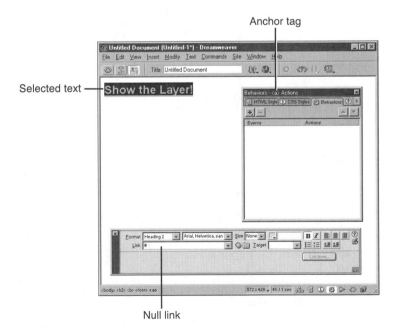

5. Click on the + button in the Behaviors panel as shown in Figure 13.5. Select the Show-Hide Layers behavior. The Show-Hide Layers dialog box appears.

+ button

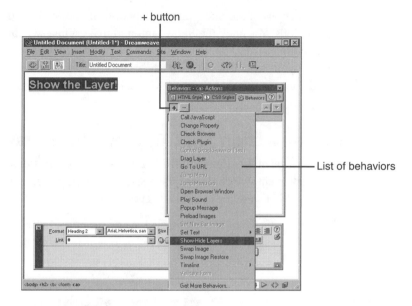

List of behaviors

FIGURE **13.5**

*The + button drops
down the Behaviors
menu with all the
actions available for
the selected object.*

6. The Show-Hide Layers dialog box, shown in Figure 13.6, lists all of the layers in
    the page. There are three buttons: Show, Hide, and Default. Highlight the correct
    layer and click on the Show button. Show will appear in parentheses next to the
    layer name.

FIGURE **13.6**

*The Show-Hide Layers
dialog box lists all of
the layers and enables
you to change their
visibility attributes.*

13

The functions of the Show and Hide buttons in the Show-Hide Layers dialog box are obvious. You click the Show button to make a layer visible and you click the Hide button to make a layer hidden. When a layer is set to show, clicking the Show button again will turn Show off (the same goes for the other buttons). The Default button restores a layer to default visibility (usually visible).

7. Click the OK button to save.

Select the Action That Triggers the Behavior

The Behaviors panel lists the Show-Hide Layers under the Actions column and defaults to the onClick event. We could use the onClick event to trigger showing the layer but that's too easy! Let's use the onMouseUp event instead:

1. Drop down the Events menu by clicking on the arrow button shown in Figure 13.7. You need to select the behavior in the Behaviors panel for this button to be available.

Arrow button for event drop-down menu

FIGURE 13.7

The arrow button beside the event drops down a menu containing the available events.

2. Make sure that the Show Events For submenu has 4.0 and Later Browsers selected.

3. Select onMouseUp in the event drop-down menu as shown in Figure 13.8.

Now that you have set up the action (Show-Hide Layers) and the event (onMouseUp), you can test your work in the browser. Preview the Web page in the browser. Click on the hyperlink and your layer should appear!

FIGURE **13.8**

The event and the action appear side by side as a behavior in the Behaviors panel.

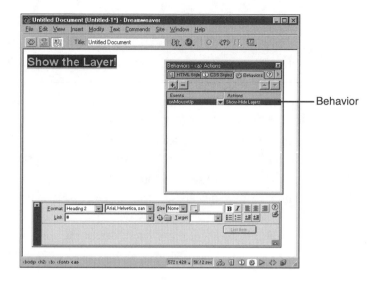

Behavior

Open a New Window

Use the Open Browser Window behavior to open a new browser window and display a URL. This time you will capture the user clicking on an image to trigger the action. When the user clicks on the image, the onClick event will fire. This then triggers the Open Browser Window event that will open a new browser window.

You can open a browser window at a specific size with specific browser attributes. Browser attributes, listed in Table 13.3, control whether the window has controls enabling the user to navigate out of the window. You set up the window attributes in the Open Browser Window dialog box.

TABLE 13.3 Browser Event Choices for Opening a New Window

Attribute	Description
Navigation toolbar	Contains the Back, Next, and other navigation buttons
Location toolbar	Displays the current URL
Status bar	Status bar is located at the bottom of the browser
Menu bar	Contains all the standard browser menus
Scrollbars	Enables the user to scroll the browser window
Resize handles	Enables the user to resize the browser window
Window Name	This name is optional. It can be used to control the window with JavaScript, so do not use spaces or punctuation in the name.

13

To open a new browser window when the user clicks on an image

1. Save the Web page. The Open Browser Window behavior needs the Web page to be saved so it knows how to build the URL that it will load in the new browser window.

2. Insert an image into a Web page. Select the image. Make sure that "<img> Actions" shows in the title bar of the Behaviors panel.

3. Click on the + button in the Behaviors panel. Select the Open Browser Window behavior and the Open Browser Window dialog box appears.

4. Fill in a URL that will load in the new window. You can use a Web page that you created previously or quickly create a new Web page to use. Or, you can load a page from anywhere on the Web into the window.

5. Set the width and height of the window. Check the window attributes (listed in Table 13.3) that you want your new browser window to have. Give the window a name.

6. The Open Browser Window dialog box should look something like Figure 13.9. Click the OK button.

FIGURE 13.9

The Open Browser Window dialog box enables you to turn on or off various attributes of browser windows.

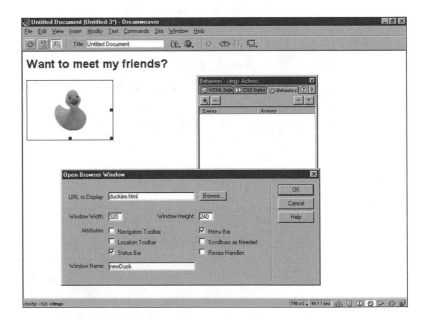

7. Select the onClick event from the Events drop-down menu as shown in Figure 13.10. Make sure that 4.0 and Later Browsers is selected in the Show Events For submenu.

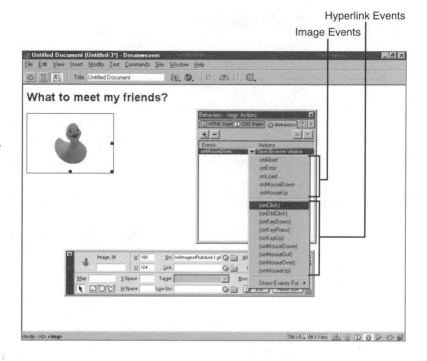

FIGURE 13.10

The Events drop-down menu shows the events available. Notice that the events list is different from the events list that appeared when we selected a hyperlink earlier this hour.

Do you notice that there are two groups of events in the Events drop-down menu in Figure 13.10? One group, including the onClick event, is contained in parentheses. The parentheses signal that Dreamweaver is going to add another tag to the object to make the event work. In this case, Dreamweaver adds a hyperlink to the image and the onClick event is actually part of the hyperlink tag, not the image tag.

Preview the Web page you created in the browser. When you click on the image, your new window should appear. To edit a behavior, simply select the object where the behavior is applied. The behavior will appear in the Behaviors panel. Double-click on the behavior to re-open the dialog box and edit the settings. Change the event by simply selecting a different event in the Events drop-down menu. Delete a behavior by selecting it and clicking the - button in the Behaviors panel.

13

Pop Up a Message

Add an additional behavior, a pop-up message, to the same image you used to open a browser window. The Popup Message behavior displays a JavaScript alert box with a message. To add the Popup Message behavior

1. Select the image, the object where you applied the previous behavior. You should see the Open Browser Window behavior listed in the Behaviors panel. Make sure that "<img> Actions" appears in the title bar of the Behaviors panel.

2. Click on the + button and select the Popup Message behavior.

3. The Popup Message dialog box includes a text box where you type your message as shown in Figure 13.11. Click OK after typing the message.

FIGURE 13.11

The Popup Message dialog box has a text box where you type in the message that will pop up for the user.

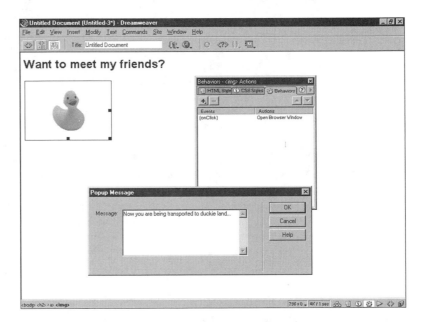

4. Select the onClick event like you did in the Open Browser Window earlier. 4.0 or better should be selected in the Show Events For submenu.

Make sure you select the onClick event and not the onMouseover event. If the Popup Message action is triggered by the onMouseover event, the browser never receives an onClick event to trigger the other actions you have attached to the object.

Preview your Web page in the browser. Does it work ideally? It would probably be better if the message popped up and then the viewer went to the new window after he clicked the OK button in the message box. You can change the order of behaviors that are triggered by the same event. To change the order of the behaviors:

1. Select the image object where the behaviors are applied. You should see both behaviors listed in the Behaviors panel.

2. Select the Popup Message behavior. Press the up arrow button to move the Popup Message behavior above the Open Browser Window behavior as shown in Figure 13.12.

FIGURE 13.12

You can change the execution order of the behaviors with the arrow buttons above the Actions column of the Behaviors panel.

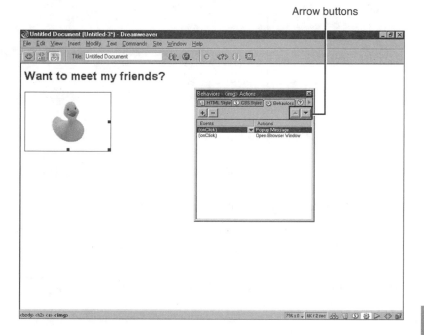

Preview your Web page in the browser. Now the pop-up message appears first. After you click the OK button on the pop-up message, the new browser window should appear.

Add a Message in the Status Bar

You can insert behaviors that write to various objects: frames, layers, text entry fields, and the browser status bar. To use the Set Text of Status Bar behavior:

1. Select an object on the page to trigger the behavior. You can add this behavior to your image after the Open Browser Window behavior.

13

2. Select the + button in the Behaviors panel. Choose the Set Text of Status Bar behavior found under the Set Text submenu. The Set Text of Status Bar dialog box appears.

3. Enter some text to display in the status bar as shown in Figure 13.13. Click OK.

FIGURE **13.13**

The Set Text of Status Bar dialog box enables you to enter a line of text to display in the browser's status bar.

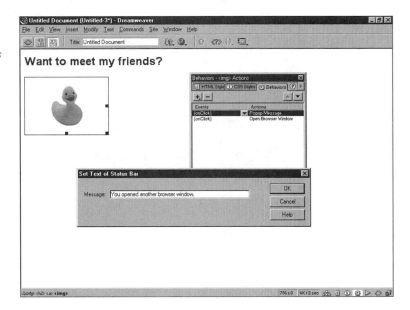

4. Select an event from the Event drop-down menu.

Preview the Web page in your browser. After the new window appears, the text you entered appears in the status bar at the bottom of the browser window as shown in Figure 13.14.

FIGURE **13.14**

All of the behaviors execute after clicking on the image. The message pops up, the new window appears, and the text displays in the status bar.

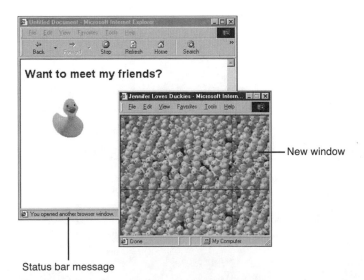

New window

Status bar message

If you don't see a status bar in your browser window, you may have it turned off in your browser preferences.

Summary

In this hour, you learned that Dreamweaver behaviors consist of an event that triggers an action. You used the Show-Hide Layers behavior, the Open Browser Window behavior, the Popup Message behavior, and the Set Text in Status Bar behavior. You captured events from a hyperlink and an image. And you used the onMouseUp and onClick events as triggers for Dreamweaver actions.

Q&A

Q How can I apply a behavior to a layer that is hidden?

A You can select a hidden layer in the Layer panel. Switch to the Behavior panel, without selecting anything else, and apply the behavior. Or, you can temporarily set the layer to visible, apply the behavior, and then re-hide the layer.

Q How can I create a button that triggers a behavior?

A We'll cover forms and buttons in Hour 16, "Creating and Using a Form to Collect Data." Place a button without a form into the Web page to trigger a behavior. Insert a button from the forms section of the Object panel. If Dreamweaver asks you if you'd like to add a form tag you can say no. The trick is to make sure the button is not a submit or reset button. Select None as the action in the Property inspector and then apply a behavior to the button.

Workshop

The Workshop contains quiz questions and activities to help reinforce what you've learned in this hour. If you get stuck, the answers to the questions can be found after the quiz.

Quiz

1. What is the equation connecting an event, an action, and a behavior?
2. True or False: You have the most behaviors and events available when you choose 3.0 and Later Browsers from the Show Events For submenu in the Behaviors panel.
3. What two events add up to an onClick event?

13

Answers

1. Event + action = behavior

2. False. Most Dreamweaver behaviors use DHTML, requiring 4.0 browsers. Selecting 4.0 and Later Browsers will enable you to use far more events and behaviors.

3. An `onClick` event consists of the `onMouseDown` and `onMouseUp` events.

Exercises

1. Create a second hyperlink for the Show-Hide Layers example that we did earlier in the hour. Type **Hide the Layer**, make it a hyperlink, and make clicking on this hyperlink hide the layer you created.

2. Try some behaviors that are similar to the behaviors we have used in this hour. Use the Set Text in Layer behavior and the Go To URL behavior.

HOUR 14

Adding Advanced Behaviors: Drag Layer

Now you will apply a more advanced Dreamweaver behavior, the Drag Layer behavior. The Drag Layer behavior enables you to create layers that the user can drag around the browser window. You can even constrain the area within which the layer can be dragged. This capability is useful for creating sliders, puzzles, dialog boxes, and other interactions.

You can use the Drag Layer behavior to let users interact with objects on your Web page. For instance, you might have a layer that contains a map legend. You could make that layer draggable so that the user could move it out of the way if it happened to be blocking part of the map. Or, you could create a blank face and let people drag different noses, ears, eyes, and so on, onto the face.

If you need to create complicated drag-and-drop interactions you should investigate Macromedia CourseBuilder. CourseBuilder builds interactive Web applications and is described in Appendix A, "CourseBuilder for Dreamweaver." The drag-and-drop interactions created by CourseBuilder have the capability to make an object return to its original position if dropped incorrectly.

You can download a free 30-day trial version for CourseBuilder at `http://www.macromedia.com/software/coursebuilder/trial/`.

In this hour, you will learn

- How to create a draggable layer
- How to create a target layer
- How to use the `onLoad` event

Use the Tag Selector to Select the `<body>` Tag

Set up a Web page to use the Drag Layer behavior by first creating four layers that will be dragged. Then create a layer that will be the target. These layers can have anything in them, such as text, images, and even other layers. Give each of these layers meaningful names. The layers should look something like Figure 14.1.

The Drag Layer behavior enables a layer to be dragged. You need to "turn on" this behavior before the layer can be dragged. This behavior can be triggered when the Web page loads by capturing the `<body>` tag's `onLoad` event. You select the `<body>` tag in Dreamweaver's tag selector. You should see `<body>` Actions in the title of the Behaviors panel.

You may notice when you select the `<body>` tag that everything in your Web page gets selected. That's because the `<body>` tag is the container within which all the objects on your Web page reside.

Target

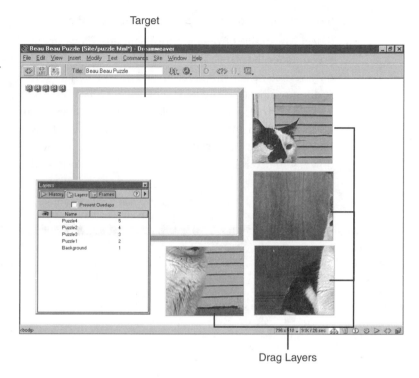

FIGURE 14.1
The user will drag layers onto the target layer to complete an interaction.

Drag Layers

Constrain the Movement of Your Layer

After you've created your drag and target layers and given them names, you're ready to apply the Drag Layer behavior. To use the Drag Layer behavior

1. Select the <body> tag from the tag selector in the Dreamweaver status bar.

2. Click the + button in the Behaviors panel and select Drag Layer. The Drag Layer dialog box appears as shown in Figure 14.2.

Basic   Advanced
tab   tab

FIGURE 14.2
The Drag Layer dialog box has a Basic and an Advanced tab.

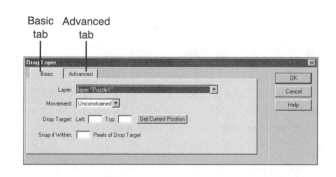

14

3. Select the name of a layer to be dragged from the Layer drop-down menu.

4. Select Constrained from the Movement drop-down menu. Four boxes appear for you to enter the pixel value of coordinates of an area. To constrain movement to only vertical, enter values for up and down but enter 0 for right and left. To constrain movement to only horizontal, enter values for left and right but enter 0 for up and down. To define a rectangular area, enter values in all of the boxes. Values are all relative to the original position of the layer. The Drag Layer dialog box should look like Figure 14.3. This layer is constrained to move 20 pixels up, 300 pixels down, 400 pixels to the left, and 20 pixels to the right of its original position.

Constrained movement area

FIGURE 14.3

When you select Constrained from the Movement drop-down menu, four new boxes appear. Enter pixel values to define the constrained movement area.

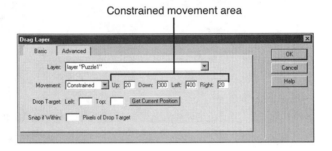

An easy way to figure out which values to enter in the Constrained Movement boxes is to calculate them ahead of time. You can use Dreamweaver and a little math to decide on the numbers before you start to apply the Drag Layer behavior. Write down the original L (left) and T (top) values for the layer. Move the layer to the edges of the constraining area and write down those L and T values. Figure out the difference and enter those values into the Constrained Movement boxes when you set up the Drag Layer behavior. To return your layer to its original position, enter the original L and T values into the Property inspector.

5. Click OK to save your changes.

Check to see that the Drag Layer behavior is working the way you want it to by previewing the Web page in a browser. The correct layer should be draggable, and other layers shouldn't be draggable yet. The drag area should be constrained the way you want it. We will go back and edit the behavior in a few minutes.

Capture the Drop Target Location

We could calculate or guess at the exact target location, which may work some of the time. But the easiest way to capture the perfect target location is to take advantage of Drag Layer behavior's built in Get Current Position button. This button will capture the position of the layer and fill in the coordinates for you.

1. Line up the layer that you set previously in the Drag Layer behavior in its final position on the target. Remember that you can use the arrow keys on the keyboard to move the layer one pixel at a time for fine-tuning.

2. Select the <body> tag from the tag selector.

3. Double-click the Drag Layer behavior you just set up in the Behaviors panel to edit it.

If you do not see the behavior attached to the <body> tag when you elect it, you've applied the behavior to the wrong tag. You will need to hunt down the object that you applied the behavior to and delete the behavior in the Behaviors panel. As you click on objects in the document window, look at the Behaviors panel to see which object has the behavior attached to it.

4. Click on the Get Current Position button. The Left and Top values will fill in automatically as shown in Figure 14.4. The Snap if Within box automatically defaults to 50 pixels.

Get Current Position Button

FIGURE 14.4

The Get Current Position button automatically fills in the coordinates with the current position of the drag layer.

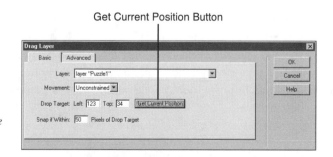

5. Accept the default Snap if Within value or change it. This value sets how close the user must drop the layer in order for it to snap and depends upon the size of your target area. Make sure that this value isn't so small that it's difficult for the user to position the layer, or so big that the user doesn't need to be accurate.

14

6. Click OK.

7. Put the layer back in its original position. Then preview the page in the browser.

 You can use the Drag Layer behavior without a target layer if the interaction you are creating doesn't require the user to drop the layers on a target.

Apply the Drag Layer Behavior Advanced Attributes

You have a functioning interaction with a Drag Layer and a target. The layer will snap when dropped within a certain distance of the target center. This interaction may work great for some situations but in other situations you may want to use some of the advanced attributes of the Drag Layer dialog box as shown in Figure 14.5.

FIGURE **14.5**

There is an Advanced tab in the Drag Layer dialog box that enables you to add advanced attributes to the Drag Layer behavior, including JavaScript.

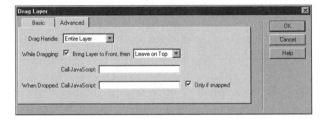

The Advanced tab in the Drag Layer dialog box enables you to define a specific area of the layer as a handle for dragging. This enables you to have finer control over what part of the layer the user actually clicks on to drag the layer and can make the interaction more realistic. For instance, if you have an image of a file drawer that the user could drag open, you could limit the user to dragging the drawer handle instead of the entire drawer.

 The coordinates for defining an area within the layer to drag are relative to the upper-left corner of the drag layer.

Another advanced attribute is the capability to control where the layer is positioned relative to other layers while dragging. You can set the layer to be on top of all other layers, regardless of its z-index value, while it is dragging. Its original z-index value can then be restored when it is dropped or it can remain on top.

The capability to call JavaScript both while the layer is being dragged and after the layer has been dropped offers many powerful options. We'll experiment in a few minutes with adding some simple JavaScript into these boxes. Knowledge of JavaScript isn't required as these settings are purely optional.

To add advanced attributes to the Drag Layer behavior

1. Re-open the Drag Layer dialog box as described above. Select the Advanced tab.

2. Select the Entire Area command from the Drag Handle drop-down menu. Optionally, if you want the user to be able to click on only a portion of the layer to drag it, select the Area within Layer command from the Drag Handle drop-down menu. Enter the Left, Top, Width, and Height coordinates.

3. Make sure that the check box beside Bring Layer to Front is checked so that the layer will be on top of all others while dragging.

4. Select Restore z-index or Leave on Top from the drop-down menu beside While Dragging, as shown in Figure 14.6. This will either put the layer back to its original z-index value after it has been on top while dragging or leave it on top.

FIGURE 14.6

The While Dragging drop-down menu enables you to choose to leave the draggable object on the top z-index or restore its original z-index.

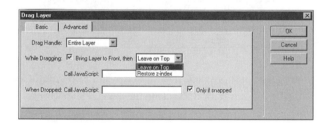

Next, place some simple JavaScript in the two boxes that will accept JavaScript under the Advanced tab in the Drag Layer dialog box. You can set the value of the browser status bar by giving a value to the `window.status` object. First, set `window.status` to "Dragging…" while the user is dragging the layer. Then, set `window.status` to "Dropped" when the user has dropped the layer on the target. To enter JavaScript in the Drag Layer dialog box

1. Carefully type this JavaScript code into the While Dragging: Call JavaScript box

```
window.status = 'Dragging...'
```

Be sure to use single quotes, not double quotes here.

14

2. Carefully type this JavaScript code into the When Dropped: Call JavaScript box:

```
window.status = 'Dropped'
```

Again, be sure to use single quotes, not double quotes here.

3. Check the Only if Snapped check box, shown in Figure 14.7, if the JavaScript should execute only if the user drops the layer on the target. Leave the Only if Snapped check box unchecked if the JavaScript should execute when the user drops the drag layer.

FIGURE 14.7

You can select whether the JavaScript executes whenever the user drops the layer or only when they drop it onto the target.

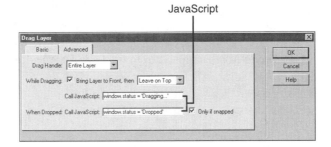

JavaScript

4. Click OK.

The Call JavaScript behavior works similarly to entering the JavaScript in the Drag Layer behavior. The Call JavaScript behavior dialog box opens a single line where you can write a JavaScript statement like you just did.

Save your Web page and preview it in the browser. You can, of course, continue to re-open the Drag Layer behavior and refine the coordinates or change settings.

Select a <body> Tag Event

After the Drag Layer behavior works the way you want it to, you need to add an event to trigger the Drag Layer action. If you apply the behavior to the <body> tag, it may have defaulted to the onLoad event. If the onLoad event is not already selected, select it from the Event drop-down menu.

You can trigger the Drag Layer behavior from other object's events too. For instance, you may require the user to click on something to show the layer that they will drag. You could place the Drag Layer behavior under the Show-Hide Layer behavior so that once the layer is visible it is also draggable.

You will not be able to apply the Drag Layer behavior to another layer with 4.0 or Later Browsers selected in the Events For drop-down menu of the Behavior panel. Netscape will not recognize layer `<div>` tag events. Internet Explorer 4.0 will recognize `<div>` tag events and you will be able to trigger the Drag Layer behavior from a layer if you have IE 4.0 selected in the Events For drop-down menu of the Behavior panel.

Summary

In this hour, you learned how to apply a behavior to the `<body>` tag. You learned how to configure the Drag layer behavior to create a drag-and-drop interaction. You set up advanced attributes of the drag layer behavior and selected an event to trigger the behavior.

Q&A

Q What if the user wants to try dragging the layer again?

A You could go through a lot of work to move all of the layers back to their original positions via a timeline (see Hour 15, "Animating with Timelines"). Or you can direct the user to simply press the Browser Refresh button to restore the look of the original Web page.

Q Where can I learn more about simple JavaScript statements?

A There are some excellent resources and tutorials on the Web where you can learn some JavaScript. You don't have to understand everything about JavaScript to use it. The short statements that we used during this hour should be easy to find in any JavaScript book or reference. Check out Appendix B, "Internet Resources," for links to helpful sites.

Workshop

The Workshop contains quiz questions and activities to help reinforce what you've learned in this hour. If you get stuck, the answers to the quiz can be found following the questions.

Quiz

1. Do you need to have a target layer to use the Drag Layer behavior?
2. True or False: The Constrained Movement coordinates in the Drag Layer dialog box are relative to the Web page.
3. How can you change the z-index of the dragging layer with the Drag Layer behavior?

14

Answers

1. No, you can simply create a layer that the user can drag either constrained or unconstrained on the screen. If it is not necessary to capture where the user drops the layer, you don't need a target layer.

2. False. The Constrain Movement coordinates are relative to the location of the layer.

3. You can make the layer come to the front by checking the Bring Layer to Front check box. Then you can leave it on top or restore it to its original z-index.

Exercises

1. Create a layer and constrain its movement to horizontal only. Check the Web page by previewing it in a browser. Then try constraining the movement to only vertical. Finally, constrain the movement to an area.

2. Make an interaction that has more than one drag layer behavior by attaching multiple behaviors to the <body> tag.

HOUR 15

Animating with Timelines

Dreamweaver's capability to create time-based animation makes it unique as a Web-based authoring tool. Those familiar with Macromedia's animation programs, Director and Flash, will quickly feel comfortable with Dreamweaver's Timelines panel. Those not familiar with animation programs will soon be creating animations after learning a few key concepts.

In this hour, you will learn

- How to record an animation
- How to create an animation in the Timelines panel
- How to change layer properties over time
- How to add behaviors to timelines

Create an Animation

Timelines change properties over time to create an animation. To make a layer move, you change the positioning properties—left and top—over time. To make objects appear or disappear, you change the visibility properties over time. To change the stacking order of objects, you change the z-index over time. You'll learn more about time-based animations in this hour.

 You can also place images into timelines and change the image source over time. You cannot make images move around the screen unless they are contained in a layer.

The animations that Dreamweaver creates play natively in the browser. You don't need any plugins to play Dreamweaver timelines. Your viewer needs to have a browser capable of viewing DHTML (either Internet Explorer or Netscape Navigator 4.0 or better) to see your timelines.

When you create a timeline, Dreamweaver inserts JavaScript into your Web page. The JavaScript defines all of the timeline functionality. If you edit the HTML source, be careful not to delete or move the JavaScript that creates the timeline.

Use the Timelines Panel

Open the Timelines panel shown in Figure 15.1. The numbered *channels* run vertically up and down the timeline. Channels enable multiple objects to be animated in the same timeline. The numbered *frames* run horizontally from left to right along the top of the timeline. The number of frames affects the pace of the animation.

There is a special channel across the top of the timeline that is labeled with a B. You can set behaviors in this channel so that behaviors execute in a certain frame. We'll add behaviors to a timeline later in the hour.

The red square with a line extending down is the *playback head*. It rests on the current frame and controls which frame is currently selected. Drag the playback head to any frame in the timeline to view a specific frame.

The playback controls at the top of the Timelines panel, shown in Figure 15.2, manage the playback head. The rewind button moves the playback head to frame one. The Back button moves the playback head back one frame. The Play button moves the playback head forward one frame. If you hold down the Back or Play buttons, you can move through all the frames. The current frame number is displayed between the Back and Play buttons.

Channels   Frames

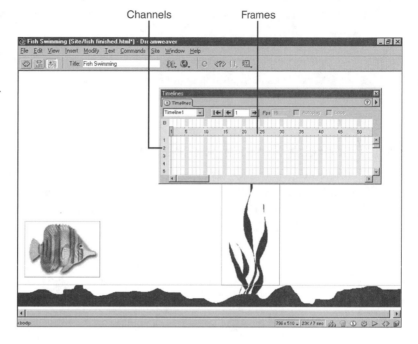

FIGURE 15.1

Use the Timeline panel to configure animations in your Web page. A timeline is made up of channels (vertical axis) and frames (horizontal axis).

15

Current
frame number

Rewind   Back   Play
button   button   button

Playback Head

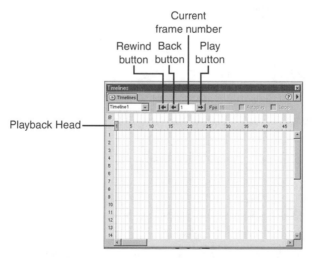

FIGURE 15.2

The playback controls, located at the top of the Timeline panel, enable you to move through all the frames in the animation both backward and forward.

You set the frames per second (fps) in the Fps box located beside the Play button. This sets the number of frames that occur per second in your timeline. The higher the fps, the faster the animation because more frames are crammed into one second. If you are moving an object around the screen, more frames will make the animation smoother. There is a certain point, however, where the browser just can't animate any faster even if you increase the fps.

> The default fps setting of 15 is a good place to start. This setting means that 15 frames will take one second to play.

Record a Simple Animation

Let's create an animation. The quickest way to make something move in a timeline is to record it. First, you will need a layer with something in it (an image, some text, or a background color). Usually animated layers contain images. All the objects that you place in your timelines need to be in layers.

> Before you begin recording the movement of a layer, you'll want to make the Timelines panel small and place it out of the way of the animation path. Dreamweaver opens the Timelines panel when you begin to record an animation if the panel isn't open already. It's also a good idea to close panels that might be in the way. Be careful not to drop the layer in the Timelines panel while animating. This has a different effect than recording an animation.

To record an animation path:

1. Select the layer that you want to animate.

2. Select the Record Path of Layer command under the Timeline sub-menu in the Modify menu.

3. Make sure that the playback head in the Timelines panel is on frame 1. If it is not, move it there.

4. Pick up the layer's move handle and drag the layer on the path that you want. A dotted line will mark your path, as shown in Figure 15.3. It's best to start out making your animation fairly short.

5. When you release the mouse button, the path becomes a solid line as shown in Figure 15.4.

FIGURE 15.3

A dotted line shows the path of your animation while you are recording it using the Record Path of Layer command.

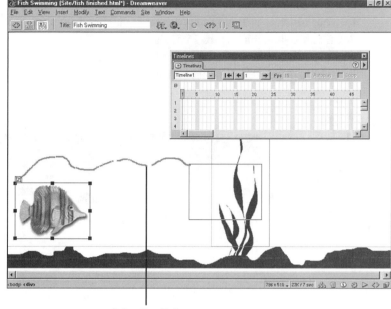

Animation Path

Animated Layer
in a Channel

FIGURE 15.4

The path of the animation becomes a solid line after you stop dragging the layer. This is what all animation paths look like.

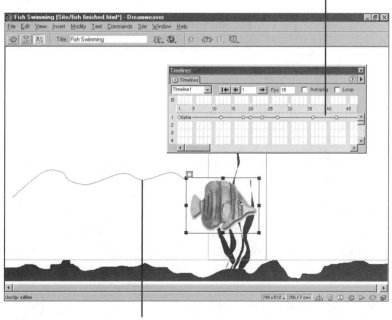

Animation Path

15

Congratulations! You've created a timeline animation in Dreamweaver. The default name for your timeline is Timeline1. To change the timeline name click in the Timelines drop-down menu shown in Figure 15.5, change the name, and press Enter. We'll talk about creating multiple timelines in a Web page later this hour. You can select different time-lines to display in the Timelines panel with this drop-down menu.

Timeline name

FIGURE 15.5

The Timelines drop-down menu lists all of the timelines in the Web page. You can change a timeline name by selecting it here and renaming it.

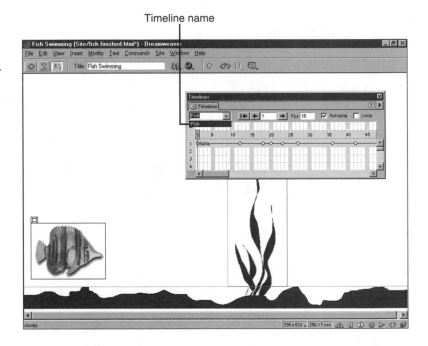

You see the name of your layer in the first channel of the Timelines panel. The line through the channel marks the duration of the animation. You can drag the playback head along the frames to see the animation in the document window.

The solid circles in the animation bar are called *keyframes,* shown in Figure 15.6. Keyframes are an important part of timeline animations because changes can **only** be defined in keyframes. Dreamweaver calculates all of the intermediate steps between keyframes. You need a keyframe every time the animation changes direction or anything else new happens. We'll explore adding and editing keyframes in a few minutes. Notice that your recorded animation probably has many keyframes. Dreamweaver added one every time the direction changed when you recorded the movement of the layer.

Keyframe

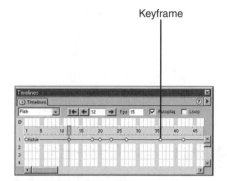

FIGURE 15.6

Keyframes appear in an animation bar as circles.

Preview the animation in the browser. Did anything happen? Probably not. You haven't yet set anything to trigger the animation to play. You'll do that next.

Turn on Autoplay and Loop Your Animation

There are two check boxes in the Timelines panel, shown in Figure 15.7, that we haven't talked about yet: Autoplay and Loop. Check the Autoplay check box to make the timeline play when the Web page loads. This setting automatically adds the Play Timeline behavior to the <body> tag, triggered by the onLoad event. After you check this setting in the Timelines panel, preview the animation in the browser. It works!

Autoplay ———   ——— Loop

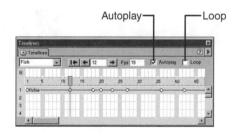

FIGURE 15.7

The Autoplay setting inserts a behavior into the <body> tag that makes the animation play when the Web page is loaded. The Loop setting inserts a behavior in the B channel that sends the animation back to the first frame.

To make the animation play continually, select the Loop check box. Dreamweaver inserts the Go To Timeline Frame behavior in the B channel of the Timelines panel. Dreamweaver inserts the behavior in the last frame of the animation. What timeline frame do you think the Go To Timeline Frames behavior is set to go to? You're right if you said frame 1.

Edit a Behavior in the B Channel

Edit the behavior that Dreamweaver inserted when you checked the Loop option. Double-click the symbol in the B channel to open the Behaviors panel (single-click if the Behaviors panel is already visible in the document window). The action and event, shown in Figure 15.8, behave just like any other behavior. Notice the onFrame event, in which a frame number is added to the event name. This event is triggered when the animation reaches the specified frame.

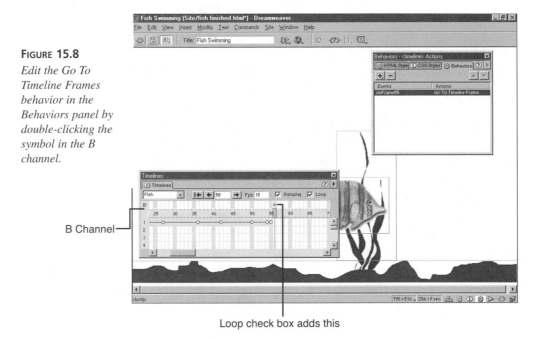

FIGURE 15.8

Edit the Go To Timeline Frames behavior in the Behaviors panel by double-clicking the symbol in the B channel.

B Channel

Loop check box adds this

Open the Go To Timeline Frame action. The Go To Timeline Frame dialog box appears, as shown in Figure 15.9. You select the timeline from the Timeline drop-down menu and set the frame to go to in the Go to Frame box. You can also set the number of times you want the animation to loop. Enter a number here (you might want to enter a small number so you don't use up the rest of this hour!) and click OK. Preview your animation in the browser. It should loop the number of times you specified.

FIGURE 15.9

You configure the number of times the animation loops in the Go To Timeline Frame dialog box.

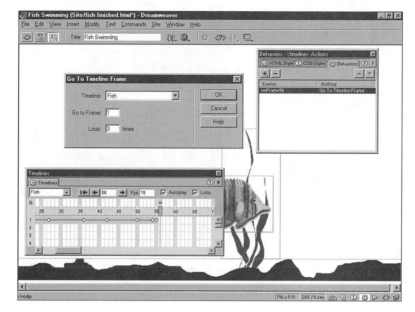

 If you change the name of a timeline after you have referenced it in the actions of Dreamweaver behaviors, you may need to edit the behavior and select the new timeline name.

Add a Layer to the Timeline

The Record Path of Layer command is nice for capturing animations that have complex movement. But most of the time you will want to set the length of a timeline and its keyframes manually. Plus, you can also add multiple layers to your animation.

Create another layer to add to the timeline that you just created. Make sure the Timelines panel is open. To add the layer to the timeline:

1. Pick up a layer, drag it into the Timelines panel, and drop it in the second channel beneath the previously animated layer as shown in Figure 15.10.

FIGURE 15.10

Another layer is dragged into the Timelines panel. The layer is placed in channel 2 beneath the other layer.

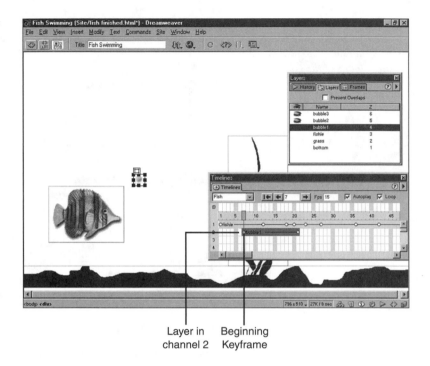

Layer in   Beginning
channel 2   Keyframe

If you see the name of an image in the timeline instead of the name of the layer that contains an image you have accidentally dragged the image into the timeline. You need to delete the image from the timeline and drag the layer onto the Timelines panel instead.

2. You might receive a message box warning you about which layer attributes Netscape does not support. We won't be using any attributes that Netscape doesn't support so you can close this box.

3. Note that the animation bar begins and ends with a keyframe. Pick up the animation bar and move it in the same channel or to a different channel if you want.

4. To increase or decrease the length of the animation, drag the end keyframe.

5. Click on the beginning keyframe. This is the position that the layer will be in at the beginning of the animation. You can adjust the beginning position **only** while you have the first keyframe selected.

6. Click on the ending keyframe. This is the position that the layer will be in at the end of the animation. Only while the ending keyframe is selected, pick up the layer and move it to its end position. When you release the mouse button you will see a line in the document window showing the animation path as in Figure 15.11.

FIGURE 15.11

A line represents the animation path when you have a timeline selected in the Timelines panel.

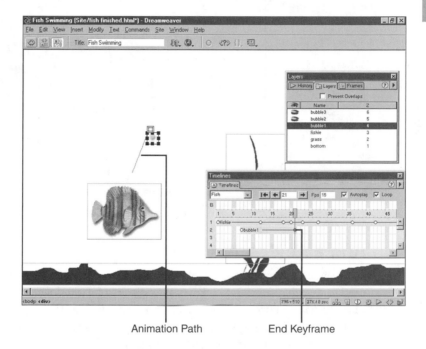

Animation Path   End Keyframe

7. Preview the animation in your browser. Note that the second layer moves in a line from one point, the beginning keyframe, to another point, the end keyframe.

If you decide to use a different object after you have created a timeline, you don't have to start from scratch. You can swap the object that you used to create a timeline with another object on the Web page. Select the Change Object command from the context menu that appears when you right-click on an animation bar in the Timelines panel. The Change Object dialog box appears, as shown in Figure 15.12. Simply select a different object from the drop-down list.

FIGURE **15.12**

*You can swap an
object in a timeline for
a different object using
the Change Object
command.*

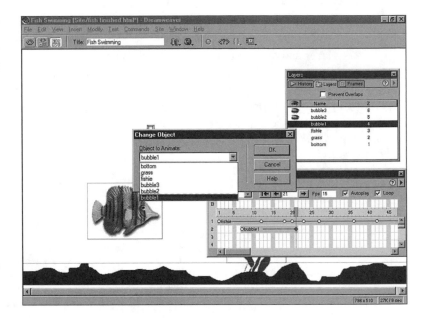

FIGURE **15.12**

*You can swap an
object in a timeline for
a different object using
the Change Object
command.*

Add a Keyframe

To create a more complex animation or make something happen at a specific frame, you
need to turn that frame into a keyframe. When you hold down the Ctrl key (⌘ on the
Macintosh) and position your cursor over an animation bar, the cursor looks like a
keyframe. Yes, you guessed it; click and you insert a keyframe at that location. You can
also access the context menu, shown in Figure 15.13, by right-clicking on a specific
frame in the animation bar. It contains the Add Keyframe command that accomplishes
the same thing.

With the newly created keyframe selected, move the layer. When you release the mouse
button, the animation path has changed as shown in Figure 15.14.

You can add as many keyframes as you want. If you need to adjust the position of a layer
at a certain keyframe, select the keyframe and move the layer. If you need to add or
remove frames, right-click on the frame in the animation bar to select either the Add
Frame or the Remove Frame commands. When you add or delete frames, they will be
added or deleted from the entire timeline, not just a single channel.

FIGURE **15.13**

The context menu contains many useful commands for manipulating timelines, including the Add Keyframe command.

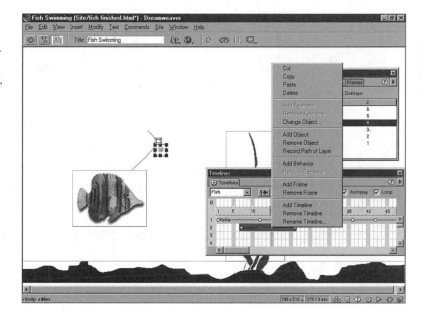

FIGURE **15.14**

After you add a keyframe and move the layer, the animation path changes.

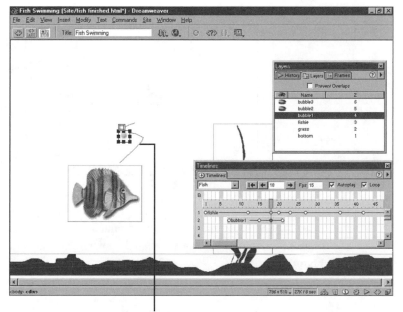

Animation Path

15

Control Layer Properties with Timelines

So far this hour you have manipulated the positioning of layers with a timeline. You can manipulate other layer attributes too. What if you wanted a number of layers to appear over a period of time? You create a timeline, add keyframes, and change the visibility attribute when a keyframe is selected. To create a timeline that changes layer visibility over time:

1. Create five layers and line them up on the page. Name them sequentially, like L1, L2, L3, L4, and L5. All of the layers' visibility should be set to visible (or default).

2. Drag each layer into its own channel in the Timelines panel as shown in Figure 15.15.

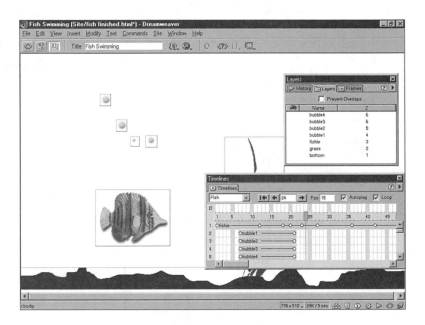

3. Drag the end keyframes so that the animation bar in a channel is five frames longer than the animation bar in the channel above it. The Timeline panel should look like Figure 15.16.

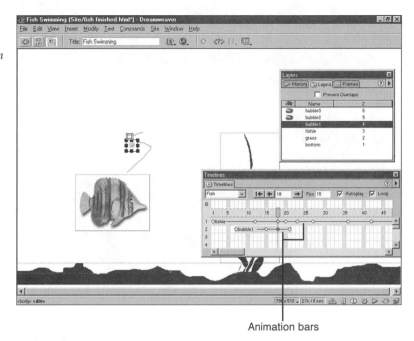

FIGURE 15.16

Each animation bar is five frames longer than the animation bar in the previous channel.

Animation bars

4. Position the playback head on the first frame. Open the Layer panel and hide all of the layers (click in the eye column until there is a closed eye).

5. Make sure you select Autoplay and then preview the timeline in the browser.

You have created a timeline where all of the layers begin as hidden and end, at varying times, as visible. You could create a similar timeline changing the z-index instead. Or, you could create a complex combination changing positioning, visibility, and the z-index all at the same time.

Place a Behavior in the Behaviors Channel

Another way to have similar results in the timeline that you just created is to place Show-Hide Layers behaviors in the B channel in the Timelines panel. To add behaviors to the timeline:

1. Do not drag any layers into the timeline. Make sure that all the layers have the visibility attribute set to hidden.

2. Open the Behaviors panel. Click in frame 5 of the B channel.

3. Click the + button in the Behaviors panel to add a behavior to frame 5. Select the Show-Hide Layer behavior. Set your first layer to show and leave the rest of the layers hidden (don't set anything). A dash appears in the B channel signaling that the frame contains a behavior.

4. Select frame 10, click the + button in the Behaviors panel, and repeat the process for the second layer.

5. Continue to add behaviors until your timeline looks like Figure 15.17.

FIGURE 15.17
This timeline contains only behaviors in the B channel.

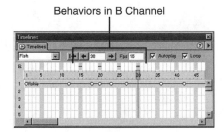
Behaviors in B Channel

6. Make sure you select Autoplay, and then preview the timeline in the browser.

This timeline should work exactly like the previous timeline. You can use combinations of the two methods. You can insert any behaviors you need into the B channel.

Use Multiple Timelines in a Web Page

Create a new timeline either by right-clicking in the Timelines panel and selecting the Add Timeline command, or selecting the Add Timeline command from the Timeline submenu of the Modify menu. Move between different timelines in a Web page by selecting them from the Timeline drop-down menu in the Timelines panel. You can delete a timeline with the Remove Timeline command.

After you create a second timeline, you need to trigger it. You can select the Autoplay check box to trigger the second timeline along with the first one. You can also trigger the second timeline by attaching the Play Timeline behavior to a generic button. You can also trigger a timeline to play immediately after another timeline by inserting the Play Timeline behavior into the last frame's B channel in the first timeline.

Summary

In this hour, you learned how to record the movement of a layer. You learned how to add layers to a timeline and change their properties. You added a keyframe so that you could add properties to an additional frame.

Q&A

Q Help! My timeline doesn't play. What's wrong?

A First, check that you dragged a layer, and not an image, into the Timelines panel. Then make sure that you have checked the Autoplay check box. Is the animation bar starting at frame one? If not, your animation may be playing empty frames before it gets to your content.

Q I'm right-clicking in the Timelines panel, but I don't see the Insert Keyframe command in the context menu. Where is it?

A You need to right-click on an individual animation bar to get the context menu to appear. You can't click on the top of the playback head or the frame numbers. If you continue to have trouble, hold down the Ctrl key (Command key on the Macintosh) and use the keyframe cursor to add keyframes.

Workshop

The Workshop contains quiz questions and activities to help reinforce what you've learned in this hour. If you get stuck, the answers to the quiz can be found after the questions.

Quiz

1. What is fps?
2. What does a keyframe do?
3. Where do you place a behavior in a timeline?

Answers

1. Fps stands for frames per second. This setting affects how fast the animation runs.
2. A keyframe is a frame where you can change properties.
3. You place behaviors in the B Channel at the top of the Timelines panel.

Exercises

1. Create a timeline similar to the timed visibility swap you did this hour, but drag images into the timeline instead of layers. With a keyframe selected, load a different source file for each image.
2. Create an animation where a layer moves around the screen. Add more keyframes. Do the keyframes change the way the animation runs? For instance, does the animation run more smoothly with more keyframes?

Part V

Collecting User Data with Forms

Hour

Hour **16**

Creating and Using a Form to Collect Data

In this hour you will create a form to collect user input. Dreamweaver gives you easy access to a number of different form elements, including text boxes, radio buttons, check boxes, lists, drop-down menus, and buttons to capture user choices. We'll cover how to submit form data in Hour 17, "Sending and Reacting to Form Data."

With forms, you can collect information, such as comments or orders, and interact with your users. In your form you can ask for your user's name and email address, or you can have them sign a guestbook or provide feedback on your Web site. You can send this information back to the Web server if you'd like. Dreamweaver enables you to validate information so that you know it's in the correct format.

In this hour, you will learn

- How to insert a form into a Web page
- How to add text fields, radio button, and check boxes
- How to add a list or a drop-down of form choices
- How to insert different types of buttons
- How to create and edit a jump menu

Create a Form

A form object is a container for other objects and an invisible element. When you add a form to a Web page, Dreamweaver represents it as a red, dashed-line box, if you have Form Delimiter checked in the Invisible Elements category in Preferences dialog box as shown in Figure 16.1. Make sure you have this option selected so you can see the outline of the form.

FIGURE 16.1

The Invisible Elements category in the Preferences dialog box enables you turn on and off the red, dashed-line box that represents the form outline.

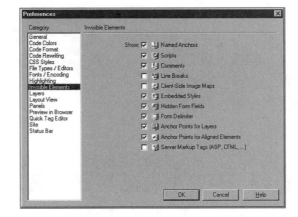

While creating a form, it might be helpful to have the Forms panel active in the Object panel as shown in Figure 16.2. The first step in creating a form is to insert a form into your Web page to hold all the form objects that will collect user input.

FIGURE 16.2

The Forms panel in the Object panel presents all of the form objects that you insert in your Web page to collect user input.

To add a form

1. Place the insertion point where you want to insert the form.
2. Select the Form command from the Insert menu or select the form object in the Forms panel of the Object panel.

3. A message box, shown in Figure 16.3, may appear telling you that you will not be able to see the form unless you view the invisible elements. Select the Invisible Elements command from Visual Aids submenu of the View menu, if necessary.

FIGURE **16.3**

A message box may appear telling you to view invisible elements to see the form you inserted into your Web page.

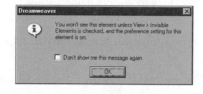

16

4. You see a red, dashed-line box that represents the form as shown in Figure 16.4.

Form Delimiter

FIGURE **16.4**

A form appears as a red, dashed-line box when invisible elements are turned on.

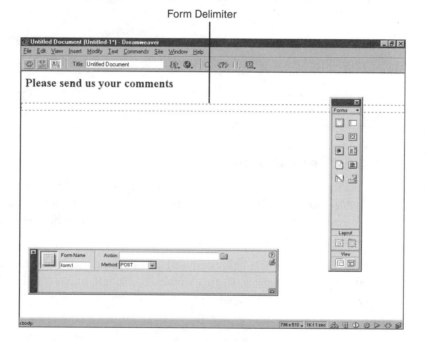

You can format the area within a form with tables, horizontal rules, text, and other items that would normally be in a Web page. The only items that will be collected, however, are the names of the form elements and the data the user enters in the form. The text and formatting objects you place within the form will not be submitted.

To select a form, click on the edge of the form outline. The Property inspector shows the three properties you can enter for a form:

- Form Name is necessary if you plan to apply any behaviors (or your own custom scripts) to a form. It's a good idea to always name forms. Dreamweaver puts a default form name in for you.
- Action is a URL that points to an application, usually a script, on the server that will process the form data.
- Method tells the application on the server how the data should be processed.

Give your form a name, as shown in Figure 16.5. We will explore the Action and Method properties in the next hour, so just leave them blank for now. To format a form, click within the form so the insertion point appears with the form outline. Now you can type or insert objects and they will be inside of the form.

FIGURE 16.5

The Property inspector shows the three attributes available to set for a form object.

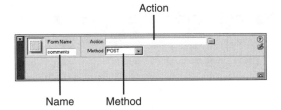

Add Text Fields

Text fields, as shown in Figure 16.6, are commonly used in forms. Single-line text fields enable you to type in a name, address, phone number, or another short piece of text information. Text fields can also have multiple lines suitable for comments or lengthy pieces of information.

Create a group of text fields designed to collect the user's first and last name, email address, and comments. Begin by inserting a single-line text field into your Web page to collect the user's first name:

1. Make sure the insertion point is within a form.
2. Select the Text Field object from the Object panel, or select the Text Field command from the Form Object submenu in the Insert menu.
3. A text field appears in the form as shown in Figure 16.7.

FIGURE 16.6

A group of text fields is used to collect user information on an order form that is submitted to the server and processed.

FIGURE 16.7

A text field is inserted within a form so that a script or an application on the server can collect the data that a user enters in the field on the Web page.

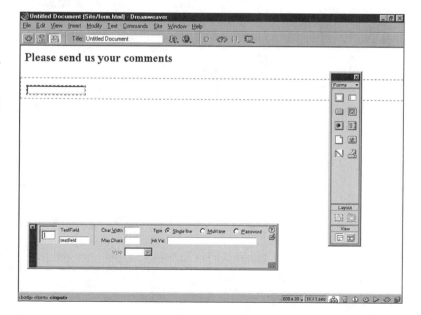

If you get a dialog box asking you to insert a `<form>` tag but you thought
that you had inserted a form object into an existing form, you do not have
the insertion point placed properly within the form. It's easiest to reply "No"
to the dialog box question, delete the newly created object, and try again. If
you are just beginning to create a form and forget to insert a form object
first, answer "Yes" to the dialog box question. A form will be inserted by
Dreamweaver around the form element you have just created.

To add another text field directly to the right of the first one, place the insertion point
after the text field and insert another text field for the user's last name. Add another
single-line text field for the user's email address; place the insertion point after the second text field you created and press the Enter key to add a new paragraph within the
form before you insert the text field. In another new paragraph, place a fourth text field
to collect user comments. The form should look like Figure 16.8.

FIGURE 16.8

*This form contains
four text fields that you
will use to collect the
user's first name, last
name, email address,
and comments.*

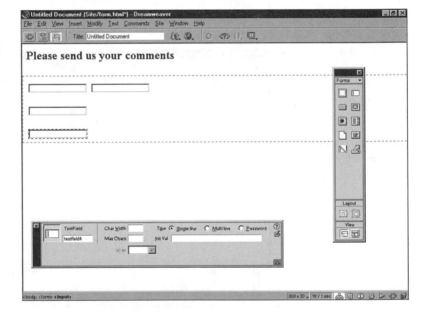

Apply Text Field Attributes

When you have a text field selected, the Property inspector presents the text field attributes as shown in Figure 16.8. Dreamweaver fills in a unique default name. Rename all
four text fields in your form with meaningful and unique names; possible names would

be firstname, lastname, email, and comments. As with other Dreamweaver objects, it is a good idea not to use spaces and punctuation in your names. Some scripts and applications are not designed to deal with form element names that contain spaces and punctuation.

You can set both the size of the text field and the number of characters a user can enter into it. There are two different width settings for a text field:

- *Char Width* sets the size of the text field and the number of characters that are visible in the field. If there are more characters in the text field than this width setting, they will be submitted but simply won't be visible.

- *Max Chars* limits the number of characters that a user can enter into the text field. The user will not be able to enter more characters than the value of Max Chars. Setting Max Chars might be useful when you know the absolute length of the data the user should enter, such as a social security number, and do not want the user to enter additional characters.

> A text field can hold up to 32,700 characters!

There are three different types of text fields:

- *Single line* text fields are useful to collect small, discreet words, names, or short phrases from the user.

- *Multiline* text fields present an area with multiple lines useful for the user to enter larger blocks of text.

- *Password text* fields are special single-line fields that mask what the user types into the field with asterisks or bullets to shield the data from other people.

The first three fields in your form should be single line text fields. The fourth field—the comments field—would be a good candidate for a multiline text field. Select the comments field and make it a multiline field by selecting the Multi line radio button, as shown in Figure 16.9.

When you select the Multi line radio button, the Max Chars box turns into the Num Lines box. Enter the number of lines that the multiline text field should have. You can think of the Num Lines settings as the height of the text field.

Multiline text field

FIGURE **16.9**

*A multiline text field
has the Num Lines and
Wrap attributes that
you can set in the
Property inspector.
Num Lines sets the
number of lines, or the
height, of the multiline
text field.*

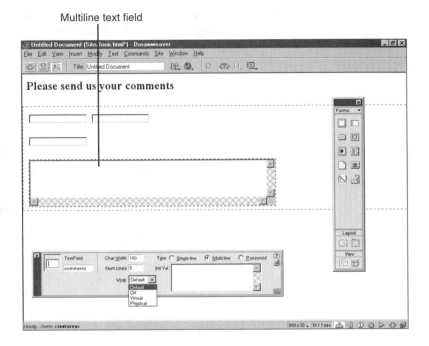

You can't resize text fields by clicking and dragging like you can other
Dreamweaver objects. You can only change the size by changing the Char
Width property in the Property inspector.

The Wrap drop-down menu also becomes active once you have created a multiline text
field. The default setting is for the text in a Multiline text field to wrap onto a new line
when the user reaches the end of a line. You can turn wrapping off by choosing the Off
command from the Wrap drop-down menu. There are two additional wrap settings: physical and virtual. *Physical* enables the lines of text to wrap at the end of the box by placing a hard return (CRLF character) there. *Virtual* enables the lines of text to wrap at the
end of the box but no character is inserted.

You can add default text that initially appears in the text field. Enter text into the Init Val box in the Property inspector so that text will be present when the user initially loads the form. This text could be instructions or a default value that the user could change if they wanted to, as shown in Figure 16.10.

FIGURE 16.10

Enter text into the Init Val box in the Property inspector so it appears when the user initially loads the form.

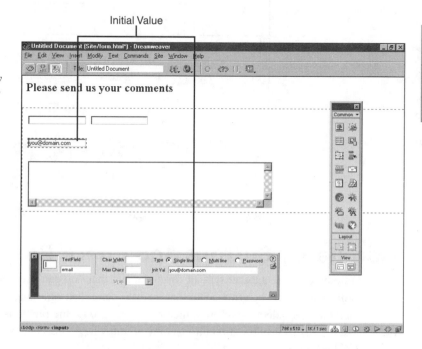

Add Labels

You've created the text fields into which the user will enter data, but you also need to add instructions, labels, and other elements to the form to make it usable. Add a label in front of each of the text fields describing what text the user should enter into the field. You might want to place the labels and the text fields into a table, as shown in Figure 16.11, to have better control over how the objects line up.

FIGURE 16.11

Placing labels and text fields into a table helps control the way all of the objects align with each other.

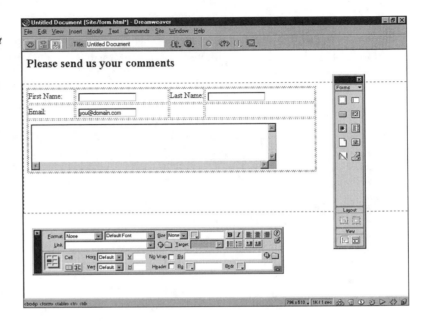

Add Radio Buttons and Check Boxes

Radio buttons are another type of form element that you can use to collect user input. Radio buttons can be grouped so that the user can select only one button of the group; when the user selects a different member of the group, the previously selected button is de-selected. To group radio buttons, they all must have the same name. To create a group of radio buttons

1. Place the insertion point within a form where the radio buttons will be located.

2. Select the Radio Button object from the Object panel or select the Radio Button command from the Form Object submenu of the Insert menu.

3. Enter the name of the radio button group into the name box in the far left of the Property inspector, as shown in Figure 16.12. Remember that all of the radio buttons in the group need to have the same name.

4. Enter a checked value for the radio button in the Checked Value box as shown in Figure 16.12. This value is sent to your script or server application that processes the form.

5. Choose whether the button will be checked or unchecked when the user first loads the form by selecting either the Checked or Unchecked options beside the Initial State setting.

Radio button

FIGURE 16.12

The name of the radio button is the same for all members of a radio button group. The user can select only one member of the group at a time.

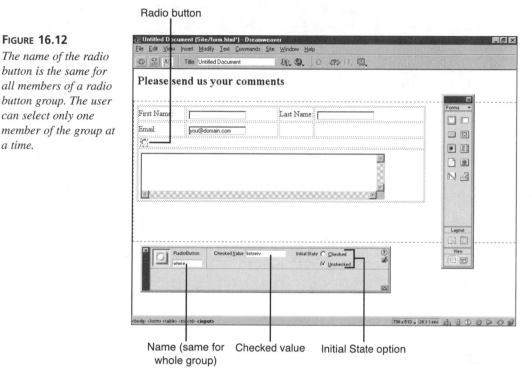

16

Name (same for whole group)   Checked value   Initial State option

6. Place a label beside the button so that it is easy for the user to tell which answer they are choosing.

7. Repeat steps one through six for all of the members of the radio button group.

Check boxes collect user input when the user either checks or unchecks the box. They differ from radio buttons because they are not grouped; instead, they act independently. To add a check box to your form

1. Place the insertion point within a form where the check box will be located.

2. Select the Check Box object from the Object panel or select the Check Box command from the Form Object submenu of the Insert menu.

3. Enter a name for the check box into the name box in the far left of the Property inspector.

4. Enter a checked value into the Checked Value box.

5. Choose whether the initial state of the check box will be checked or unchecked in the Initial State setting.

6. Add a label beside the check box. The setting should look like Figure 16.13.

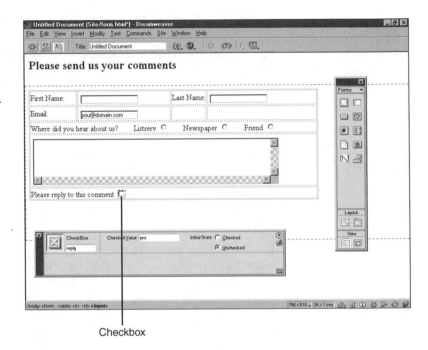

Checkbox

Add a List or a Menu

Radio buttons are a great way to give the user set choices. However, sometimes they're not appropriate, such as when you're selecting one of the 50 United States. Allowing the user to select from a drop-down menu helps you collect consistent data. If you allowed the user to enter a state in a text field, you might get some users entering the full name, like Washington, other users entering the correct postal abbreviation, like WA, and other users entering anything in between.

The List/Menu object inserts a list of values. You create the List/Menu object as either a list, displaying a set number of lines, or a menu, a drop-down menu displaying all the list values. Figure 16.14 shows a list and a menu in a form displayed in the browser.

To create a list

1. Place the insertion point within the form where the list will be located.

2. Select the List/Menu object from the Object panel or select the List/Menu command from the Form Object submenu of the Insert menu.

3. Enter the name of the list into the name box in the far left of the Property inspector.

4. After you select List as the Type, the Height and Allow Multiple attributes become active.

FIGURE 16.14

Lists display a certain number of values. A menu drops down when the user clicks on it, allowing the user to select a value.

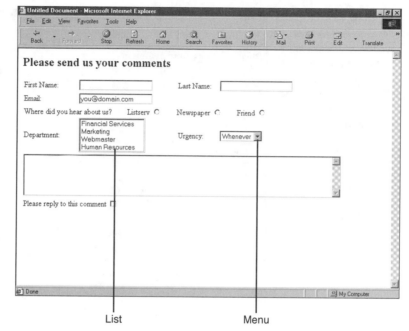

List   Menu

5. Set the Height to the number of list items that you want visible at one time (shown in Figure 16.15). If there are more list items than can be shown, scrollbars will automatically appear.

6. Check the Allow multiple check box beside Selections if you want to allow the user to select multiple values in the list. You might want to add instructions telling the user they can select multiple entries by using the Ctrl key (Command key on the Macintosh) and clicking on multiple selections.

7. Set up the list values by selecting the List Values button. The List Values dialog box appears as shown in Figure 16.16.

8. Enter an item label and a value for each item in the list. The item label is what the user will see and select. The value is what will be sent back for processing. They can be the same, if appropriate. To add an item click the plus sign, enter the item label, tab to the value field, and enter a value. You can tab forward and shift-tab back if you want. Use the - button to delete entries and use the arrow keys to rearrange entries.

9. Click the OK button in the List Values dialog box.

10. Select an item from the Initially Selected box if one of the items should be selected by default. Otherwise, the first item will appear.

11. Add a label beside the list.

FIGURE 16.15

Set the list's height in the Property inspector. You can also allow the user to select multiple values in the list by checking the Allow multiple check box.

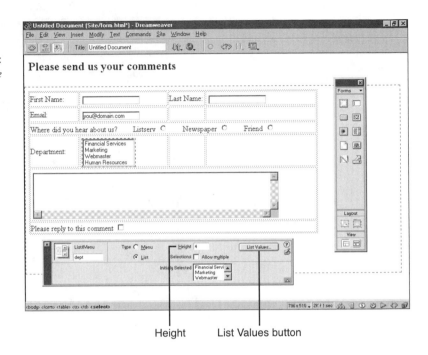

Height   List Values button

Item Labels   Values

FIGURE 16.16

Select the + button in the List Values dialog box to add an item to the list. The Item Label is what the user sees and the Value is submitted to the script or the application on the server for processing.

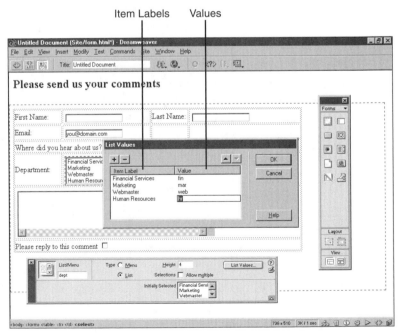

Some people like to create a blank name and value pair as the first item in a list or menu. This keeps the first choice from being a default choice.

While a list can show a number of lines, a menu shows only one until the user drops the menu down by clicking. Menus use less space than lists because the menu can drop down over other objects on the page when clicked but shrinks to only one line when it is inactive. You create a menu exactly like you do a list except that you don't set the height and you cannot allow the user to select multiple entries. Turn your list into a drop-down menu by selecting the Menu option as the type.

16

There isn't an attribute to control the width of a list or a menu. But, to your advantage, the list or menu will expand to the width of the widest object. To make the list wider than the widest object, you need to add non-breaking spaces to one of the list items to make it wider. Unfortunately, you cannot do this in the List Values dialog box. You need to add it directly to the HTML for the page.

Select the list or menu object and then open the HTML Source inspector. Since you have the list or menu selected, the HTML code for that object will be automatically selected in the HTML Source inspector. Place your cursor after one of the labels and insert some non-breaking spaces. You can insert a non-breaking space by using the keyboard shortcut Ctrl+Shift+Space (Option+Space for the Macintosh). The code for a non-breaking space is . The HTML code will look like this:

```
<select name="select">
      <option
value="1">1         </
option>
      <option value="2">2</option>
      <option value="3">3</option>
      <option value="4">4</option>
      <option value="5">5</option>
      <option value="6">6</option>
   </select>
```

Add Push Buttons and Picture Buttons

There are four different types of buttons that you can add to your forms:

- The Submit button triggers sending the data the user has entered into a form to a script or an application on the server. The Submit button triggers the action that you've set in the form's Action box in the Property inspector.

- The Reset button erases all of the data the user has entered in the form. It also reloads any initial values.

- An Image button acts like a Submit button. All of the data in the form is submitted, and the coordinates of where the user clicked are sent too.

- A generic button has no automatic function. You can add functionality to a generic button by applying a behavior to it.

Add Submit and Reset Buttons

First, add a Submit and Reset button to your form. Usually the Submit button is on the left and the Reset button is beside it on the right. Add a button to the form by positioning the insertion point and then selecting the Button object from the Object panel (or the Button command from the Form Object submenu in the Insert menu). Select Submit form as the action for the left button and select Reset form as the action for the right button. The buttons should look like those in Figure 16.17.

FIGURE 16.17

The Submit button is usually placed on the left of the Reset button. You need one Submit button per form if you are sending the form data to a script or application on the server.

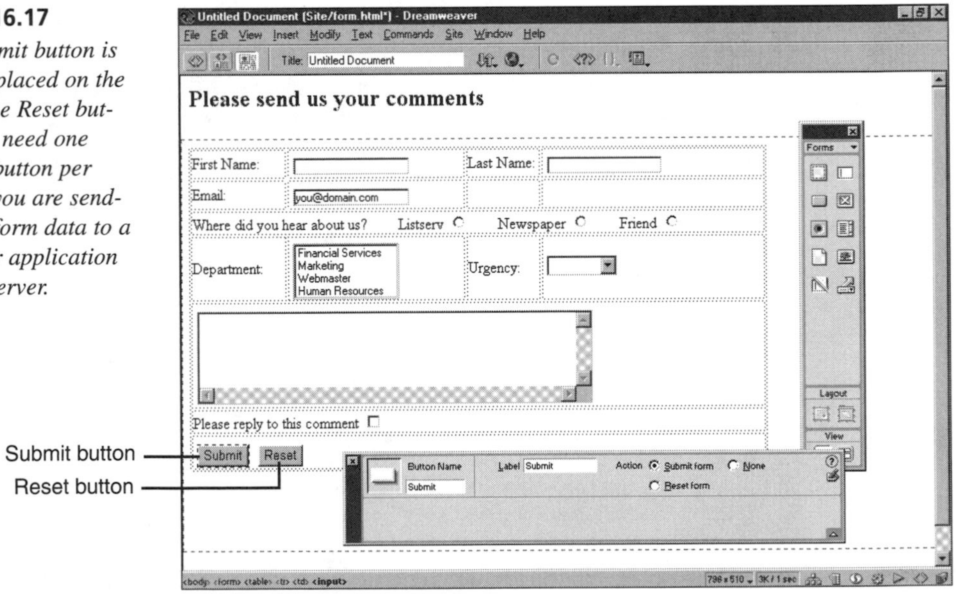

You can accept the default names that Dreamweaver gives the Submit and Reset buttons, or you can give them new names. You can change the label of either button; a button does not need to say "Submit" to function as a Submit button. Each form must have a Submit button to send the form data. The Reset button is optional. You only want to have one Submit button per form.

Add an Image Field to Submit a Form

You can replace a Submit button with an image field. When the user clicks on the image, the form contents are submitted and the coordinates of the location where the user clicked on the image are sent too. You could capture and process the coordinate information if you wanted to.

First, make sure the insertion point is inside of a form. Add an image field by selecting the Image Field object from the Object panel or the Image Field command from the Form Object submenu of the Insert menu. The Select Image Source dialog box enables you to navigate and select a standard Web image file. The Property inspector displays the name, width, height, source, alt text, and alignment attributes. You set these attributes as you would for any image.

16

Add a Generic Button

You can add a generic button anywhere on your Web page. It does not have to be within a form because it cannot submit form contents. Add a generic button by selecting the Button object from the Object panel or the Button command from the Insert menu. Name the button, give it a label, and select None as the action. Now you can apply a behavior to this button that can be triggered by a button click.

> Sometimes it is difficult to delete a form from the page. The easiest way to delete a form is to right-click on the form to view the context menu. Choose the Remove Tag <form> command. If the Remove Tag command does not say <form>, you have the wrong object selected. You could, of course, always select the <form> tag in the tag selected to delete the form.

Create a Jump Menu to Navigate to Different URLs

A jump menu is a list of links that allows the viewer to jump to other Web sites or different Web pages within the current site. Dreamweaver's Jump Menu object makes it easy to set up this type of jump menu. You can create a jump menu of email links, images, or any object that can be displayed in a browser.

Dreamweaver's Jump Menu object inserts a drop-down menu similar to the one you created a few minutes ago. You set up the list values in a special dialog box. The item labels appear in the drop-down menu and the values contain the URL to the Web pages where the user will jump. If you need to edit the jump menu after you have created it in the special dialog box, you will need to brush up on the form skills you've learned in this hour and the behavior skills you've learned in previous hours.

To create a jump menu

1. Place the insertion point on the page where you want the jump menu to appear. You don't need to insert a form because the Jump Menu object will do that for you.

2. Select the Jump Menu object from the Object panel or the Jump Menu command from the Form Object submenu of the Insert menu. The Insert Jump Menu dialog box appears as shown in Figure 16.18.

FIGURE 16.18

The Insert Jump Menu dialog box enables you to create a drop-down menu where the user can select an item to link to.

Menu items——

Insert Go Button check box

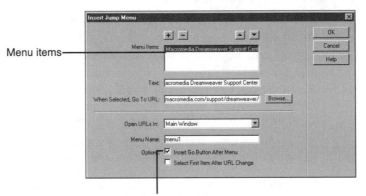

3. Type a name for the first item that will appear in the jump menu in the Text box. The item text is highlighted when you first open the Insert Jump Menu dialog box.

4. Enter a URL that will be launched when the item is selected. You can either type it in or use the Browse button to navigate to a local file.

5. Select the + button to add another item.

6. Repeat steps 3 through 5 until you have entered all of the items for the jump menu.

7. Select a target for the links in the Open URLs In drop-down menu. You will only have target options if your current Web page is part of a frameset that is open in Dreamweaver.

8. Give the menu a unique name in the Menu Name box.

9. Select the appropriate options. Click the check box beside Insert Go Button After Menu if you would like to have a button with the label Go that the user can press to jump. Even if the button is present the user will still automatically go to the link once they have chosen it. The Go button enables the user to launch the first link without having to first launch another link. This is caused by form processing idiosyncrasies.

10. Select the check box beside Select First Item After URL Change if you want the first item to be reselected after each jump selection.

11. Click OK. The jump menu within a form is inserted into your Web page.

A common way to create a jump menu is to have the first item be the text "Choose One..." and leave it without a link. Because you never want to select this item, the inability to select the first item in the drop-down menu won't be a problem. Select the check box that makes the first item always selected after you have jumped somewhere and the "Choose One..." selection reappears.

You can edit the jump menu by editing the Jump Menu behavior. Select the List/Menu object that the Jump Menu command creates and double-click the Jump Menu behavior in the Behaviors panel. Add or remove list items with the + and - buttons. Rearrange the list with the up and down arrow buttons. You can turn on or off the Select First Item After URL Change setting.

You cannot add a Go button by editing the Jump Menu behavior. You can add it manually, though. Create a generic button by inserting a button into the form, giving it the label "Go", and setting its action to None. Apply the Jump Menu Go behavior to the button triggered by the onClick event. Select the jump menu name from the drop-down menu as shown in Figure 16.19.

FIGURE **16.19**

You can create your own Go button by inserting a generic button into a form and applying the Jump Menu Go behavior.

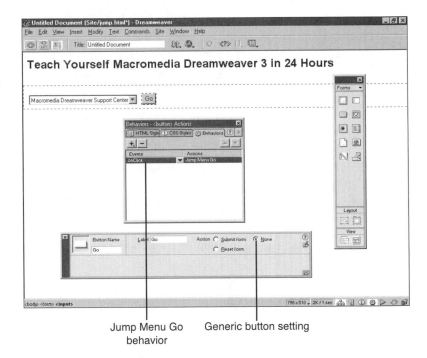

Jump Menu Go   Generic button setting
behavior

Summary

In this hour, you learned how to insert and configure a form. You learned how to add text fields, radio buttons, check boxes, lists, and menus to the form. You learned how to add submit and reset buttons to the form, and create a generic button. You learned how to use the Dreamweaver Jump Menu object to create a menu consisting of a bunch of URLs that the user can jump to.

Q&A

Q I just want to email my form contents. I know that in the next hour I'll learn about CGI and other scripting methods, but isn't there a quick and dirty way to do this?

A You can email form contents by putting in your email address as the action. Your email address needs to be prefaced with "mailto" so that it looks like "`mailto:you@yourdomain.com`". Additionally, you may need to add the attribute `ENCTYPE="text/plain"` to the `<form>` tag.

This way of submitting a form may be fine for collecting form data on where your co-workers want to go to lunch on Friday. They all know and trust you (at least I hope they do), and they probably all have their email programs set up in a similar fashion to yours. An email program must be set up properly with the browser for this method to work. And, some browsers put up a warning when submitting forms in this fashion.

Q Why can't I see my form elements in Netscape?

A If your form elements aren't showing up, they must not be inside of <form> tags. Netscape hides form elements that are not inside a form.

Workshop

The Workshop contains quiz questions and activities to help reinforce what you've learned in this hour. If you get stuck, the answers to the quiz can be found after the questions.

Quiz

1. What do you need to do to make a number of radio buttons act like they are a group?

2. How do you create a generic button?

3. What's the difference between a list and a menu?

Answers

1. All of the radio buttons in a group have the same name.

2. After you insert a button, select None as the action. You can then attach Dreamweaver behaviors to the button if you like.

3. A list displays a configurable number of items and allows the user to select more than one item to submit. A menu displays only one line and drops down when the user clicks on it so they can select an item. The user can only select one item from a menu.

Exercises

1. Create a form to collect the user data of your choice. Format the form objects and labels with a table so that they line up nicely. Place the Submit and Reset buttons in the bottom row or the table, merging the cells so that the buttons are centered under the entire table.

2. Create a jump menu in a frame at the top of the page. Enter all of your favorite URLs into the menu. Have the URLs load into a frame in the bottom of the page.

HOUR 17

Sending and Reacting to Form Data

In Hour 16, "Creating and Using a Form to Collect Data," you learned how to create a form. In this hour, you'll decide what to do with the data that the user enters into your form. You need to send the data to a script on the server to process the form data. The script on the server can store data in a database, send it to an email address, send results back to the browser, or process it any way you want.

> You also can have client-side scripts created in JavaScript to process form data, but those scripts will not have access to server resources and will not be able to email data or insert it into a database.

Some of the types of information you might want to receive in a form can include orders, feedback, comments, guest book entries, polls, or even uploaded files. Creating the form and inserting form elements is usually the easy part. The difficult part is installing and configuring the scripts that will process the data.

In this hour, you will learn

- How to use the Validate Form behavior
- How to set up a page to submit to a CGI script
- How to create secure Web pages
- How Dreamweaver edits and displays ASP, PHP, and CFML code

Validate a Form's Data Using the Validate Form Behavior

Before you receive and process information from a form, you want to make sure the information is complete and in the right format. Dreamweaver has a Validate Form behavior that will force the user to enter data into a field, figure out whether an email address has been entered, or make sure the user enters a number correctly.

The Validate Form action requires the user to enter the form data correctly before they can submit the data to a script or an application on the server. You can validate the form in two ways:

- Attach the Validate Form action to the Submit button to validate the entire form when the Submit button is clicked. The onClick event triggers the behavior.
- Attach the Validate Form action to individual text fields so that the data they entered is validated after the user leaves the field. The onBlur event triggers the behavior when the user's focus leaves the field.

You must have a form with form objects in your Web page before the Validate Form behavior is active in the + drop-down menu of the Behaviors panel. Create a new form with various text fields, or use the comments form you created in Hour 16. To validate a form:

1. Select the Submit button or a text field in the form.
2. Open the Behaviors panel. Click the + button and select the Validate Form behavior.
3. The Validate Form dialog box appears as shown in Figure 17.1. A list of all of the text fields appears in the dialog box.
4. If you have selected the Submit button and are validating the entire form, set up validation settings for every text field that requires them. If you are validating an individual text field, you set up the validation settings for that field.

FIGURE 17.1

The Validate Form dialog box enables you to set validation settings for text fields in your form.

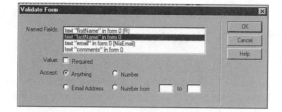

5. Check the Required check box if an entry in the field must be filled in by the user.

6. There are four settings in the Accept category:

   • Select the Anything setting if the user needs to enter data into the field but that data can be in any format. For instance, if you are asking for a phone number, you do not want to limit the user to just entering numbers because phone numbers are often formatted with other characters.

   • Select the Number setting if the user needs to enter data that is numeric.

   • Select the Email Address setting if the user needs to enter an email address. This setting checks for an @ symbol.

   • Select the Number setting to check for a number within a range of specific numbers. Fill in both the low and high ends of the range.

7. Notice that your settings appear in parentheses beside the name of the text field (shown in Figure 17.2). Repeat steps 4 through 6 if you are validating more than one text field.

FIGURE 17.2

The validation settings appear in parentheses beside the text field in the Validate Form dialog box.

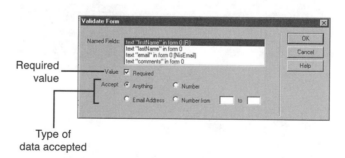

Required value

Type of data accepted

8. Click OK. Select the onClick event if your behavior is attached to the Submit button. Select the onBlur event if your behavior is attached to an individual text field.

When the Validate Form behavior is triggered, the behavior will check the data in the field or fields against the settings you have entered. You will want to make sure that the labels and instructions for your form clearly tell the user what type of data to enter and

17

which fields are required. You want to give the user the information to fill out the form properly so he doesn't get frustrated with error messages.

> A standard way to signal that a form element is required is to place an asterisk next to it. You'll want to tell your users somewhere on the page that the asterisk indicates that they need to enter data in that field.

If the user enters incorrect data, the dialog box appears as shown in Figure 17.3. The message box tells the user that errors have occurred and lists the text fields' names and why the data was not entered correctly. This is another place where a meaningful name for a Dreamweaver object is important. If you are validating a form, it is a good idea to name the text fields the same name as the label beside the field so the user can easily locate and change the field data.

FIGURE 17.3

After the form is validated, the user sees this message telling her which fields have either been omitted or filled out incorrectly.

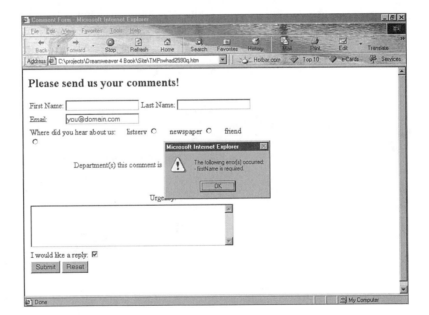

Receive Information from a Form

The standard way to process a form is to have an application on the server that parses the data and performs an action on it. *Parsing* data is the act of dividing and interpreting the name and value pairs that are sent to the server.

Each name and value pair contains the name of the form element entered in Dreamweaver, and the value that the user has entered or selected for that field. A text field will have a name and value pair that contains the name of the text field and the value that was entered into the text field. A radio button group will send a name and value pair with the name of the radio button group and the value of the button that was selected when the user submitted the form. A list or a drop-down menu will send the name of the object and which item or items the user selected.

A popular way of processing forms on a server is with a *CGI script*. Usually these scripts are written in Perl or other programming languages. Later in this hour we will discuss other ways of processing forms with Active Server Pages (ASP), Java Server Pages (JSP), Hypertext Preprocessor (PHP), and ColdFusion Markup Language (CFML)— proprietary processing systems that are powerful in creating Web applications.

Luckily, there are a number of places on the Web to download CGI scripts that are already written. Since programming CGI scripts is beyond the scope of this book, the examples will use an existing script that processes form data and sends it to a specific email address.

The Web is an incredibly generous place and you can download all sorts of free scripts to use. If you don't know how to program CGI scripts and you are willing to process your forms generically, you'll find a number of great scripts available from

Matt's Script Archive

http://www.worldwidemart.com/scripts/

Freescripts

http://www.freescripts.com/

CGI stands for *Common Gateway Interface,* which is the definition of the standard method of communication between a script and the Web server. The CGI script resides in a specific directory on the Web server. It is common for access to this directory to be limited to Webmasters for security reasons. You can contact your Webmaster and ask if a script is already available on your server to do what you want to do, or whether they will install one for you. You may have a directory within your own Web directory that can hold CGI scripts. Often this directory is called cgi-bin or has cgi in the directory name.

If you are signing up with a hosting service and using this type of script, make sure before you confirm that your account supports CGI scripts. Sometimes you can only use the scripts that the service has available, and they may not do what you want to do.

Carefully review the features of the type of account you are signing up for and ask questions, if necessary.

> CGI scripts may expose a server to hackers on the Web. That is why access to the scripts directory is usually limited. If you don't have access to CGI scripts you might want to use a form hosting site (search for "free form hosting" at Yahoo! or any other search engine).
>
> These sites allow you to create forms that are processed at the form-hosting site. You simply link to the page with the form located on the hosting service's server. The disadvantage of using these services is that they usually display advertising on your form page.

Enter the path to the CGI script as the Action of a form as shown in Figure 17.4. The URL needs to be an absolute URL and should not be relative even if the script resides in a directory relative to your Web site. The documentation for the script will tell you whether the script expects the form name and value pairs to be submitted via the GET or the POST methods.

FIGURE 17.4

Enter the URL to the CGI script that will process your form in the action box of the Property inspector with the form selected.

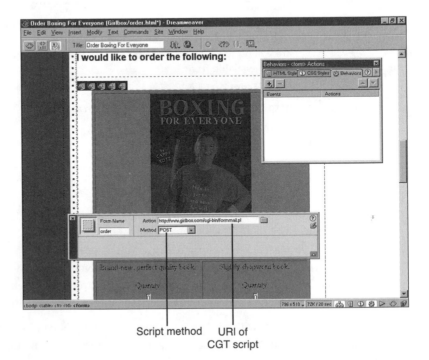

Script method   URI of
CGT script

- The GET method adds a limited number of name and value pairs to the end of a URL of CGI script. You may have seen URLs that have extra characters appended to them. These characters are being sent to the server for processing.

- The POST method sends unlimited encoded name and value pairs, along with other information, to the script.

Download Matt's FormMail script from www.worldwidemart.com/scripts/ to use with the rest of this chapter. This script takes the contents of a form and sends them to an email address. The script has a number of different ways it can be configured. If you are going to test the script, you will need to install the script first. The script comes with a "readme" file that describes all of the functions and parameters you can set in the script. The process to set up and call the FormMail script is similar to what you will do to submit a form to any CGI script.

There are various operating systems that Web server applications reside on. UNIX and Windows NT are the most popular operating systems for servers. It's important to know which operating system your Web server is located on. Scripts are written to run on certain operating systems. For instance, Matt's FormMail script is written to run on UNIX. Other people have translated the script to other operating systems. Also, UNIX file names are case-sensitive so you must be careful that you reference links and image files with the proper case.

To use the FormMail script, you must add hidden fields to your form that contain parameters telling the script what to do. If you open up the FormMail script in a text editor, such as Notepad, there are instructions at the top of the file. The scripted processes are also contained in the file so be careful what you change.

There are two variables that you need to configure at the top of the FormMail script before it is loaded onto the serve r:

- The $mailprog variable needs to point to the UNIX server's sendmail program. Leave it as the default; if it doesn't work, your Webmaster can give you the address. You do not need this variable if you are running the Windows NT version of the script.

- The @referers variable contains the domains that are allowed access to the script. This setting keeps unauthorized domains from using the script and the resources on your server.

Add a Hidden Field

Hidden fields are sent along with all of the other form fields. The user cannot change the contents of these fields nor can they see the fields unless they view your HTML source. Create hidden fields for the recipient of the emailed form data, the subject that appears in the email subject field, and the URL to redirect the user to after they have filled out the form. You can explore many other settings on your own.

Make sure that your form has the URL to the FormMail script on the server as its Action. The FormMail script can accept either the GET or POST methods of submitting the data. I suggest the POST method because it is more common and you do not risk exceeding the amount of data that the GET method can handle. To add hidden fields to your form:

1. Place the insertion point anywhere inside your form. It does not matter where the hidden fields are located.

2. Select the Hidden Field object from the Object panel or the Hidden Field command from the Form Object submenu of the Insert menu.

3. Dreamweaver displays the Hidden Form Field symbol in your Web page as shown in Figure 17.5. You must have Invisible Elements checked in the Visual Aids submenu of the View menu and the Invisible Elements category in Dreamweaver preference must have Hidden Form Fields checked.

FIGURE 17.5

The Hidden Form Field symbol appears when you insert a hidden field into a form. The Property inspector shows a hidden field name-value pair.

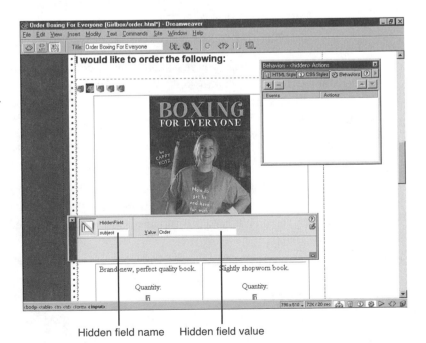

Hidden field name   Hidden field value

4. Enter the name of the hidden field and the value of that field as shown in Figure 17.5. These name and value pairs are documented in the script documentation.

Create three hidden fields using the steps listed above. Enter the following name and value pairs into the hidden fields:

- Name a hidden field "recipient" and give it your email address as a value.

- Name a hidden field "subject" and enter some text that you will see in the subject field of the email that you receive with the data.

- Name a hidden field "redirect" and enter a URL of a pre-built Web page that the user will see after they have submitted the form.

> When you are naming your own objects in Dreamweaver you can afford to make an occasional typo or misspelling. Scripts and applications, however, are not forgiving of typos. Adding hidden fields requires you to enter the names exactly as they are listed in the documentation.

When the user submits the form, the name and value pairs are sent to the email address specified in the hidden field named recipient, with the subject specified in the hidden field named subject. The browser will automatically load the URL that is specified in the hidden field named Redirect.

This is the simplest processing possible for a form. Other scripts can save data to databases, process and validate credit card information, and perform all sorts of complex actions.

Explore Submission Security

When your users submit form information, it travels in *packets* across the Internet along with millions of other packets. Packets are electronic bundles of information that carry your data to the server. These packets of information can be intercepted and read by people who understand how to intercept and reassemble data taken from the Web. Even though this is not a common occurrence, you still should take steps to assure your users that sensitive data is secure.

Again, this is a Web server issue. The Web server on which your site is located must have secure sockets enabled. Many ISPs offer this service. Ask your Webmaster whether you have access to secure Web pages.

A user accesses a secure URL exactly like they would a regular URL. The only difference is the protocol that changes from http to https. The user must have a browser that is capable of accessing secure pages. The browser displays a graphic of a lock in the status bar, as shown in Figure 17.6, when it is in secure mode.

FIGURE 17.6

The browser displays a lock in the status bar when the page is served via secure sockets.

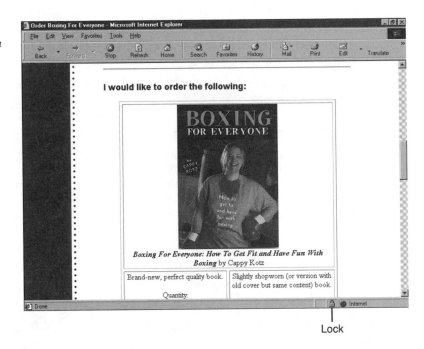

Lock

You only need to worry about secure submissions when the user enters sensitive information, such as credit card numbers or other financial data. For polls, guest books, or feedback forms, you don't need to shield the information from potential thieves. Customers will only expect you to protect their sensitive data.

You need a *certificate* to add security to your form submissions. Sometimes you can use your Web host's certificate or you can purchase your own. One of the major certificate vendors is Verisign, and you can learn more about certificates at their Web site www.verisign.com/. The certificate is an electronic document that verifies you are who you say you are.

Upload a File from a Form

You may need to add a file field to your form, enabling users to upload files. You can collect images, homework assignments, or any type of file that you may need a user to send to you with a file field object. The user selects the Browse button, shown in Figure 17.7, to select a file from their local drive. When they press the Submit button, the file is sent to the server.

FIGURE **17.7**
*Use a file field to
enable uploading a file
to the server. Make
sure your server
allows it, however,
before you create your
form.*

File field

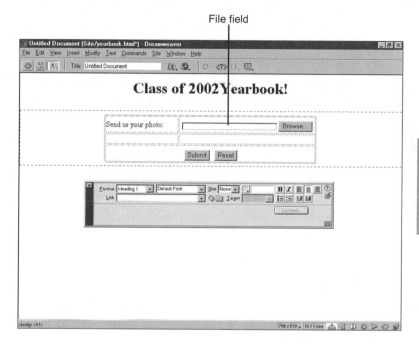

A file field has attributes similar to a text field that you used in the last hour. You can set the size of the file field by putting a value in the Char Width box of the Property inspector. You can also set the Max Chars attribute and Init Val attributes. You will need to give the file field a unique name.

The important question you need to answer before you use a file field is whether or not your server allows anonymous file uploads. You will also need to manually enter ENCTYPE="multipart/form-data" into the <form> tag so that the file is encoded correctly. You'll learn about editing your Web page's HTML in Hour 23, "HTML Is Fun! Viewing and Modifying HTML." Also, you should use the POST method to submit your form; the GET method does not work with file fields.

Prepare Your Page to Interact with Active Server Pages (ASP), JSP, PHP, or CFML

Besides CGI scripts, there are other ways to process forms and create dynamic Web applications. Like CGI scripting, these technologies interact with the Web server to process Web page information. Dreamweaver is great at handling the code that these server-side processing technologies add to a Web page.

The Dreamweaver program has XML files that define how Dreamweaver deals with any third-party tags that scripting technologies insert. In Dreamweaver 4, definitions already exist for

- Microsoft's Active Server Pages, or ASP, combines client-side scripting with processing on the server to create dynamic Web pages. The capability to process ASP comes with Microsoft's IIS 4+ (Internet Information Server) that runs on Windows NT. (You can add the capability to process ASP to IIS 3.) There are third-party applications, like ChiliSoft, that interpret ASP on UNIX servers. ASP code begins with <% and ends with %>.
- JSP (Java Server Pages) is a Java-based way to dynamically build Web pages. JSP scripts interact with a JSP-enabled server and, like ASP, JSP scripts begin with <% and end with %>.
- PHP (Hypertext Preprocessor) is a server-side scripting language that sends dynamic Web pages after interpreting PHP code. PHP code begins with <? and ends with ?>.
- Allaire's ColdFusion server interprets ColdFusion Markup Language, or CFML, to create dynamic Web pages. The ColdFusion server application can run on many different operating systems. Dreamweaver recognizes around fifty different CFML tags.

Check Appendix B, "Internet Resources," for links to sites where you can learn more about these scripting methods.

If you use scripting tags other than the ones defined in Dreamweaver, you can create a custom tag database to tell Dreamweaver how to display the tags. The definitions exist in Dreamweaver's configuration/ThirdPartyTags directory. Check Dreamweaver's extensive help system for more information.

You can embed ASP, JSP, PHP, and CFML into your Web pages and Dreamweaver represents the code with special icons shown in Figure 17.8. Server Markup Tags needs to be checked in the Invisible Elements category in Dreamweaver preferences, as shown in Figure 17.9, for you to see and access the code within your Web pages. Of course, Invisible Elements must also be checked under the Visual Aids submenu of the View menu.

ASP Script Icon

FIGURE 17.8

Special icons, in this case an ASP Script icon, appear when viewing invisibles that represent code.

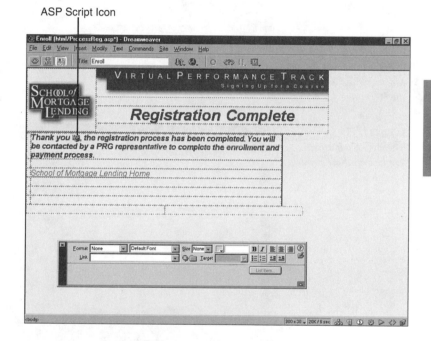

17

FIGURE 17.9

Server Markup Tags must be checked in Dreamweaver preferences to be able to view the special tags that represent this code.

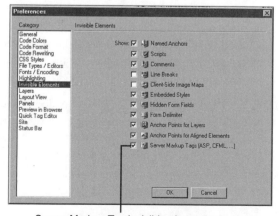

Server Markup Tag invisible element

To edit the ASP, JSP, PHP, or CFML code you select the representative icon on your Web page. The Property inspector appears as shown in Figure 17.10. Click the Edit button to display the Edit Contents dialog box shown in Figure 17.11. You edit your code directly in this dialog box.

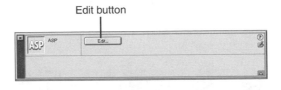

Edit button

FIGURE 17.10

The Property inspector displays the Edit button when you select one of the Server Markup Tags icons on the Web page.

FIGURE 17.11

The Edit Contents dialog box enables you to edit code.

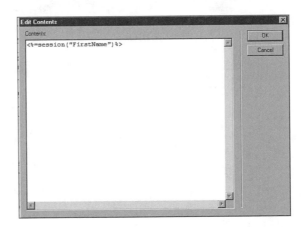

You can use ASP, JSP, PHP, or CFML scripts contained in an external script file to process a form. The script will act like the CGI script that we used earlier this hour. You reference the script's URL as the form's action in the Property inspector. Again, the script's directory must have the proper permission for the script to execute. Figure 17.12 shows a form submitting its contents to an ASP script.

Dreamweaver UltraDev, shown in Figure 17.13, is a version of Dreamweaver that you can use to create ASP, JSP, or CFML. Dreamweaver UltraDev enables you to hook up your Web content easily to databases. UltraDev's WYSIWYG environment is exactly like Dreamweaver and enables you to visually add ASP, JSP, or CFML components. Dreamweaver UltraDev generates the code for you behind the scenes. You can even see how your Web page will look with real data from the database right within Dreamweaver UltraDev.

FIGURE 17.12

You enter the URL of an ASP script if the script will process your form when the user submits it.

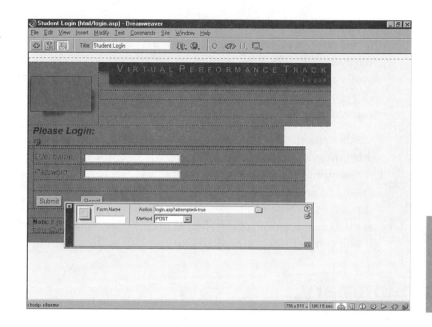

FIGURE 17.13

Dreamweaver UltraDev is a version of Dreamweaver designed to create dynamic Web pages based on data from databases.

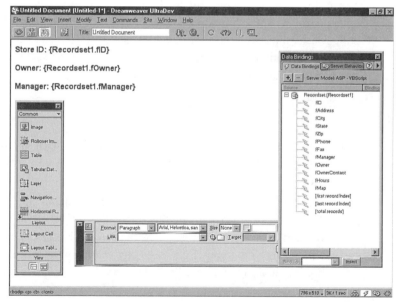

The Macromedia Web site has a tutorial on using UltraDev that you can download at `http://www.macromedia.com/support/UltraDev/documentation/db_dwtutorial/`. Make sure you follow the instructions for installation. To use this database technology locally on your computer, you will need to have a Web server installed, such as Microsoft's Personal Web Server. The tutorial also requires Microsoft Access to be installed.

Another product that you might want to use is BlueWorld's Lasso Studio for Dreamweaver. Lasso enables Dreamweaver to create ASP. The software creates a couple of new panels in the Object panel that enable you to drop objects onto the document window that can interact with databases. You configure the objects in the Property inspector just like any other Dreamweaver object. Very cool! You can find out more (and download an evaluation copy of the software) at `http://www.blueworld.com/blueworld/products/LassoStudio/Dreamweaver/`.

Summary

In this hour, you learned how CGI scripts work and how form data is submitted to them. You learned how to use the Validate Form behavior to validate the data that the user enters into your form. You inserted hidden fields in a form that contain a name and value pair. You set the action for a form and learned the difference between the GET and POST methods of submitting data. You learned about secure transactions. You learned how to edit and call ASP, PHP, JSP, and CFML code.

Q&A

Q I know an ASP programmer that will help me with my Web pages. What do I need to tell her about my Web pages so that she can write a script to process them on the server?

A She needs to know what you have called the items in your form and how you want them processed. If she is sending the data to a database she will need to know what you call them in your form so that she can parse the data into the correct place. She will also need to know if you need any validation or processing applied to the data. For instance, you may need to have individual prices added together as one total price.

Q Should I learn Perl, ASP, PHP, JSP, or CFML?

A It depends what you want to do when you grow up! Do you have a knack for coding? If so, having skills in any of these technologies might be fun and look great on your resume. Find out what technologies people at your work are using. If you learn those technologies your colleagues might be a good support system for your learning endeavor.

If you aren't that interested in coding but want to expand your Web skill set, maybe it's a better idea to specialize in something Dreamweaver excels at like Timeline animations or DHTML. On the other hand, you can always learn more about databases. If you don't really enjoy coding, it can be a real chore. More and more tools are now available, such as UltraDev and Lasso, that do the coding for you.

Workshop

The Workshop contains quiz questions and activities to help reinforce what you've learned in this hour. If you get stuck, the answers to the quiz can be found after the questions.

Quiz

1. What pair of items is sent when a user submits a form?
2. What is a hidden text field?
3. True or False: Dreamweaver allows you to add tag definitions for any type of code that can be inserted into Web pages.

Answers

1. The name of the form object and the value the user either entered or selected is submitted. This is called a name and value pair.
2. A hidden text field contains a name and value pair that the user cannot change. Generally, this data is required by the script to properly process the form.
3. True. You can create a custom definition for any type of code you use in your Web pages so that Dreamweaver will recognize it.

Exercises

1. Experiment with the FormMail fields that we did not explore in this hour. The script also offers validation functionality that you could use instead of using Dreamweaver Validate Form behavior.

2. Find a form on the Web and look at it critically. Select the View Source command to see the HTML. Does the form have any hidden fields? Where is the form being submitted? You should look for the `<form>` and `</form>` tags that contain the code for the form.

PART VI

Making Your Development More Efficient and Collaborating with Others

Hour

HOUR 18

Managing and Uploading Your Projects

Web sites usually reside on a server where many people can access the Web pages that the site contains. While you are working on your Web sites, you will want to move them onto the server both for testing and for final production. There are different ways to move the files onto a server and different methods for ensuring that the version of the files is correct and not accidentally overwritten.

Dreamweaver has a number of commands that are useful to manage your entire Web site. You can create (and even save) a site map that is a visual representation of the relationships of all of the files in your Web site. There are commands to update links site-wide, as well as search and replace text in either the text or the HTML of the Web page.

In this hour, you will learn

- How to synchronize your files on the local and remote sites
- How to create a site map
- How to manage links

- How to add Design Notes to document your project and share ideas with others
- How to generate reports about your Web site

Move Your Site onto a Remote Server

If your server is located on a LAN, you normally connect to the server when you log on to your computer and stay connected all day. If you access the remote server over the Internet using FTP, you connect while getting and putting files onto the server and then you disconnect. Even if you don't disconnect on your end, your connection will most likely time out on the server and you will need to reconnect if you have been inactive for a period.

The Current sites drop-down menu enables you to select which site you are currently working on. The menu lists all of the sites you have defined. To the right of the Current sites drop-down menu are four buttons or six buttons, depending on whether Check In/Out is turned on. Additionally, a Stop Current Task button appears during a file transfer in the lower-right corner of the Site window. These buttons, shown in Figure 18.1, enable you to view and move files to and from the remote site.

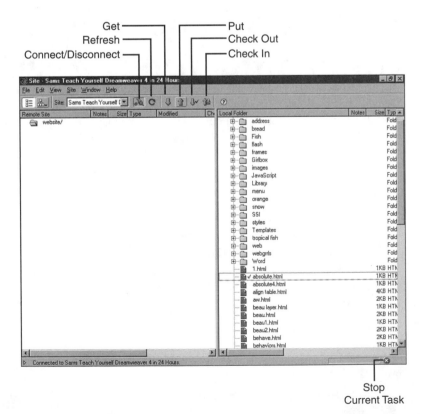

FIGURE 18.1

The buttons at the top of the Site window help you transfer files between the local and remote sites.

- The Connect/Disconnect button establishes a connection to a FTP server. This button is always connected when you have LAN access to your remote site.

- The Refresh button manually refreshes the local and remote Site windows. If you did not select the Refresh Local File List Automatically or the Refresh Remote File List Automatically when setting up your site, you can use this button to manually refresh the list of files.

- The Get button retrieves files from the remote site and moves them to your local site.

- The Put button places files from your local site onto the remote site.

- The Check Out button checks out the file or files you have selected. You select the files in either the remote or the local Site window.

- The Check In button checks in files you have previously checked out.

- The Stop Current Task button only appears when you are transferring files. It issues a Stop command, but the server may take some time to actually stop the current process.

Understand Dreamweaver's Web Site Management Capabilities

You can get a file from or put a file on a remote site. That's why Dreamweaver's buttons are called Get and Put. These buttons work the same way when you are accessing the remote server via a LAN, FTP, or a source control system. You can choose to enable the automatic Check In/Out functionality Dreamweaver while using FTP or LAN access. Source control systems, such as Microsoft SourceSafe, require you to check out files to change them.

Use the Check In/Out capabilities of Dreamweaver to make sure that only one person is working on a file at a time. When you have a file checked out, no one else can check that file out until you check it back in—just like when you have a video checked out from the video store. Dreamweaver marks the file as checked out by you so that your collaborators know who to bug if they also need to make changes to the file!

You'll explore some of the automated capabilities of Dreamweaver to decide whether files are newer on the remote site later this hour. Since you overwrite files when you transfer them from site to site, you need to be careful which files you are transferring. The Check In/Out functionality should be used so that you do not overwrite files newly edited by others on the remote site.

18

When you check out a file from the remote site, Dreamweaver retrieves a copy of that file from the remote server to ensure that you have the most up-to-date version of the file in your local site. When Dreamweaver gets the file, it overwrites the file that exists on your local drive. The checked out file appears to Dreamweaver users with your name beside it on the remote server, signaling your collaborators that you have checked it out. The file has a green check mark beside it in your local site, showing you currently have that file checked out (refer to Figure 18.1). If you entered your email address while setting up the site, your name will be a link that launches an email message to you.

When you check in a file to the remote site, Dreamweaver transfers the file back to the remote server to make it available for others to work on or view. The file will no longer appear to other Dreamweaver users with your name beside it. Dreamweaver sets the file to read-only in your local site and there is a little lock beside the file (refer to Figure 18.1).

Dreamweaver creates a file on the remote server with the .lck (for lock) file extension. This file contains the name of the person who has checked out the file. You don't need to worry about creating these .lck files. If you look at your remote site with an application other than Dreamweaver, you may see these .lck files and you will know what they are.

You can drag and drop files back and forth between the local and remote sites. However, you need to be careful where you drop the files. You might drop them in an incorrect directory. Dreamweaver automatically transfers files into the mirror image location when you select a file and use the buttons to transfer the file. This way the file remains in its correct location.

The Check In and Check Out process is designed to help you manage a collaborative environment. The process forces you to download the most recent version of the file during the check out procedure. While you have the file checked out, others cannot work on it. After you check the file back in, you can open the file but cannot save any changes because Dreamweaver marks it as read-only.

Remember to check files back in when you are finished with them! Don't go on vacation with a bunch of files checked out if you want your co-workers to happily welcome you back when you return.

Dreamweaver enables you to circumvent some of the Check In/Out safeguards. You can, for instance, override somebody else's checked out file and check it out yourself. You can also turn off the read-only attribute of a file and edit it without checking it out. However, why would you want to do any of these things? Dreamweaver's Check In and Check Out process is fine for a small environment where you don't expect mischief. If you need tighter security and version control, there are products on the market, such as Microsoft Visual SourceSafe, that enable very tight control.

Your project will work more smoothly if everyone who is collaborating on the project turns on the Check In/Out functionality for the site. Otherwise, it's too easy to overwrite a file that someone else has updated.

You can still use Get and Put when you have Check In/Out enabled. The Get command will move a file from the remote server, overwriting the local file. The file will be read-only on your local machine because you won't have it checked out. If you try to put a file onto the remote server that someone has checked out, Dreamweaver warns you that changes to the remote copy of the file may be lost if you put the file. You can choose to do the action anyway or cancel the action.

To get only the files on the remote site that are more recent than the files on the local site, use the Synchronize command that will be discussed in a few minutes.

To get or put files

1. Open the Site window and select the site on which you want to work from the Current sites drop-down menu.

2. If you access your site via FTP, click the Connect button. If you are already connected or are accessing the files on a LAN, skip this step.

To get, or check out, files

1. Select the files you want to transfer to your local site. You can select the files on the remote site, or on the local site if they exist there. Usually you'll want to select the files in the remote site.

2. Click either the Get command, or click the Check Out command if you have Check In/Out enabled for this site.

3. Dreamweaver may display a dialog box, shown in Figure 18.2, asking if you would also like to download dependent files. Dependent files are images and other assets that are linked to the files you are transferring. You can disable this dialog box by checking the Don't Ask Me Again check box.

FIGURE 18.2

Dreamweaver prompts you to transfer dependent files, such as images, when you transfer a file. Disable this box by checking the Don't Ask Me Again check box.

To put, or check in, files

1. Select the files you want to transfer to the remote site. You can select the files on the remote or the local site if they exist there. Usually you'll want to select the files in the local site.

2. Click either the Put command, or click the Check In command if you have Check In/Out enabled for this site. If you transfer a file that is currently open, Dreamweaver will prompt you to save the file before you put it on the remote site.

3. Dreamweaver may display a dialog box asking if you would also like to upload dependent files. You can disable this dialog box by checking the Don't Ask Me Again check box.

Continually getting and putting dependent files will slow down your transfers. Image files are usually much larger than HTML files and take longer to transfer. If the files haven't changed, you don't need to transfer them. Coming up, you'll learn how to use the Synchronize command to make sure all of your files are up-to-date on both the local and remote sites.

You can view the FTP Log by selecting the Site FTP Log command from the Window menu in the Site window. This log shows all of the FTP commands and replies for the current site. This log can be useful if you need to troubleshoot your FTP connection.

Transfer the Current File from the Document Window

Dreamweaver enables you to Get, Put, Check In, Check Out, and issue other site management commands from the document window while working on a file. The Site menu, shown in Figure 18.3, enables you to issue all the transfer commands without opening the Site window.

FIGURE 18.3

The Site menu in the document window contains many of the file management commands that you use in the Site window. These commands only apply to the file currently open in the document window.

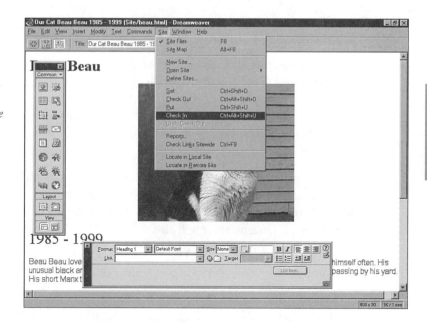

18

Edit an Entire Site

Dreamweaver has a number of useful commands that can help you make site-wide changes. In the next few minutes, you will use commands that are very powerful and can save you a lot of time. You'll want to be careful when changing items site wide in case you make a mistake. Of course, you could just change it site wide again!

Synchronize Your Files on the Local and Remote Sites

Synchronize your files on the local and remote sites so that you are assured you have the most up-to-date files in both places. Dreamweaver has three commands that are useful in determining which site has the newer files. Select the Synchronize command to automatically synchronize files between the local and the remote sites, bringing both sites up to date with the most recent files. If you want to check whether new files reside on the remote or the local sites, use either the Select Newer Local or the Select Newer Remote commands in the Edit menu.

To see which files are newer on the remote

1. Connect to the remote site by clicking on the Connect button if you are using FTP to access the remote site.

2. Select either the root directory or a section of files in the local site.

3. Select the Select Newer Remote command from the Edit menu.

Dreamweaver searches through the files on the remote site to see if any of them are newer than the same files on the local site. The files that are newer on the remote site are all selected. If files exist on the remote site that don't exist on the local site, Dreamweaver selects those, too. With all the files selected, you simply get the files from the remote site to update your local files. Follow the same steps to select files that are newer on the local site using the Select Newer Local command.

When you synchronize files, Dreamweaver analyzes the files on both the local and remote sites and gives you a report on which files need to be copied to synchronize the sites. You have total control over the process and can deselect any files that you do not want transferred. Dreamweaver will also tell you if files are completely up to date and if there is no need to synchronize.

To synchronize the files in the local and remote sites

1. Open the Site window and select the site you want to synchronize.

2. If you only want to synchronize certain files, select those files.

3. Select the Synchronize command from the Site menu.

4. The Synchronize Files dialog box appears as shown in Figure 18.4.

FIGURE 18.4

The Synchronize Files dialog box enables you to select which files to synchronize.

5. Choose to synchronize the entire site or just the files you have selected in the Synchronize drop-down menu.

6. Select how you want to transfer the files in the Direction drop-down menu. You can put the newer files to the remote site, get the newer files from the remote site, or get and put newer files in both directions.

> Because I often collaborate with groups of people on Web sites, I usually am interested in what files are newer on the remote site. Others on the team may have changed files and uploaded them while I was doing something else. I like to make sure I'm looking at the most recent files in the project by synchronizing to get the newer files from the remote site.

7. Check the check box beside Delete local files not on remote server if you want to get rid of any extraneous local files.

> Be very careful checking the Delete local files check box because you don't want to delete files you will need later. You will be deleting the files from your hard drive. If the files do not exist anywhere else, you will not be able to restore them. Checking this box is a quick way to clean your site of files that are not being used.

8. Click the Preview button.

9. If your files are up to date, you will get a message that no synchronization is necessary. If there are files that need to be synchronized, Dreamweaver will display the Site dialog box, shown in Figure 18.5, listing all of the files that either don't exist or are older.

FIGURE 18.5

*The Synchronize dia-
log box lists the files
that need to be syn-
chronized.*

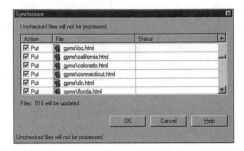

10. Look through the list and deselect any actions that you do not want. When you are ready to transfer the files, select the OK button.

11. During the transfer, Dreamweaver displays a completion bar in the lower-right corner of the Site dialog box. After the synchronization is complete, the Site dialog box displays the message "Synchronization complete" and gives the status of each file.

12. If you'd like to save a log of the synchronization, select the Save Log button and save the file on your hard drive. Otherwise, select the Close button.

Create a Site Map

Create a site map to visually represent the layout of your site. Up to this point we have only viewed the remote and local sites in the Site window. Before you view the site map, you need to define a home page for your site. To define a home page, single-click on the home page file in your local site and select the Set as Home Page command under the Site menu in the Site window.

You can configure other attributes of the site map by opening the Site Map Layout category in the site definition dialog box. For instance, you can change how many icons (columns) appear per row in the site map.

You can change the home page with the New Home Page command in the Site menu.

Select the Site Map icon to display the site map. The site map appears in the Site window along with the files in your local site. Files appear as icons in the site map with lines drawn between related files representing links as shown in Figure 18.6. Symbols appear next to the icons that describe the files:

- A broken link appears as red text with a small picture of a broken link of chain.
- A link appears as blue text with a small globe beside it.
- A file that is checked out to you appears with a green check mark beside it.
- A file that is checked out to someone else appears with a red check mark beside it .
- A file that is read-only appears with a lock beside it.

FIGURE 18.6

The site map shows the files in your site along with icons that represent links, check out information, and the read-only attribute.

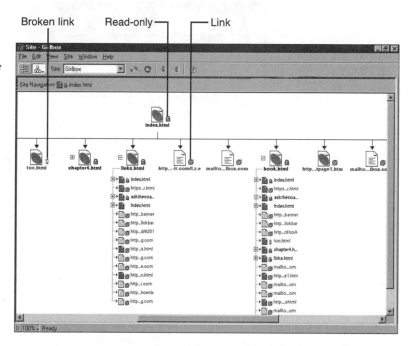

18

The site map can be used as a storyboarding tool to quickly add files and lay out the structure of a Web site.

By default, dependent files (usually images) and hidden files (we'll explore these in a minute) are not displayed in the site map. The View menu contains a number of commands to turn on different views in the site map. You can view dependent files, show files marked as hidden, display page titles instead of file names, and turn on or off tool tips. You can go directly to the Site Map Layout section of the Site Definition dialog box with the Layout command.

When you view dependent files you will see links to all of the files that load along with your Web page, as shown in Figure 18.7. Displaying dependent files can make your site map much more cluttered.

FIGURE 18.7

Viewing dependent files greatly increases the number of icons in your site map. Notice that the images are now shown in the map.

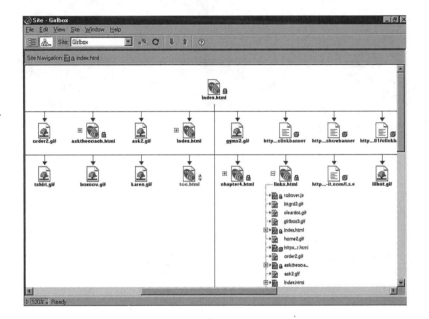

If you do not want to display certain files in the site map, you can mark them as hidden by clicking on the icon and selecting the Show/Hide Link from the View menu. The icon disappears from the site map if Show Files Marked as Hidden is not selected. When you view files marked as hidden, the icon appears with text in italics. You can show the files normally again by re-selecting the Show/Hide Link command.

You can link an HTML file to a Web page by dragging it into the site map. Open both the site map and the Windows Explorer (or Macintosh Finder). Drag an HTML file and drop it on an icon in the site map. A hyperlink is added to the page represented by the icon; the hyperlink links to the new page. You can use the site map to open files in Dreamweaver by double-clicking on an icon.

Create a new file and link an existing file to it in one step in your site map. Right-click on an icon in the site map to bring up the context menu. Select the Link to the New File command and the Link to New File dialog box appears as shown in Figure 18.8. Enter the file name for the new file, the title of the Web page, and the link text that Dreamweaver will automatically insert into the icon you originally clicked.

FIGURE 18.8

Create a new file and a link to the new file by right-clicking on an icon in the site map and selecting the Link to New File command.

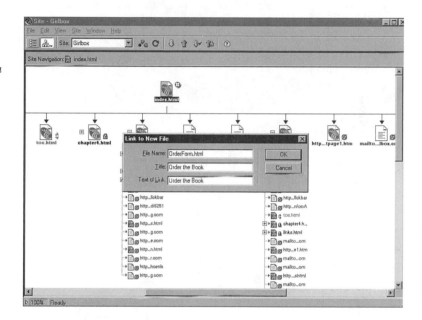

You can also change the view in the site map by clicking on any icon and selecting the View as Root command in the View menu. This places the icon you selected at the top of the site map. The files that are between the currently selected icon and the actual site root are displayed in the bar directly above the site map. You can click on these files to jump to that level.

You can save your site map as either a bitmap (.bmp) or a PNG file. You cannot view bitmaps in a browser, but you can embed a site map saved as a PNG file into a Web page to share it with others over the Web. You can embed a bitmap representation of your site map into a text document to send to a client or save as documentation. You can also print the file as a reference.

Manage Your Links

Dreamweaver automatically updates links when you move or rename a file within the current Web site. Make sure that you create a cache when you define the Web site to speed up the update process. When you move or rename Web pages, Dreamweaver displays the Update Files dialog box. A list of linked files, shown in Figure 18.9, is displayed in the dialog box. Click the Update button to update all the links or select individual files to update.

You can also change the URL of a certain link throughout the site. For instance, if you displayed links in your site for today's menu in the cafeteria you would need to change the link to a new Web page every day. On Tuesday morning you could select the Monday Web page and then select the Change Links Sitewide command from the Site menu. The Change Link Sitewide dialog box, shown in Figure 18.10, displays the old Web page and enables you to enter the path to the new Web page.

FIGURE **18.10**

You can use the
Change Link Sitewide
dialog box to search
your Web site and
change one link to
another.

Use the Link Checker, shown in Figure 18.11, to check all of the links in your site. Select the Check Links Sitewide command from the Site menu. The Link Checker displays three different categories: broken links, external links, and orphaned files. External links are links that Dreamweaver cannot check. Orphaned files are files that do not have any files linking to them.

Dreamweaver might say a file is an orphan even when that file is used in your site. The file may be referenced in a behavior, for instance, an image file used with the Swap Image behavior.

FIGURE **18.11**

The Link Checker displays broken links, external links, and orphaned files.

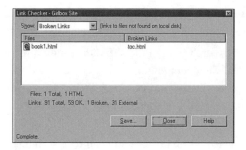

Broken links need to be fixed. Fortunately, Dreamweaver makes that easy. Select the broken link, click on the folder icon, and navigate to the correct file to fix the link.

You can save the report from running the Link Checker by selecting the Save button at the bottom of the dialog box. Then you can easily refer to it as you fix any problems with your site.

Use Find and Replace

Dreamweaver has the powerful capability to search through your entire site for text, text between certain HTML tags, HTML tags, and tag attributes. You can search through the local site, the remote site, or both.

The Find and Replace command is available under the Edit menu in both the document window and the Site window. This command can search for text or source code. To search for text or source code in your Web site

1. From the Edit menu, select the Find and Replace command to display the Find and Replace dialog box (see Figure 18.12).

FIGURE **18.12**

Use the Find and Replace dialog box to search for text or code and replace it with something else.

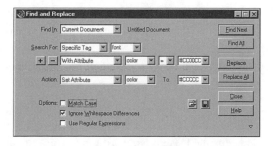

2. Select the file or files for which you want to search from the Find In drop-down menu. You can select the current file, the current site, or a certain folder.

3. Specify the type of search in the Find What drop-down menu. Choose Text to search in the text of the document, ignoring any code. Choose Source Code to search for specific text in the Source Code. Select Text (Advanced) to search for text either within or not within specific HTML tags. Select Tag to search for an HTML tag with certain attributes.

4. Check the Match Case check box if you need to match a specific case in your search.

5. Select Ignore Whitespace Differences if the number of spaces in your search does not matter.

6. Use Regular Expressions enables you to search for patterns. Look in the Dreamweaver Help index for a list of character expressions you can search for such as a carriage return (\r) or beginning of line (^).

7. Once you have created your *query*, click either the Find Next or the Find All button. When you find a match, you can click the Replace or the Replace All button.

> To see all of the matches, expand the Find and Replace dialog box by clicking on the small arrow in the lower-right corner.

After you have refined a search, wouldn't it be nice to save it or share it? You can save queries to use again by clicking on the Save Query button. Load a query by clicking on the Load Query button.

Add Design Notes to Your Pages

Design Notes enable you to add notes to your Web pages. You can use Design Notes to document your design process, share information with others, and keep any extra information that would be useful. Since Design Notes are not actually part of the Web page, you can record sensitive information that you might not want people who view the Web page to be able to read.

You can add a Design Note to any file in your Web site, including templates, images, and movies. Web pages based on templates do not have the design notes attached; only the original template file keeps the Design Note. You may want to add design notes to images listing the name and location of the original image file.

You first need to enable Design Notes in your Web site. Select the Design Notes category in the Site Definition dialog box for the site, as shown in Figure 18.13. Make sure that Maintain Design Notes is checked. Check Upload Design Notes for Sharing if you want to share your notes with others. The Clean Up button deletes any Design Notes that are associated with files that no longer exist.

FIGURE 18.13

You turn on Design Notes and sharing in the Site Definition dialog box.

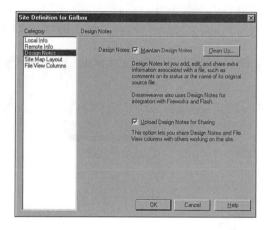

To attach a Design Note to a file

1. When a file is open in the document window, select the Design Notes command from the File menu. Or, click on a file in the Site window and select the Design Notes command.

2. The Design Notes dialog box appears as shown in Figure 18.14. Select the type of Design Note from the Status drop-down menu.

FIGURE 18.14

Select the type of Design Note from the Status drop-down menu.

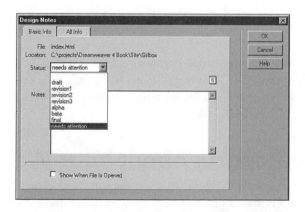

18

3. Click on the Date icon to insert today's date in the Notes field. Type a note in the field after the date.

4. Check the Show File When Opened check box if you want this Design Note to appear when someone opens the file next.

5. Select the All Info tab in the Design Notes dialog box to see a list of the information in the current Design Note, as shown in Figure 18.15. Add a record to the list by clicking the + button, entering a name, and entering a value.

FIGURE 18.15

You can add additional data to the Design Notes by selecting the All Info tab.

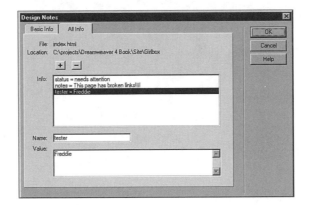

6. Click OK.

A useful name and value data pair to add to your Design Note when in a collaborative environment is the name of the author of the note. First, select the All Info tab in the Design Notes dialog box and click the + button. Name your new record "Name" and put your name in the value field.

The Design Note remains associated with the files even if it is copied, renamed, moved, or deleted. Dreamweaver saves your Design Notes in a directory in your site root called _notes. This directory doesn't appear in the Site window. Notes are saved as the name of the file plus the .mno extension.

Generate Reports About Your Web Site

Dreamweaver comes with reports that you can run on your site. The reports that come with Dreamweaver enable you to compile information about your site such as when files were created or errors in your site. These reports are useful for examining, troubleshooting, and documenting your Web site. You can also save and print the results of the reports. The following reports are available in Dreamweaver:

- Checked Out By
- Design Notes
- Combinable Nested Font Tags
- Missing Alt Text
- Redundant Nested Tags
- Removable Empty Tags
- Untitled Documents

To run a report

1. Select the Reports command from the Site menu in either the Site Manager or the document window.

2. The Reports dialog box appears as shown in Figure 18.16. Select what you want to report on (either the current document, current site, selected files, or a certain folder).

18

FIGURE **18.16**

Many reports are available that give you information on either your current document or an entire site.

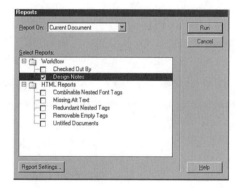

3. Select one of the reports.

4. Some reports have additional settings that can refine the search. If the Report Settings button is active at the bottom of the dialog box, there are additional settings available for that report.

5. Select the Run button to run the report.

6. A results window appears with a list of files. You can save this report and open the individual files that are referenced.

Summary

In this hour, you learned how to import an existing Web site, whether or not it was created in Dreamweaver. You learned how to synchronize files between local and remote sites. You also learned how to find and replace text and HTML. You learned how to manage links in your Web site. And, you learned how to create site maps, add Design Notes, and run reports on your Web site.

Q&A

Q Am I really going to goof up my files if I use the Synchronize command?

A Using Synchronize can be daunting. You might want to run the Select Newer Local and the Select Newer Remote commands first. Jot down the file names that are selected. Then, when you run Synchronize, check to see if that command comes up with the same file names. This will hopefully reassure you so you can confidently use the Synchronize command in the future!

Q Why does Dreamweaver list some of my files as "orphaned files" when they really aren't?

A Dreamweaver checks whether files are linked to other files. The files that Dreamweaver lists as orphaned may be used in behaviors. For instance, you may have a Web page loaded with the Open Browser Window behavior. Since the file is not actually linked to another file, Dreamweaver will show it as orphaned.

Q One of my co-workers left for a two-week vacation with a bunch of files checked out in his name. How can I work on these files while he is gone?

A When you attempt to check out the files, Dreamweaver will warn you that someone else has them checked out. It will then ask you to override your co-worker's checkout. If you select the Yes button, the files will now be checked out to you. Just hope that your co-worker hasn't made any changes to the files that he forgot to move onto the remote site.

Workshop

The Workshop contains quiz questions and activities to help reinforce what you've learned in this hour. If you get stuck, the answers to the quiz can be found following the questions.

Quiz

1. How can you tell which images in your entire site are missing the alt text?

2. True or False: When working in a collaborative environment-using FTP, it doesn't matter if everyone is using Dreamweaver's Check In/Out functionality.

3. True or False: Dreamweaver can attach a Design Note to any file, whether it's a Web page or another type of file, in a Web site.

Answers

1. Run the Missing Alt Text report on the entire site.

2. False. It's too easy for one member of your group to overwrite the work of another member if not everyone is using the Check In/Out functionality. The only time you don't need to use this functionality when working with a group is when you are using a third-party program to manage version control.

3. True. Dreamweaver can attach a Design Note to any file in a Web site.

Exercises

1. Create a site map of a site you have set up and experiment by setting various pages as the root of the site. Try saving the map as a PNG and inserting it into Dreamweaver. Try adding a new Web page in the site map.

2. Run the Link Checker on a site that you created or imported. Do you have any broken links? If so, fix them! Do you have any orphaned files? If you no longer need these files, delete them. If your site has external links, you should periodically check to see that they are still valid.

18

HOUR 19

Managing Your Assets with the Asset Panel

After you have designed your Web page, you will populate it with page elements. The elements that make up your individual Web pages will come from various sources and will be different types of objects. You might include Flash movies, images created in Fireworks, various colors, links, clip art, and photographs in your Web pages.

You'll gather and organize these page elements before you start to create a Web page. Dreamweaver 4's Asset panel enables you to organize the elements of your Web site to quickly access and re-use items. The Asset panel can help you become more efficient and better organized!

In this hour, you will learn

- How to manage assets
- How to create favorite assets
- How to add assets to your Web site

What Are Assets?

Web pages are not just made out of text and code. You use images, movies, colors, and URLs to present information in Web pages. These Web page elements are called *assets*.

The Asset panel organizes these elements, enabling you to quickly find an image or a color that you want to use. You can preview assets in the Asset panel. You can also create a list of favorite assets—ones that you use often.

The Library and Template Panels are part of the Asset panel. These panels are covered in the next two hours.

Manage Assets in the Asset Panel

Dreamweaver automatically catalogs the assets for your entire site. When you open the Asset panel, you can select one of the category buttons from along the left side of the panel to display a list of all of the assets of that type in the site. The Asset panel includes several categories:

- Images
- Colors
- URLs
- Flash Movies
- Shockwave Movies
- Movies
- Scripts
- Templates
- Library

You can browse the assets category, previewing the assets until you find the one you want. The Asset panel enables you to quickly add a selected asset to your current page. Later this hour you'll learn how to set some assets as favorites so you can find them even quicker.

Assets are specific to the current site that you are working in. Often you'll use certain page elements in multiple Web site that you are working in. You can copy your assets to another Web site defined in Dreamweaver to use in that Web site.

List Assets in a Site

When you open the Asset panel, Dreamweaver goes through the cache and automatically catalogs all of the assets. It places the assets into the correct categories by examining the file extensions of the files in your Web site. The Asset panel only lists the assets that are in the currently selected site. When you change sites, you may see a message box appear briefly while the Asset panel is being updated.

View all the assets in a category by selecting a category button along the left side of the Asset panel. All of the categories except for the Library and Templates categories have two radio buttons at the top of the panel, as shown in Figure 19.1, enabling you to select whether you want to see all of that type of asset or just your favorites. We'll discuss how to create a favorite asset in a few minutes.

FIGURE 19.1

The Asset panel has buttons for the different categories along the left side and radio buttons at the top to select whether you view all of the assets or just your favorites.

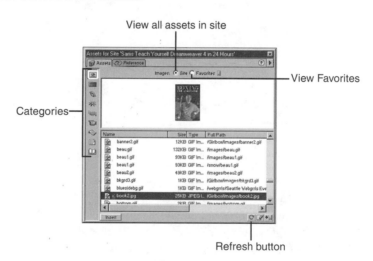

View all assets in site

View Favorites

Categories—

Refresh button

If you add an asset to your site, you may need to select the Refresh button to see it listed in the Asset panel. You can refresh the list of assets anytime.

The title in the Asset panel tells you the name of the site that the current page belongs to. When you open the Site window, it may show a different site.

19

Preview Assets

When you select a category in the Asset panel, the first asset in the list of that category is selected on the lower half of the panel and a preview of that asset appears in the upper half. You can preview the assets by selecting them in the list, shown in Figure 19.2.

The items listed in the Asset panel are sorted alphabetically by default. You can sort the items by any of the available column headings by clicking on the column heading. For instance, you might want to sort your image assets by file size, which is one of the column headings that appears for the image assets category, instead of the filename default sort.

Sometimes you may want to locate the original asset file in the Site window. Dreamweaver has a command that opens up the Site Manager window with the asset file highlighted. Right-click on an asset item and select the Locate in Site command from the context menu. This command only works on assets that are individual files, such as movies or images, and not on assets that are elements of Web pages, such as URLs or colors.

Image Assets

The images category of the Asset panel displays all of the images in your defined Web site (see Figure 19.1). Dreamweaver catalogs images in either the GIF, JPG, or PNG formats. Dreamweaver displays a preview of the selected image in the top half of the Asset panel.

Color Assets

The colors category of the Asset panel, shown in Figure 19.3, displays all of the colors used in the defined Web site. The colors are catalogs and are displayed in hexadecimal format. Dreamweaver displays a preview of the selected color, along with both its hexadecimal and RGB definition, in the top half of the Asset panel. Beside the color name Dreamweaver displays whether or not the color is part of the Web-safe palette.

FIGURE 19.3

The colors category shows the hexadecimal and RGB definition of the colors in the Web site and tells whether the color is part of the Web-safe palette.

 You explored the Dreamweaver palettes when you learned about the color picker in Hour 2, "Creating a Basic Web Page with Text." One of the available palettes available is the Web-safe palette containing the 216 colors that work on all browsers on both Windows and the Mac. The Asset panel tells you whether the colors listed in the color category are within those 216 colors by marking them as Web-safe or Non-Web-safe in the Type column.

Link Assets

The URLs category of the Asset panel holds all of the hyperlinks contained in the currently defined Web site (shown in Figure 19.2). This category lists all URLs in the site including FTP, mailto, gopher, JavaScript, HTTP (Web), and HTTPS (secure Web).

19

 You should not use URLs that begin with file:/// because those URLs will not work when you move your site anywhere other than on your computer. Find those locally referenced URLs in your site and change them.

Movie Assets

There are three different movie asset categories: Flash movies, Shockwave movies, and movies. The movies category will catalog movie types other than Flash or Shockwave movies, such as Quicktime or MPEG movies. There is a play/stop button in the upper-right corner of the preview window (see Figure 19.4) that enables you to play the movie in the preview window.

Play button

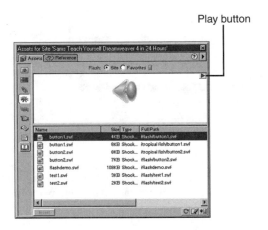

Script Assets

The script category of the Asset panel catalogs all of the external script files in your Web site, as shown in Figure 19.5. External script files end with the .js extension. These script files contain JavaScript functions that you can call from your Web pages. The preview window shows the actual code in the script.

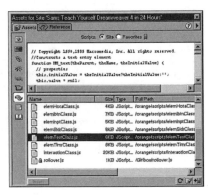

JavaScript that is contained in individual Web pages is not included in the
scripts category of the Asset panel.

You reference an external script in the head section of your Web page. If you call a func-
tion that is contained in an external script, you need to link the external script file to your
Web page by dragging it from the scripts category of the Asset panel into the Head
Content section of the Dreamweaver document window as shown in Figure 19.6.

linked external script   Head content

FIGURE 19.6

*Drag an external
script from the scripts
category of the Asset
panel into the Head
Content of the Web
page.*

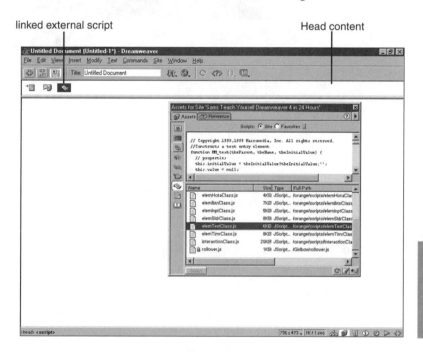

19

Add Assets to a Web Page

Use the Asset panel to add assets to your Web page. To add an asset to your Web page

1. Select the category.

2. Find the asset you want to add by scrolling through the list for the name or viewing the preview in the preview window.

3. Place the insertion point into your Web page where you want the asset located.

4. Select the Insert button and the asset is inserted into your Web page as shown in
   Figure 19.7.

FIGURE **19.7**

*An asset is inserted
into the Web page with
the Insert button.*

Insert button   Refresh Site
                       List button
                       Edit button
                       Add to Favorites button

You can also use assets from the Asset panel to affect other objects on the Web page.
For instance, you can apply a color asset to some text on your Web page:

1. Select some text on the page.
2. Drag a color from the Asset panel by picking up the name in either the preview
   window or the category list.
3. Drop the color on the selected text.

Instead of dragging and dropping, you can simply press the Apply button to apply the
color to the text.

To quickly jump to a section of the item list, first select one of the items in
the list and then type the first letter of the name of the item you are looking for. You will jump to the first item beginning with that letter.

Create Favorite Assets

There are often assets in your Web site that you use repeatedly. You can assign these assets to the favorites list so that they are easy to pick out of the Asset panel. The favorites list is displayed when the Favorites radio button is selected at the top of the Asset panel.

To create a favorite asset, select the asset in the Asset panel and then select the Add to Favorites button. When you select the Favorites radio button, the favorite assets that you just added should be listed as shown in Figure 19.8. You can give a favorite a different name by right-clicking on it, selecting the Edit Nickname command, and typing in a name that is easier to remember.

FIGURE 19.8

You can list only your favorite assets in a certain Asset panel category instead of all of the assets in the site.

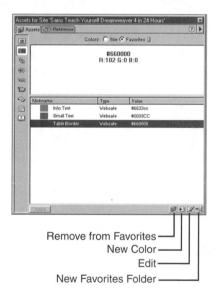

Remove from Favorites
New Color
Edit
New Favorites Folder

Favorites are not available for the Templates and Library categories of the Asset panel.

You can organize your favorites into groups by creating new folders within the favorites list. The New Favorites Folder button (shown in Figure 19.8) enables you to create a folder within the favorites list. After you create a folder, drag and drop items into the folder. Figure 19.9 shows favorite items organized into folders. Expand the folder to view the contents by selecting the + button next to the folder name. Collapse the folder view by selecting the – button next to the folder name.

FIGURE 19.9

Organize your favorite assets by creating folders in the favorites list.

Remove items from the favorites list by selecting the Remove from Favorites button. The item is only removed from the favorites list and is not deleted from the Web site. You can also right-click on an item and select the Remove from Favorites command from the context menu.

Create New Assets in the Asset Panel

You can use the Asset panel to help design your Web site. Dreamweaver enables you to create new assets in certain asset categories. You can add a new color, URL, template or library item. The next two hours will describe how to create new templates and library items.

When you begin creating a Web site, you can organize your development effort with the help of the Asset panel. Organize your image assets into favorites so that commonly used images are easy to find. Define commonly used links and colors so that they can be applied to Web pages quickly.

The Asset panel catalogs the assets that already exist in your site. When you are in the favorites view, you can actually add new assets. These new assets are then available even though they haven't yet been used in your Web site.

To create a new color or link asset

1. Select the Favorites radio button at the top of the Asset panel. Select either the colors or the link categories.
2. Right-click to launch the context menu.
3. Select the New Color or New URL command. Either the color picker appears, as shown in Figure 19.10, or the Add URL dialog box appears, as shown in Figure 19.11.

FIGURE **19.10**

*Use the color picker to
create a new color in
the favorite colors list
of the Asset panel.*

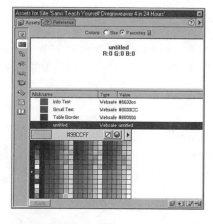

FIGURE **19.11**

*Create a new favorite
link in the URLs cate-
gory of the Asset
panel.*

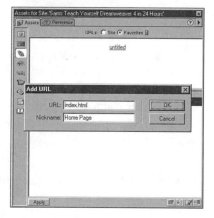

19

4. Pick a color from the color picker or fill in the URL and nickname in the Add
   URL dialog box.

Copy Assets to Another Site

The Asset panel displays the assets of the current site. Sometimes you might want to
share assets between different Web sites defined in Dreamweaver. You can copy a single
asset, a group of assets, or a favorites group to another site.

To copy a single asset to another site, simply right-click on the item name and select the
Copy to Site command. Select the defined site you want to copy to. Dreamweaver copies
the exact folder structure and the file for an image or movie asset.

To copy a group of assets to another site, select multiple asset items by either Shift-clicking or Ctrl-clicking on the item names. Right-click on the group and select the Copy to Site command from the context menu. All of the assets will be copied to the other site. You can also copy a group of favorites to another site by following these same steps.

Summary

You learned how to use assets from the Asset panel. You also learned how to sort, add, and organize assets. You explored the various types of assets and how to create favorites. And you learned how to copy assets from site to site.

Q&A

Q What is the best way to organize images?

A Many Web developers divide images into logical directory structures so that they can more easily find the image they want. The Asset panel can help you organize images so that you may not need to use various directories for organization. You might want to use a naming convention trick so that you can sort your images. For instance, all of the images for section 1 of a Web site can begin with the number 1 (1_image1, 1_image2, and so on). After you've sorted the images, you can create favorites and folders to organize the favorites so that you can quickly find the images you need.

Q I have some URLs listed in the Asset panel that begin with file:///. How can I find and fix these?

A When you notice in the Asset panel that you have links that begin with file:///, you know that you have a problem with your site. The way to identify the pages that contain these links is to run the Check Links report from the Site window. Select the files that show in the report as having links that begin with file:/// and run a Find and Replace on the page to change the URL to a document relative address.

Workshop

The Workshop contains quiz questions and activities to help reinforce what you've learned in this hour. If you get stuck, the answers to the quiz can be found following the questions.

Quiz

1. Which assets categories list individual files?

2. How can you organize favorite assets?

3. True or False: When you copy assets to another site Dreamweaver creates the exact same folder structure in the site that the assets are copied to.

Answers

1. The images and movies categories (include Flash movies, Shockwave movies, and the generic movies categories) list actual files that are referenced in Web pages.

2. You create and name folders to organize your favorite assets so they are easier to find and use.

3. True. The assets are stored in the exact same folder structure.

Exercises

1. Create some favorite assets and then create folders. Organize the favorites in the folders you created.

2. Practice copying image assets to another site. Open up the Site window and confirm that Dreamweaver created a new directory and copied the images to that directory.

19

Hour 20

Re-Using Items in Your Web Site with the Library

You can create library items from objects that you use often when creating your Web pages. If you update a library item, it can update everywhere throughout your site. This is very handy!

Library items help you maintain consistency in your Web site. They also allow you to share design elements with other Web developers. When you are in the design phase of your Web site you should be thinking about common elements that would be appropriate to create as Dreamweaver library items.

You can turn all sorts of objects into library items. For instance, a navigation bar that is present in many of the pages in your Web site would be an excellent candidate for a library item. When you need to add a new button to the navigation bar, it will be a simple matter to add the button to the original library item and then update your entire site automatically with the change.

In this hour, you will learn

- How to create a library item from both existing content and from scratch
- How to add a library item to a Web page
- How to edit the original library item and update linked library items
- How to use behaviors and styles with library items

Create a Library Item

You can create a library item, save it to the Library category of the Asset panel, and then apply it to any Web page within your Web site. Others who are working on the same Web site can use the library item, too, and you can use library items created by others. You can include a library item multiple times in a Web page. Library items can be created from any object contained in the body of the Web page, such as forms, tables, text, Java applets, plug-ins, or images.

You need to define a Web site before Dreamweaver can insert a library item. Dreamweaver creates a directory called Library in the root of your Web site where it stores all of the library items. When you insert a library item into your Web page, Dreamweaver inserts a copy of everything contained in the library item into the page.

 Library items differ from Dreamweaver templates because library items are portions of a page while a template is an entire page. Libraries and templates are similar, though, because they both can automatically update all of the linked items and pages. You'll learn about templates in the next hour, "Creating and Applying a Template."

Use the Library Category of the Asset Panel

When you are creating and applying library items, open the Library category of the Asset panel, shown in Figure 20.1. The Library category of the Asset panel shows all of the library items that exist in the current Web site. Each Web site that you create can have a different set of library items.

FIGURE 20.1

The Library category of the Asset panel displays all of the library items in the current Web site. There are buttons at the bottom of the panel to insert, create, open, and delete library items.

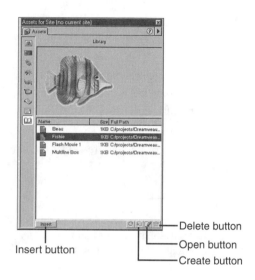

Delete button

Open button

Create button

Insert button

The Library category of the Asset panel is divided into two halves. The bottom half lists the names of the library items in the Web site. The top half displays the contents of a library item that you have selected in the bottom half. The buttons at the bottom include

- The Insert button inserts the currently selected library item at the location of the insertion point in the Web page.

- The New Library Item button creates a new, blank library item.

- The Open Library Item button opens the library item in its own Dreamweaver document window for editing.

- The Delete Library Item button removes the original library item from the library. This doesn't affect any instances of the library item (although the item can no longer be updated throughout the site).

Create a Library Item from Existing Content

There are two ways to create library objects:

- From an existing object or group of objects—After you decide to create a library item out of a group of objects on a Web page, you select the objects and save them into the library.

- From scratch, as a new, empty library item—You can create a new library item, open it up, and add objects to the library item just like it was a regular Web page.

Create a library item from an existing object or group of objects on your Web page:

20

1. Select an object or group of objects. Select multiple objects either by dragging your cursor over them or holding down Shift and clicking to add objects to the selection.

2. To add the selection to the library, drag and drop it onto the bottom half of the Library category of the Asset panel. Alternatively, select the Add Object to Library command under the Library submenu of the Modify menu.

3. Give the library object a meaningful name. The name field is selected immediately after you create the library item or you can re-select the name with a long single-click on the name field.

> Dreamweaver creates an individual file for each library item. The file extension for library items is .lbi. If you look in the Library directory of your Web site, you will see one .lbi file for each library item you have in your Web site.

When you select a library item name you will see the contents of the library item in the top half of the Library category of the Asset panel, as shown in Figure 20.2. The contents may look different from how they will look in the Web page because the Library category of the Asset panel is small and the objects wrap. Also, because the library item is only a portion of a Web page it appears with no page background color.

FIGURE 20.2

The Library category of the Asset panel displays the contents of a library item in its top half and the names of all of the library items in the bottom half.

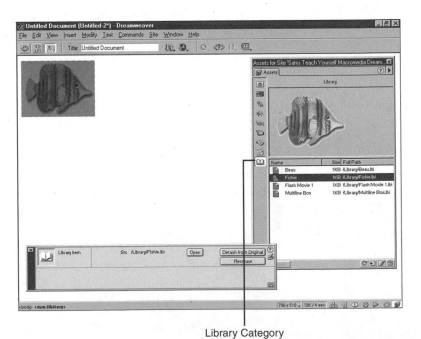

Library Category

Create a Library Item from Scratch

Create a new, empty library item and add objects to it:

1. Click the New Library Item button at the bottom of the Library category of the Asset panel.

2. Dreamweaver creates a new, blank library item as shown in Figure 20.3. A message appears in the top half of the Library category of the Asset panel telling you how to get started adding content to the blank library item.

FIGURE 20.3

A message appears in the Library category of the Asset panel after you create a new blank library item. The message tells you how to add content to the new item.

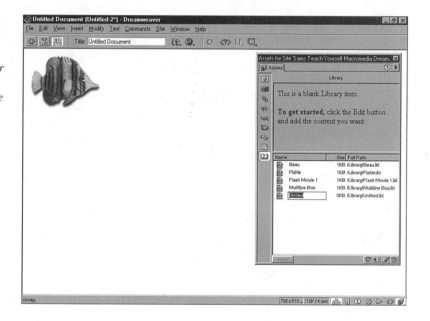

3. Give the library item a name. For example, create a copyright statement that will go at the bottom of each of your Web pages. The name "Copyright" would be a good choice.

4. Double-click the library item in the Library category of the Asset panel. Dreamweaver opens the library item in a separate document window. You can tell that you have a library item open because Dreamweaver displays <<Library Item>> along with the name of the library item in the title bar as shown in Figure 20.4.

5. Insert objects into the library item's document window just like you would any Web page. Insert the copyright symbol (from the Characters panel in the Object panel), a year, and your name.

20

Shows you are in Library items

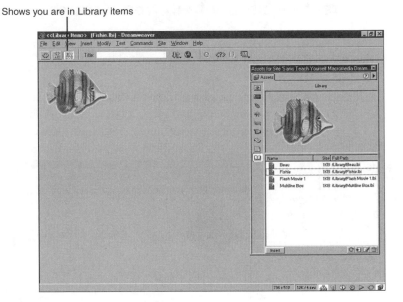

FIGURE 20.4

To add content to a library item, you open it in a separate Dreamweaver document window. The window shows <<Library Item>> in the title bar.

6. Close the document window and save the library item. Your changes will be reflected in the Library category of the Asset panel.

The Library category of the Asset panel has a pop-up menu that contains useful commands, shown in Figure 20.5. The New Library Item command is only active when objects are selected in the document window; this is yet another way to create a library item. This same menu also pops up when you right-click on a library item in the Library category of the Asset panel.

FIGURE 20.5

The Library category of the Asset panel pop-up menu has a number of commands to add, rename, open, and delete library items.

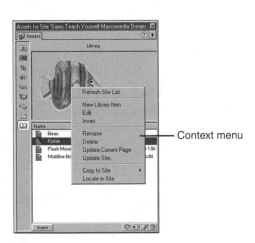

Context menu

Add a Library Item to a Page

Once you have created a library item, you simply drag it from the list in the Library category of the Asset panel and drop it into your Web page, as shown in Figure 20.6. You can pick the library item up and move it to a different location in the document window. You will not be able to select individual objects contained in the inserted library item. When you click on any of the objects, you select the entire library item; the group of objects in a library item is essentially one object in your Web page.

FIGURE 20.6

Drag a library item from the Library category of the Asset panel and drop it on your Web page.

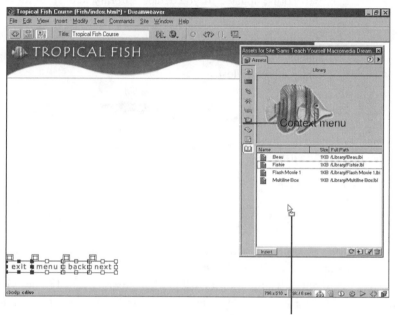

Dragging items into Library

When you insert a library item into your Web page, a copy of all its content gets inserted. You no longer need to have the original library item present. When you upload your Web page onto a remote Web site you do not need to upload the library directory. You'll want to kccp the directory in case you want to make changes to library items throughout your Web site.

20

You might want to upload the library onto your server so that others can use the library items, too.

The Property inspector, shown in Figure 20.7, displays the library item attributes when a library item is selected in the document window. The Src box displays the name of the library item (which you cannot change here). Three buttons in the Property inspector help you manage the library item:

- The Open button opens the library item to edit.
- The Detach from Original button breaks the link between this instance of a library item and the original item. If the original library item is changed, a detached item will not be updated. If you detach a library item from the original, the individual objects contained in the item will now be editable.
- The Recreate button overwrites the original library item with the currently selected instance of the library item. This is useful if the original library item was inadvertently edited or lost.

FIGURE 20.7

The Property inspector contains buttons to manage a library item. You can detach the item from the original or overwrite the item as the original.

You can apply a highlight to library items so that they are easy to pick out in the document window. The highlight only appears in Dreamweaver and not in the browser. The highlight only appears if Invisible Elements is checked in the View menu. Set the highlight color in the Highlighting category in Dreamweaver preferences, as shown in Figure 20.8.

FIGURE 20.8
Set a highlight color for all library items in Dreamweaver preferences. The highlight only appears in Dreamweaver and not in the browser.

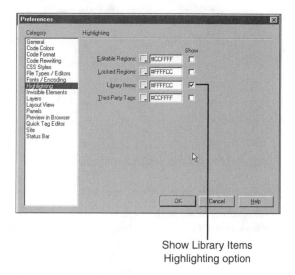

Show Library Items
Highlighting option

Make Changes to a Library Item

Edit library items by opening the item to add or change objects in the document window. Don't worry about the page background color when editing library items; the item will appear on the background color of the page it is inserted in. After you've inserted your previously created library item into a page, open the library item to edit it. Apply different formatting to some of the objects in the item.

Update Pages That Contain the Library Item

After you are finished editing, save the library item. Dreamweaver will ask you whether you want to update all of the documents in the Web site that contain the library item. Select the Yes button to automatically update all linked library items. The Update Pages dialog box, shown in Figure 20.9, displays statistics on how many files were examined, how many were updated, and how many could not be updated. The Show Log check box needs to be checked to display these statistics. Select the Close button to close the Update Pages dialog box.

20

FIGURE 20.9

With Show Log checked, the Update Pages dialog box shows how many files were examined, how many were updated, and how many could not be updated.

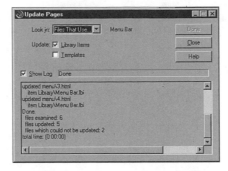

 Certain library items in the Web site may not be updated because you do not have these items checked out. When you have check in/check out turned on in your Web site, files that are not checked out to you are marked as read-only. Dreamweaver will not be able to update any library items in files marked read-only. Make sure you have all the appropriate files checked out before you update a library item.

You can manually update linked library items at any time. Right-click on the library item in the Library category of the Asset panel and select either the Update Page command to update the current Web page, or the Update Pages command to update the entire Web site. The Update Page command acts immediately and no dialog box appears. When you issue the Update Pages command, the Update Pages dialog box appears as shown in Figure 20.10. Click the Start button to begin updating all of the linked library items in the Web site.

FIGURE 20.10

Select the Start button to begin updating all of the library items in your entire Web site linked to the selected library item.

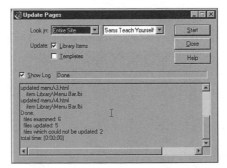

Use Behaviors and Styles in Library Items

When you apply a Dreamweaver behavior to an object, Dreamweaver inserts JavaScript in the <head> of the HTML document. A library item does not have a <head> section.

So, what happens to the JavaScript when you drag an object into the Library category of the Asset panel that has a behavior applied to it? When a library item with an attached behavior is inserted into a Web page, Dreamweaver cleverly inserts any necessary JavaScript into the <head> section of the Web page.

Problems arise if you want to change the behavior associated with a library item. You cannot use the Behavior panel while editing a library item because only the event half of the behavior is present. To edit a behavior attached to a library item, you must first detach the item, edit the behavior, and then recreate the library item. It's easier to be sure of how you want the library item to work before you put in the library!

You can apply styles to library items but you will need to either manually copy the style definition into every page that uses the library item or use a linked style sheet. It's easiest to use a linked style sheet for this purpose. Make sure that every Web page that includes the library item is linked to the style sheet that contains the style definitions used in the library item. If you edit a style in the linked style sheet, all the library items will reflect any changes to the style.

You cannot save timelines to the library. If you save objects in a timeline to the library, the object will be saved in the library item but not the JavaScript that runs the timeline.

Summary

In this hour, you learned how to create library items, both from existing content and from scratch. You learned how to use the Library category of the Asset panel to manage library items and how to open and edit the items. You learned how Dreamweaver will automatically update all of the linked library items in your Web site and how you can launch that process manually.

20

Q&A

Q How can I apply edits I made to library items in only some of the linked files?

A Well, first I have to caution you to be careful when maintaining various pages, some with the newest version of the library item and some with an old version. You can select only the pages you want to update. But why not instead open the library item, save it with a different name, apply your edits, and then replace it in the selected pages?

Q What types of objects are appropriate to put in the library?

A Some examples of objects that you may want to put in the Dreamweaver library: the company logo, a group of layers that appear on each page as a background, a search box (small form), a frequently used button, a custom bullet image, or a placeholder for content that isn't finalized (you can detach it later). I'm sure you will find plenty of uses for the library.

Workshop

The Workshop contains quiz questions and activities to help reinforce what you've learned in this hour. If you get stuck, the answers to the quiz can be found following the questions.

Quiz

1. What is the file extension for library item files?
2. True or False: Dreamweaver will not insert the necessary JavaScript into a Web page when you insert a library item that has a behavior attached.
3. How do you unlink an instance of a library item from the original library item?

Answers

1. The file extension for a library item is .lbi.
2. False. Dreamweaver inserts the JavaScript required for a behavior attached to a library item into every page the library item is inserted into.
3. Select the Detach from Original button from the Property inspector with the library item selected.

Exercises

1. Create a library item and add it to a page. Experiment with re-opening the library item, editing it, and then updating the page it's connected to.
2. Place a button in a Web page and add the Go To URL behavior to it. Drag the button into the library. Open the library item and view the HTML. Do you see any JavaScript in the <head> section? You shouldn't because there isn't one! Open a new blank Web page. Add the button to the page. View the HTML of the new page and you should see the JavaScript that Dreamweaver added automatically to the <head> section.

HOUR **21**

Creating and Applying a Template

You create templates to use as a base for consistent, controlled Web pages. Templates contain objects that you mark as editable; the rest of the template is locked. You can update the original template and it will update throughout your site.

In this hour, you will learn

- How to create a template from both existing content and from scratch
- How to apply a template to a Web page
- How to edit the original template and update linked templates
- How to mark a selection as editable
- How to use behaviors, styles, and timelines with templates

Create a Template

First create a template, save it to the Template category of the Asset panel, and then use it to create a new Web page within your Web site. Others that are working on the same Web site can use the template, too, and you can use templates created by others.

You need to define a Web site before Dreamweaver can insert a template. Dreamweaver creates a directory called Templates in the root of your Web site where it stores the original template files. Dreamweaver keeps the code of a template in a file in the Template directory and inserts a copy of the code when you insert a template in a Web page.

A template differs from a library item because the template is an entire Web page, not just a portion of one.

Use the Template Category of the Asset Panel

When you are creating and applying templates, open the Template category of the Asset panel, shown in Figure 21.1. The Template category shows all of the templates that exist in the current Web site. Each Web site that you create can have a different set of templates.

Does the Template category of the Asset panel look bare? Copy one or more of the sites available in the templates directory of the Dreamweaver CD-ROM to your hard drive and set it up as a site in the Site Window. These templates are also available for download from the Macromedia Web site at: http://www.macromedia.com/software/dreamweaver/download/templates/.

The Template category of the Asset panel is divided into two halves. The top half displays the contents of the template. The bottom half lists the names of the templates in the Web site. The buttons at the bottom include the following:

- The Apply button applies the currently selected template to the Web page.
- The New Template button creates a new, blank template.
- The Open Template button opens the template in its own Dreamweaver document window for editing.

- The Delete Template button removes the template from the Templates directory. This doesn't affect any instances of the templates except that the template can no longer be updated site wide.

FIGURE 21.1
The Template category of the Asset panel displays all of the templates in the current Web site. There are buttons at the bottom of the panel to apply, create, open, and delete templates.

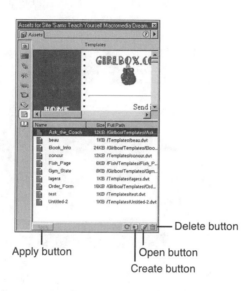

Apply button   Open button   Create button   Delete button

Create a Template from an Existing Web Page

There are two ways to create templates:

- From an existing Web page—after you decide to create a template out of a Web page, you save the page as a template.
- From scratch, as a new empty template—you can create a new template, open it up, and add objects to the template just like it was a regular Web page.

Once you apply a template to your Web page a copy of all of the content that the template contains gets inserted into the page. You no longer need to have the original template present for the Web page to display. When you upload your Web page onto a remote Web site you do not need to upload the Templates directory. You might want to upload the template onto your server so that others can use the templates too. You'll want to keep the directory in case you want to make changes to templates throughout your Web site.

21

Keeping the templates on the server ensures that you have a backup copy in case you accidentally change a template and need to restore the original.

Create a template from an existing Web page:

1. Select the Save As Template command under the File menu.

2. The Save As Template dialog box appears as shown in Figure 21.2. Enter a meaningful name for the template.

FIGURE 21.2

Give a template a meaningful name in the Save As Template dialog box. You'll see a list of existing templates in the current Web site displayed.

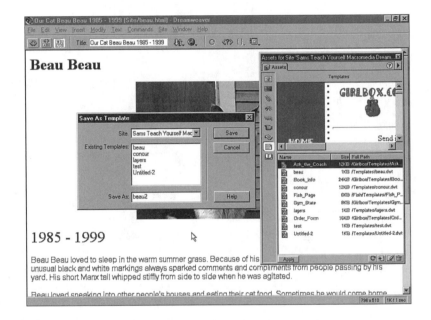

 Dreamweaver creates an individual file for each template. The file extension for templates is .dwt. If you look in the Templates directory of your Web site you will see one .dwt file for each template you have in your Web site.

Create a Template from Scratch

To create a new empty template and then add objects to it

1. Click the New Template button at the bottom of the Template category of the Asset panel.

   Dreamweaver creates a new blank template as shown in Figure 21.3. A message appears in the top half of the Template category of the Asset panel telling you how to get started adding content to the blank template.

FIGURE 21.3

A message appears in the Template category after you create a new blank template. The message tells you how to add content to the new template.

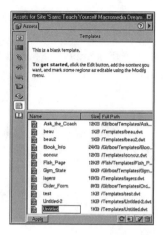

2. Give the template a name. For example, create a template for displaying your CD or book collection and call it "CD" or "book".

3. Double-click the template in the Template category of the Asset panel. Dreamweaver opens the template in a separate document window. You can tell that you have a template open because Dreamweaver displays <<Template>> along with the name of the template in the title bar as shown in Figure 21.4.

FIGURE 21.4

To add content to a template you open it in a separate Dreamweaver document window. The window shows <<Template>> in the title bar.

Templates

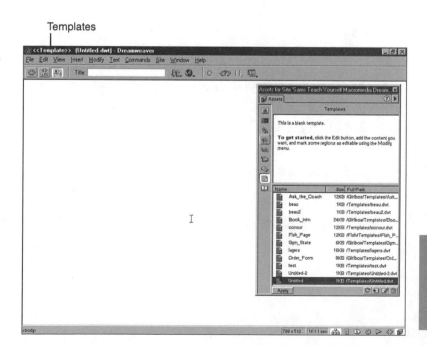

21

4. Insert objects into the template's document window just like you would any Web page.

5. Close the document window and save the template. Your changes will be reflected in the Template category of the Asset panel. Don't worry right now about the message you receive about your template not having any editable regions. You'll add some editable regions in a few minutes.

The Template category of the Asset panel has a pop-up menu that contains useful commands, shown in Figure 21.5. Different commands are available depending on what is currently selected.

FIGURE 21.5

The Template category of the Asset panel context menu has a number of commands to apply, rename, open, and delete templates.

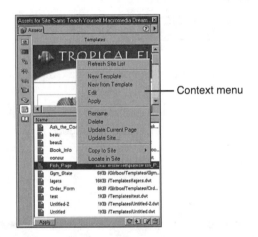

— Context menu

Make an Existing Region Editable

Before you apply a template to a Web page, you need to mark regions of the template as editable. By default, all regions in the template are locked. Mark regions as editable if you will need to change, add, or update the content in the region.

Leave all regions locked that do not need to be changed. If you need to make changes to a locked region, you can change the original template file and update all of the Web pages that are linked to that template. The Template commands to manipulate Editable Regions are located in the Templates submenu in the Modify menu, shown in Figure 21.6.

FIGURE 21.6

The Templates submenu in Dreamweaver's Modify menu contains all of the commands to manipulate editable regions.

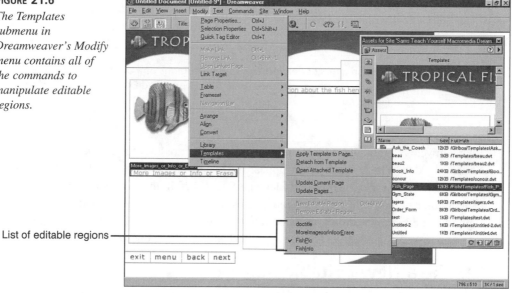

List of editable regions

To make an existing region editable

1. Open a template and select the region that needs to be editable.
2. Select the Mark Selection as Editable command from the Templates submenu in the Modify menu.
3. The New Editable Region dialog box appears as shown in Figure 21.7. Give the region a meaningful name.

FIGURE 21.7

When you apply the Mark Selection as Editable to a region, you name the region in the New Editable Region dialog box.

After you create an editable region, the name of the region is listed at the bottom of the Templates submenu in the Modify menu while you are working on the template. Select one of the region names in the menu to highlight that region in the document window.

Dreamweaver gives you the ability to create editable regions on various objects in a template. For instance, you can make a layer editable. You will be able to move the layer or change any of its properties after you apply the template to a Web page. Or, you can leave the layer locked and create an editable region within the layer. Then you can't

21

move the layer or change the layer properties when you've applied the template but you can put content within the layer.

 You can import or export the editable regions of a Dreamweaver template as XML. Use the commands under the Import and Export submenus of the File menu.

Dreamweaver highlights editable regions so that they are easy to pick out in the document window. The highlights only appear in Dreamweaver and not in the browser. The highlights only appear if Invisible Elements is checked in the View menu. Set the highlight color in the Highlighting category in Dreamweaver preferences. The editable regions are highlighted only while editing the original template file. Just the opposite is true in a Web page with a template applied: The locked regions are highlighted.

Make a New Editable Region

You can create a new, blank editable region in a template. Select the New Editable Region command from the Templates submenu in the Modify menu. Name the new region in the New Editable Region dialog box. The editable region appears in a highlighted rectangular outline as shown in Figure 21.8.

Editable regions

FIGURE 21.8

After you insert a new editable region into the template, it appears as a highlighted rectangular outline.

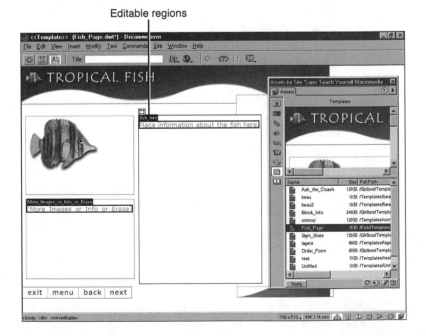

> If Dreamweaver displays the message that the selection is already a part of an editable region, then you need to move the selection. Examine the tag selector for the tag `<mm:editable>`. If you see this tag, you need to modify your selection until that tag is no longer part of the selection.

To lock a region that has previously been marked as editable, select the Unmark Editable Region command from the Templates submenu of the Modify menu. Select the name of a region to lock and click OK. If you have entered information into previously editable regions in Web pages, you will lose that information after locking the region and updating the Web pages.

Apply a Template to a Web Page

You can apply templates in three different ways:

- Simply drag the template from the Template category of the Asset panel and apply it to a new Web page.

- Select the Apply Template to Page command from the Templates submenu in the Modify menu.

- Select a template in the Template category of the Asset panel and click the Apply button.

Apply a template to a Web page or open a new Web page with the New from Template command in the File menu. If a Web page already has a template applied to it, Dreamweaver attempts to place existing content into editable regions with the same name in the new template. If there is content that Dreamweaver cannot reconcile between the two templates, you can direct Dreamweaver to either save the extra content into new regions or delete it.

> If you apply a template to a page with an existing template and content entered into the editable regions, make sure the new template's editable regions have the same names as those in the original template. That way you won't lose the content you have already entered.

21

Make Changes to a Template

Edit templates by opening the template to add or change its contents. You can open the template from the Template category of the Asset panel or you can open the template from the Site Manager. Edits to locked objects are applied to all of the Web pages that use the template. Edits to editable objects have no effect on Web pages that use the template.

Update Pages That Contain the Template

After you edit and save a template, Dreamweaver will ask you whether you want to update files. Select files and then the Update button to automatically update the linked templates. The Update Pages dialog box displays statistics on how many files were examined, updated, and could not be updated. The Show Log check box needs to be checked to display these statistics. Select the Close button to close the Update Pages dialog box.

> Certain files in the Web site may not be updated because you do not have these files checked out. When you have check in/check out turned on in your Web site, files that are not checked out to you are marked as read-only. Dreamweaver will not be able to update any files marked read-only.

You can also manually update files linked to templates. Right-click on the template in the Template category of the Asset panel and select either the Update Page command, to update the current Web page, or the Update Pages command, to update the entire Web site. The Update Page command acts immediately and no dialog box appears. When you issue the Update Pages command, the Update Pages dialog box appears as shown in Figure 21.9. Click the Start button to update all of the linked templates in the Web site.

FIGURE **21.9**

Select the Start button in the Update Pages dialog box to start updating all files in your entire Web site linked to the selected template.

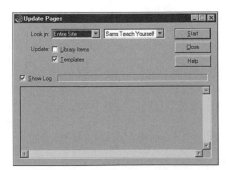

Use Behaviors, Styles, and Timelines in Templates

You can use behaviors, styles, and timelines in templates. Styles and JavaScript will be applied to a Web page based on the template, as shown in Figure 21.10. To edit styles and behaviors in the Web page, objects they are applied to must be editable. Select an object with a style or behavior and edit the style or behavior in the CSS Style panel or Behavior panel. Even though you can edit behaviors and styles in a Web page linked to a template, you can only apply behaviors and styles to objects in the original template.

FIGURE 21.10

Apply a style to objects in the template. If those objects are editable, you can change them in the Web page that is based on the template.

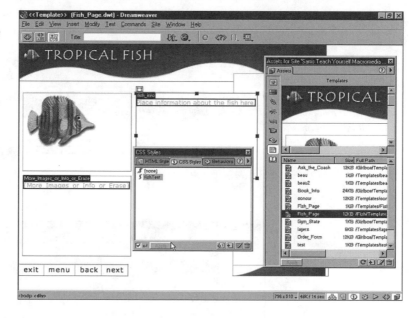

 Everything in the <head> section of a Web page created with a template is locked except the title. That's why you can't add styles or behaviors. Both need to add content to the <head> section. The <body> tag is also locked.

You can add timelines to a template. The layers or images in the timeline must be marked as editable if you intend on allowing them to be changed. If you don't need the timeline content to be changed, leave the layer or image locked and it will still animate.

21

To add a timeline to a Dreamweaver template

1. Create a timeline as you normally would in an open template.

2. Mark objects as editable if you want to be able to change them after the template is applied.

   Since the <body> tag is locked when a template is applied you can't trigger the timeline to play by checking the Autoplay check box in the Timeline panel. That adds JavaScript to the <body> tag that will be removed.

   Instead, attach the Play Timeline behavior (under Timelines in the Behaviors inspector) to any image on the page. Have the Play Timeline action triggered by the image's onLoad event. When the image loads, the timeline will play! See Figure 21.11 for an example.

FIGURE 21.11

Create a timeline in your template and trigger it with the onLoad *event attached to an image on the page.*

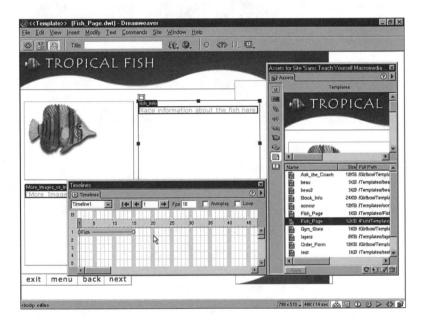

3. Create a new Web page with the template. Change any objects that need to be edited.

If you do not have an image in your template, insert a small transparent gif (1 x 1 pixels) somewhere in your Web page and attach the behavior to it.

Summary

In this hour, you learned how to create templates, both from existing content and from scratch. You learned how to use the Template category of the Asset panel to manage templates and how to open and edit the templates. You learned how to make regions of a template editable. You learned how Dreamweaver will automatically update all of the linked templates in your Web site and how you can launch that process manually. And, you learned how to insert a timeline into a template.

Q&A

Q Is there any way I can use templates without having locked and editable regions?

A You can create a template with everything layed out perfectly, apply it to a Web page, and then detach it. That way you have a standard beginning point but have the freedom to do what you want with the page.

Q Why can't I change the background or link colors in a page created with a template?

A When you apply a template to a Web page, the <head> section (except for the title) and the <body> tag are locked. The background and link colors are attributes of the <body> tag and will need to be defined in the original template, either in the <body> tag or as styles.

Workshop

The Workshop contains quiz questions and activities to help reinforce what you've learned in this hour. If you get stuck, the answers to the quiz can be found following the questions.

Quiz

1. What is the file extension for template files?

2. Which regions, editable or locked, are highlighted when you are editing the original template file?

3. What happens when you apply a template to a Web page that already has a template applied to it?

21

Answers

1. The file extension for a template is `.dwt`.

2. The editable regions are highlighted when you are editing the original template file. The locked regions are highlighted when you are in a Web page linked to a template.

3. Dreamweaver will match up the content when the regions have the same name in both templates. If there is content that doesn't fit into the new template, Dreamweaver will ask you if you want to delete it or create a new region.

Exercises

1. Create a template and practice marking various objects as editable. Apply the template and see which objects can be marked as editable and which cannot. What properties can you edit?

2. Open a template that you have already applied to a page, edit it, and practice updating the linked page. Open the page. Do you see the edits you made?

Hour 22

Using Server-Side Includes and Adding a Date

Server-side includes (SSI) can save you time and effort when developing a Web site. You create files that are inserted into your Web page by the server when the user accesses a Web page. The server, where the final Web site is stored, processes a command that you've inserted into your Web page.

Using server-side includes enables the Web server to place information dynamically into your Web pages. Since the processing of the included information happens on the server, you cannot view the file properly without loading it onto the server. Dreamweaver simulates the final appearance of your Web page by displaying the included information in the document window. Also, Dreamweaver displays the server-side include when you preview your Web page in the browser.

You can also add a last modified date to a Web page. These dates are a courtesy to your viewers, enabling them to see how current the information is that they are viewing. Dreamweaver can automatically update the last modified date when you make changes to your Web page.

In this hour, you will learn

- How to insert a comment
- How to insert any server-side include
- How to insert files into Web pages using server-side includes
- How to insert a last modified date into a Web page

What Is a Server-Side Include?

A server-side include (SSI) enables the server to place external data into your Web page. The data placed in the page can be either a data string or the contents of a file. Dreamweaver's capability to handle many types of code without mangling it is exemplary and it won't mess with your server-side includes. However, even nicer is that Dreamweaver can actually simulate the processing of some of these server directives.

In this hour, we will explore how to use Dreamweaver to include other files in your Web page. But server-side includes can also insert information that Dreamweaver won't be able to display. You might want to include instances of the many types of server-side includes in your Web pages.

Here are the five main things that server-side includes do:

- Insert another file into the current Web page. Dreamweaver simulates the appearance so you don't have to always check how your page looks by transferring and viewing it from the server.
- *Echo* back information from the server to display a date, the user's IP address, the URL of the previous Web page, or other information that the server has available.
- Configure information in another include. For instance, add an include before another include to make a date appear in a certain format.
- Execute a CGI script. For instance, if you use a server-side include to add forward and back buttons to your Web page, the include calls a CGI script to figure out what the hyperlink is for the next and previous pages.
- Display the file size of the current Web page.

To make server-side includes work, you will have to know a little about your server. First, the directory in which you are going to place your Web page needs to be configured to allow server-side includes. Second, you need to know what file extension your server recognizes as potentially containing server-side includes. Your network or Web administrator can give you this information or set it up for you.

You'll want to check with your Web administrator before you design server-side includes into your Web site. Some accounts simply do not allow the use of server-side includes.

The server needs to know which files to look through for server-side includes. If your server is set up to look for SSI in all files, it adds a lot of processing overhead and may slow down the entire server. Often servers are configured to only look for SSI in files ending with .shtml, .shtm, .stm, or other extensions that signal the server that a server-side include is present in the page. The server parses through only those pages, looking for server-side includes and processing them.

Extensive server-side includes that require processing of code can be a drain on the resources of a Web server. If your Web site resides on a server with a lot of traffic, server-side includes may increase the time the server takes to send your Web page to the viewer.

For the same reasons you might use Dreamweaver library items, you might also want to use server-side includes. You can update an included file and change every page in your site that references it. Dreamweaver inserts the contents of the library item into the Web page, but the contents of the file that is referenced in a server-side include are inserted by the server when the file is requested.

Insert a Server-Side Include

Server-side includes look like HTML comments. You can insert a comment into your Web page by selecting the Comment object in the Invisibles panel of the Object panel or the Comment command under the Invisible Tags submenu of the Insert menu. The Insert Comment dialog box appears as shown in Figure 22.1. A comment is usually some text that describes your Web page or explains some of the code.

FIGURE 22.1

The Insert Comment dialog box enables you to insert a comment that is only visible in the HTML.

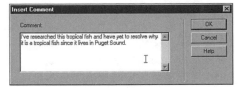

A comment appears in Dreamweaver as an invisible element. You can edit a comment in the Property inspector. If you select the Quick Tag editor in the Property inspector when a comment is selected, as shown in Figure 22.2, you can see the HTML for a comment. The comment will not be visible to people viewing your Web page (unless, of course, the user views the HTML).

Comment tags are commonly used around some code or HTML, like JavaScript, to hide the code from older browsers. Newer browsers recognize the JavaScript but the older browsers ignore it because it is in a comment. And, the browser doesn't show an error message.

FIGURE 22.2

The HTML of a comment viewed with the Quick Tag Editor.

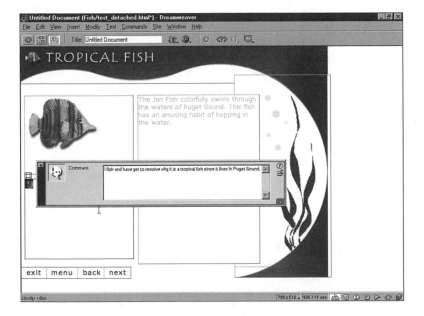

Turn a Comment into a Server-Side Include

A server-side include looks like a comment. There's a # (pound sign) before the code for the server-side include. The server replaces the server-side include with the appropriate text (or whatever the server-side include inserts). Table 22.1 lists some server-side include commands.

TABLE 22.1 There Are a Number of Different Server-Side Include Commands You Can Put in Your Web Page

Code	Description
#echo var="HTTP_REFERER"	Displays the URL of the Web page you just came from.
#echo var="DATE_LOCAL"	Displays the date and time.
#echo var="REMOTE_ADDR"	Displays the viewer's IP number.
#echo var="DOCUMENT_NAME"	Displays the name of the current Web page.
#echo var="HTTP_USER_AGENT"	Displays the viewer's browser and operating system.
#fsize file="my_file.shtml"	Displays the size of the file.
#flastmod file="my_file.shtml"	Displays the last modified date of the file.

If your server recognizes these commands, you can enter them into the comment field as shown in Figure 22.3. Save the file (remember, there may be a special file extension), transfer the Web page onto the remote server, and view the Web page.

FIGURE 22.3

You enter the server-side include code into the Comment dialog box, save the file, and then load it on the server.

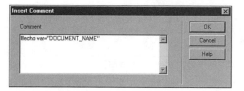

Include a File

You can insert a comment to add any of the server-side includes described above. However, Dreamweaver has a specialized object that enables you to insert an included file. Dreamweaver's Server-Side Include object inserts a reference to an external file into your Web page.

Dreamweaver processes server-side includes that do not contain *conditionals*. Conditionals are bits of code that make the command dependent upon a certain outcome. For instance, the statement "if you are good you get some candy" bases whether or not you get candy on whether or not you are good. You can use this type of conditional statement in server-side includes but Dreamweaver will not display the results.

First, you need to create the external file that will be included in your Web page. The included file is a fragment of HTML, not an entire page. This makes sense when you realize that the file is being placed inside of another Web page. To create an external file and insert its contents into a Web page with a server-side include

1. Open a text editor, such as the Windows' Notepad or Macintosh's SimpleText, and enter some text into it as shown in Figure 22.4.

FIGURE 22.4

Create the included file in a text editor such as Notepad or SimpleText. You can edit the file later in Dreamweaver.

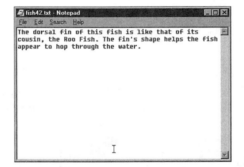

 You can create the included file in Dreamweaver but it will then be a complete HTML page, meaning it will have <head> and <body> tags. Since the Web page that you will insert the included file into already has these tags, you must not have them in the included file. If you create the file in Dreamweaver, you will need to go into the HTML and remove the entire <head> section and both the opening and closing <body> tags.

2. Save the text file in the same directory that your Web page will reside in. You can give the file any extension; you might want to use .txt, .html, or .htm.
3. Open a Web page in Dreamweaver.
4. Place the insertion point where you would like the text from the file to appear.

5. Select the Server-Side Include object from the Common panel of the Object panel or select the Server-Side Include command from the Insert menu.

6. The Select File dialog box appears. Select the text file that you created a moment ago.

The text that you added to the separate file now appears in your Web page as shown in Figure 22.5. The Property inspector displays the server-side include file name, file type, and an edit button. Notice that when the contents of the external file are selected they cannot be edited in the Web page.

FIGURE 22.5

The text from the separate file appears in the Dreamweaver document window where the server-side include is.

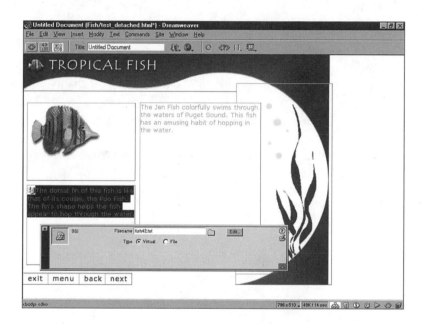

There are two different ways to enter the address of the external file that you are including in your Web page. Select either Virtual or File in the Property inspector beside Type. Select File to create an address that is relative to that of the current file, similar to document relative addressing. Select Virtual to reference the file relative to the root of your Web server, similar to site root relative addressing. We explored document relative and site root addressing in Hour 4, "Setting Lots o' Links: Hyperlinks, URLs, Anchors, and Mailto Links."

If you use virtual addressing in your server-side include you will need to know which directory is set as the root of your Web site on the server. You will also have to have the proper permissions to save your file there.

The Virtual setting always works when you are using an Apache server. Select the File setting when using IIS as your Web server software. You need to only reference files that are either in or below the current folder in the file hierarchy.

Unlike library items, Dreamweaver does not actually insert the HTML for the server-side include into the Web page. If you look at the HTML, you will see a tag that looks like this:

```
<!-- #include file="header.txt" -->
```

Edit the Server-Side Include File

Edit your included file right in Dreamweaver. When you have the server-side include selected, click on the Edit button. Dreamweaver opens the contents of the included file in a separate document window, as shown in Figure 22.6.

FIGURE 22.6

The included file can be edited in a separate window by clicking on the edit button in the Property inspector.

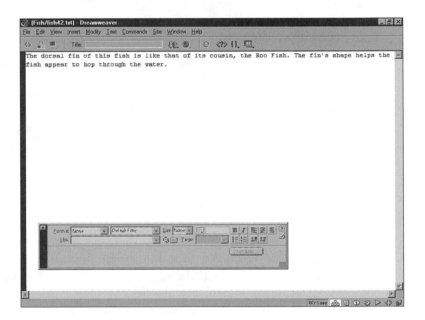

Use Dreamweaver to edit and add content to your included file. When you save the file, your changes will be reflected in all Web pages that reference the file. Since the file doesn't need page attributes, such as background color, link colors, or background image, they will not appear when you are editing the included external file.

We've used a text file here but you can include a file with HTML tags, including references to images and any other object that a Web page can contain.

22

Add a Last Modified Date

There are two ways you can add a last modified date to your Web page: a server-side include and Dreamweaver's Date object. A server-side include takes the last modified date from the file attributes of the page. Dreamweaver's Date object simply updates the date (and time) every time you edit and save the Web page in Dreamweaver. Earlier in this hour you saw the code that can be included to add a last modified date via a server-side include. Now you will learn about Dreamweaver's Date object.

When you select the Date object in the Object panel or the Date command from the Insert menu, the Insert Date dialog box appears as shown in Figure 22.7. Select from the various day, date, and time formats. If you select the Update Automatically on Save checkbox, Dreamweaver will update the date every time you save the Web page. Click OK to insert the date.

FIGURE 22.7

Set the format of a Date object in the Insert Date dialog box. You can format the day, date, and time.

You edit the format of a date you've inserted into a Web page by first selecting the date object in the document window and then clicking on the Edit Date Format button in the Property inspector. Once you have set the date to automatically update, you cannot undo it; you'll need to either delete the date and insert a new one or edit the HTML.

Summary

In this hour, you learned how to add a comment to your Web page. Then, you learned how to turn a comment into a server-side include. You learned how to insert a file into your Web page using Dreamweaver's Server-Side Include object. You learned how to edit an included file. You learned how to insert a date and set it to update automatically whenever you save the Web page.

Q&A

Q **When I view a Web page that has a server-side include from the server, I get the message "An error occurred processing this directive". What am I doing wrong?**

A It looks like your server is trying to process the server-side include but it can't. This is most likely a problem with the path to your included file. If you are using document relative addressing for the SSI, you must select File as the type of addressing in the Property inspector. And if you are using site root relative addressing, make sure you select Virtual as the Type and that the file resides in the site root directory.

Q **Which browsers support server-side includes?**

A Any browser will work fine with server-side includes. Server-side includes have already been processed by the time the Web page gets to the browser so it's the server that has to support server-side includes not the browser.

Workshop

The Workshop contains quiz questions and activities to help reinforce what you've learned in this hour. If you get stuck, the answers to the quiz can be found following the questions.

Quiz

1. What signals the server that a comment is a server-side include instead of just a comment?

2. What type of server-side includes does Dreamweaver translate so that you can preview the results in Dreamweaver and your local browser?

3. What are some common file extensions for Web pages that contain server-side includes?

Answers

1. A server-side include is a comment that begins with a # (pound sign).

2. Dreamweaver translates included files, displaying them both in the document window and when you preview in a browser.

3. Common file extensions for Web pages that contain server-side includes are .shtml, .shtm, and .stm.

Exercises

1. Create a file in a text editor to be included in a Web page. Make it content that you would update often such as a weekly menu, weather, or stock information. Add a reference to the file into a Web page using Dreamweaver's Server-Side Include object. Edit the included file, adding formatting. Preview your page in a browser.

2. Insert a date and time into a Web page and check the Update Automatically on Save. Save the file, after noting the time that was inserted, and wait a minute or two. Open the file, change something in the file, and then save the file again. When you reopen the file is the time different?

22

PART VII

Using External Editors and Changing Dreamweaver to Suit You

Hour

HOUR 23

HTML Is Fun! Viewing and Modifying HTML

Can you believe you've already learned 22 hours worth of Dreamweaver 4 and you're just now starting to poke into HTML (HyperText Markup Language)? Even though Dreamweaver handles HTML behind the scenes, you might occasionally want to look at HTML. Dreamweaver also makes the transition easier for those stoic HTML hand coders who are making a move to a WYSIWYG (What You See Is What You Get) HTML development tool.

Dreamweaver offers several ways to access the code. During this hour you will explore the HTML editing capabilities of Dreamweaver. In addition, you will learn how to launch your Web pages directly from Dreamweaver in your favorite code editor. If you don't already know HTML, viewing HTML that Dreamweaver creates is a great way to learn.

Included with Dreamweaver 4 is the capability to debug JavaScript code. As you remember from previous chapters, JavaScript is a common scripting language. The Dreamweaver Debugger can debug JavaScript code in both Microsoft Internet Explorer and Netscape Navigator by checking syntax and logic.

In this hour, you will learn

- How to use the Quick Tag Editor
- How to view and edit HTML in the Code inspector
- How to clean up Word HTML
- How to configure and launch external HTML editors
- How to debug JavaScript code.

View and Edit HTML Tags with the Quick Tag Editor

Dreamweaver 4's Quick Tag Editor is the quickest and easiest way to look at a single HTML tag and edit it. There are different ways you can access the Quick Tag Editor:

- Click on the Quick Tag Editor icon on the Property inspector, shown in Figure 23.1.

FIGURE 23.1

Click on the Quick Tag Editor icon to view and edit the tag of the object that is currently selected.

 —— Quick Tag Editor

- Right-click on any object and select the Edit Tag command from the drop-down menu, shown in Figure 23.2.

FIGURE 23.2

The Edit Tag command in the drop-down menu launches the Quick Tag Editor.

- Select the Quick Tag Editor command from the Modify menu.

When you select the Quick Tag Editor icon from the Property inspector, the tag pops up beside the Quick Tag Editor icon. When you select the commands from the context menu or Modify menu, the tag pops up directly above the object in the document window.

When the Quick Tag Editor is open, you can use a keyboard shortcut to move up and down through the tag hierarchy. The Ctrl+Shift+< key combination (⌘+Shift+< on the Macintosh) selects the parent tag of the currently selected tag. As you press this key combination, the contents of the Quick Tag Editor change and the Tag Selector does too, as shown in Figure 23.3. Use Ctrl+Shift+> (⌘+Shift+> on the Macintosh) to move down through the tag hierarchy. These same commands are found in the Edit menu: Select Parent Tag and Select Child.

23

FIGURE 23.3

Press Ctrl+Shift+< to move up the tag hierarchy. The tag changes in the Quick Tag Editor and you can see which tag is selected in Dreamweaver's Tag Selector.

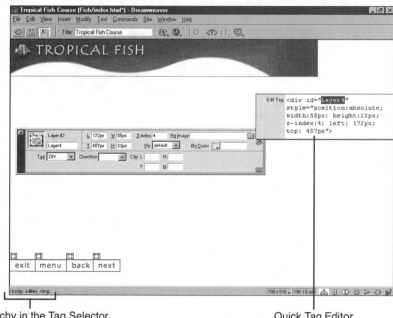

Tag hierarchy in the Tag Selector   Quick Tag Editor

The Quick Tag Editor has three modes:

- The Insert HTML mode enables you to insert HTML into the tag.
- The Edit Tag mode enables you to edit the existing tag contents.
- The Wrap Tag mode wraps another HTML tag around the selected tag.

When the Quick Tag Editor opens, you can toggle between the three modes by pressing Ctrl+T (⌘+T on the Macintosh). You'll explore each of the three modes next.

Use the Insert HTML Mode

The Quick Tag Editor's Insert HTML mode, shown in Figure 23.4, shows a pair of empty tag angle brackets with the insertion point between them. You can either enter text into the brackets, select from the tag drop-down menu, or both. Dreamweaver adds the closing tag automatically. The Quick Tag Editor starts in this mode when you do not have an object selected.

Tag menu

FIGURE 23.4

The Insert HTML Mode in the Quick Tag Editor presents empty tag brackets. You can enter a tag name and attributes or select from the tag drop-down menu.

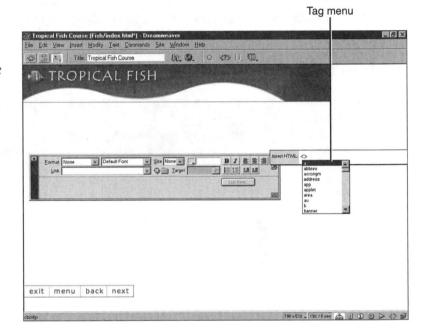

The Quick Tag Editor panel of Dreamweaver's preferences, as shown in Figure 23.5, enables you to set up the way the Quick Tag Editor works. Select whether or not you want edits to be applied immediately by selecting or de-selecting the Apply Changes Immediately While Editing check box. If this option is not selected, you must press Enter to apply your edits. You can also set the time delay for the tag drop-down menu.

Use the Edit Tag Mode

The Quick Tag Editor's Edit Tag Mode enables you to edit the HTML of an existing tag and the tag's contents. To add attributes of the selected tag, place the insertion point at the end of the tag contents in the Quick Tag Editor and add a space. The tag drop-down menu appears, as shown in Figure 23.6, with attributes appropriate for the tag.

FIGURE 23.5

The Quick Tag Editor category of Dreamweaver preferences enables you to select whether edits in the Quick Tag Editor are applied immediately. You also set the delay for the tag drop-down menu.

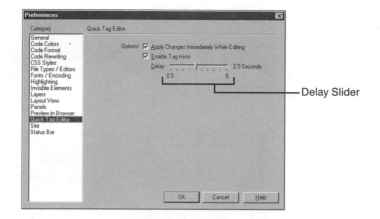

Delay Slider

23

Image Attributes

FIGURE 23.6

The tag drop-down menu presents attributes appropriate for the current tag. It appears automatically after a delay that is set in preferences.

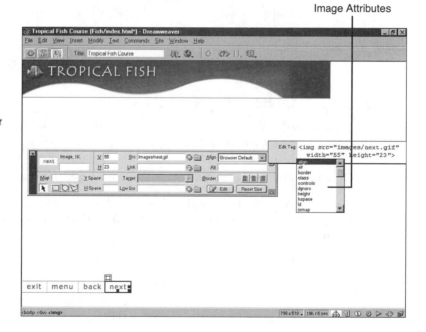

Use the Wrap Tag Mode

The Quick Tag Editor's Wrap Tag Mode, shown in Figure 23.7, enables you to wrap HTML around the current selection. For instance, when you have text selected you can wrap a hyperlink (<a href>) or text formatting (<h1>) around the text. Dreamweaver adds the opening tag before the selection and the closing tag after the selection.

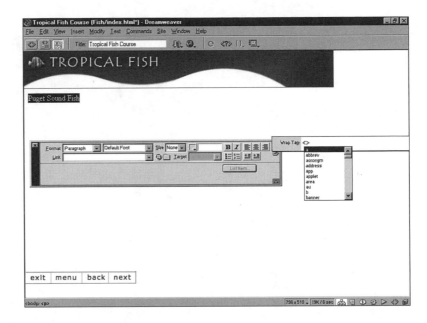

FIGURE 23.7

The Wrap Tag Mode wraps an HTML tag around the current selection.

Use the Code Inspector

The Dreamweaver document window enables you to view your Web page in either the Design view or the Code view. You can see Design and Code views at the same time by selecting the Show Code and Design Views button in the toolbar. You can also open up the Code inspector to display the Code view in a separate window.

The Code inspector displays the HTML source of the current Web page. Launch the Code inspector, shown in Figure 23.8, from the Window menu, the Launcher, or the Mini-Launcher. Since all HTML tags are contained within < and >, the symbol for the Code inspector in the Launcher is a set of these empty tag angle brackets.

If you select an object in the document window, the code for that object will be selected in the Code inspector. This is a quick way to get to the code of the selected object. If your Web page is large, there may be a lot of HTML to go through and it might not be easy to find the code that you are looking for.

The toolbar appears at the top of the Code inspector. The View Options menu is one of the toolbar choices that displays attributes of the Code inspector. The following options are available:

- Word Wrap—Wraps the lines of code so that you can view it all without scrolling horizontally. This setting does not change the code but simply displays it differently.

- Line Numbers—Displays line numbers in the left margin.
- Highlight Invalid HTML—Turns on highlighting of invalid that Dreamweaver doesn't understand.
- Syntax Coloring—Colors your code so that elements are easier to discern. Set the colors in the Code Colors category of Dreamweaver preferences.
- Auto Indent—Makes the code automatically indent based on the settings in the Code Format category of preferences.

23

FIGURE 23.8

The Code inspector displays the HTML of the Web page, enabling you to view or edit it.

Selected Object

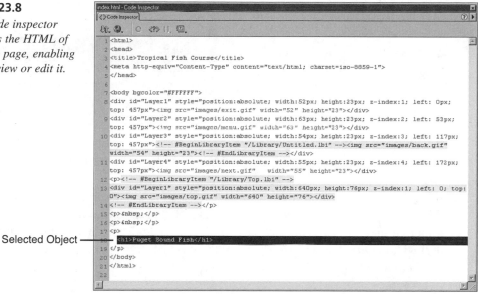

If you receive a JavaScript error when previewing a Web page in the browser, the error often displays the line number in the code that is causing the problem. View the code in the Code inspector with the line numbers displayed to troubleshoot the error.

If you make changes to the code in the Code inspector, Dreamweaver doesn't display the changes in the document window until you select the Refresh button in the toolbar. If you enter invalid HTML, Dreamweaver will highlight the invalid tags in bright yellow in both the Code inspector and the document window, as shown in Figure 23.9.

Invalid tags

FIGURE 23.9
Invalid tags appear highlighted in yellow in the document window and the Code inspector. The Property inspector may offer insight into why the tags are invalid and what to do about it.

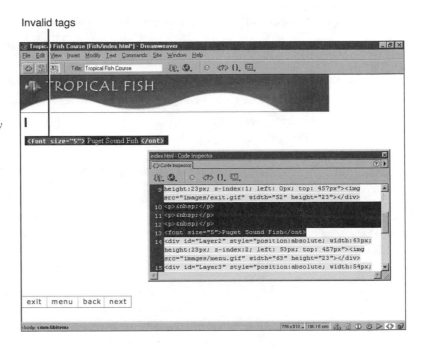

If highlighted tags appear in your Web page, you'll know that something is wrong with the HTML. When you select a highlighted tag, the Property inspector calls the tag invalid. It may give a reason why the tag is invalid and offer some direction on how to deal with it. Often, you can simply select and delete the highlighted tags and everything will be fine.

Set Your Code Preferences

There are a number of preferences you can set for HTML. The three categories in Dreamweaver preferences that apply to HTML—Code Colors, Code Format, and Code Rewriting—help control the way Dreamweaver creates and displays the code in your Web pages.

Don't change a setting in preferences if you aren't sure what it does. Many of Dreamweaver's default settings reflect the standard way of creating Web pages. Change them if you need to but know that you could inadvertently cause a problem if you change them blindly.

Set the Code Colors Preferences

The tags in the Code inspector display color coded according to the settings in Dreamweaver preferences. Select the Code Colors category in preferences. The panel enables you to set the background, text, comments, and tag default colors at the top. Either enter a color in hexadecimal format or use the color picker to select a color.

The bottom half of the Code Colors category enables you to individually set a color for each HTML tag. Most of the tags are set to the default color. The tags that you commonly use, such as <table>, <img>, <div>, and others, have a custom color to set them apart from the rest of the HTML.

To change a tag color, select the tag, as shown in Figure 23.10. Select either Default, to apply the default color selected above, or select a new color. If you want the tag contents (such as the text in a hyperlink) to also share the tag color, check the Apply Color to Tag Contents check box.

FIGURE 23.10

Select a tag and set its color in the Code Colors category. You can set the tag to have a default or custom color. You can also set the tag contents to have the same color as the tag.

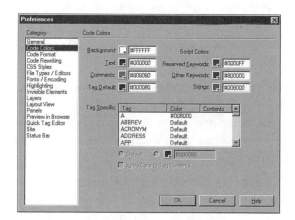

Set the Code Format Preferences

In the Code Format category of Dreamweaver preferences, shown in Figure 23.11, you set how Dreamweaver will create code. Dreamweaver indents the code to make it easier to read. You can change the size of the indent in the preferences. You can also select or de-select whether you want Dreamweaver to indent the code for tables and frames.

FIGURE 23.11

The Code Format category of Dreamweaver preferences enables you to set indentation, wrapping, and tag case.

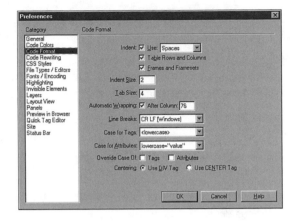

The Code Format options apply only to new documents created in Dreamweaver. However, you can select the Apply Source Formatting command from the Commands menu to apply the same formatting to an existing Web page.

If automatic wrapping is selected, Dreamweaver will wrap a line after the column width entered in the After Column field. Some lines may end up a little longer because Dreamweaver will not wrap lines that will affect the appearance of the Web page. You can also set the type of line break that Dreamweaver uses. This can affect the way your code looks on different operating systems.

Set the case of tags and attributes with the Case for Tags and Case for Attributes drop-down menus. Since the W3C standards are moving toward lowercase tags, it's a good idea to stick to that unless there is a compelling reason not to. If you want to be able to override the case for tags or attributes, select one of the Override Case Of check boxes. For instance, if you do not want Dreamweaver to change the tag case of an existing document, check the Override Case Of Tags check box and Dreamweaver will leave the tag case as it exists.

The last setting is whether Dreamweaver will use <center> tags to center objects or <div> tags with the align="center" attribute. The standards are moving toward using <div> tags but the <center> tag has been around for quite a while and is widely supported in both old and new versions of browsers. You might stick with the default and use <div> tag. If you expect your audience will not have newer browsers (that handle the <div> tag), use the <center> tag. This tag has been in use for some time but is not the correct tag to use to comply with W3C standards.

The options you set in the Code Format section of Dreamweaver preferences only apply to changes made in the document window. The automatic formatting will not occur when you edit the HTML in the Code inspector.

Set the Code Rewriting Preferences

The Code Rewriting preferences, shown in Figure 23.12, set what changes Dreamweaver makes when it opens a Web page. Dreamweaver automatically fixes certain code problems, but only if you want it to. If you turn off the Rewrite Code options, Dreamweaver will still display invalid code that you can fix yourself if you need to.

FIGURE 23.12

The Code Rewriting category of Dreamweaver preferences enables you to set the changes that Dreamweaver makes when it opens a Web page.

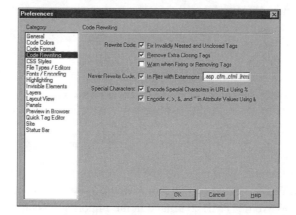

The Fix Invalidly Nested and Unclosed Tags setting tells Dreamweaver to rewrite tags that are invalidly nested. For instance, `<b><i>hello</b></i>` will be rewritten as `<b><i>hello</i></b>`. Dreamweaver also inserts a missing closing tag, quotation marks, or closing angle brackets. The Remove Extra Closing Tags option enables Dreamweaver to remove any stray closing tags that are left in the Web page.

If you would like more control over the automatic changes that Dreamweaver makes, select the Warn when Fixing or Removing Tags option. Dreamweaver displays a summary of problems it attempted to correct. You can view the summary and double-check that the code appears as you want it to.

By default, Dreamweaver is set up not to rewrite HTML in files with the following file extensions: .asp, .cfm, .cfml, .ihtml, .jsp, and .php. You can add any additional file extensions that contain third-party tags. Dreamweaver's default is to not rewrite these files since they contain extra tags that Dreamweaver may not understand. The Never Rewrite Code check box controls this functionality.

If you enable Dreamweaver to rewrite files that contain ASP, CFML, JSP, PHP, or other code, you may end up with a mess on your hands. It's not Dreamweaver's fault that it doesn't understand these languages. Either leave Dreamweaver's default setting of not rewriting these files or do your own thorough testing before you uncheck the Never Rewrite Code check box. It's always a good idea to make backup copies of your files before you test.

Clean Up HTML Created with Microsoft Word

Dreamweaver can clean up the extra HTML tags that are left behind when you save a Word document as HTML. All of the extra information that is useful in Word formatting is not necessary when the document is saved as HTML. Dreamweaver can clean up HTML saved in Word 97, Word 98, and Word 2000.

When you save a Word document as HTML, Word closes the original document and leaves the HTML version open. Dreamweaver will not be able to open and convert the HTML document while it is open in Word.

You can either import a Web page created by Word or apply the Clean up Word HTML command to a Web page that you already have open in the document window. To import, select the Import Word HTML command in the Import submenu of the File menu. To apply the Cleanup Word HTML command to a Web page in the document window, select the command from the Commands menu. Both methods launch the Clean Up Word HTML dialog box, shown in Figure 23.13.

FIGURE 23.13

When you import a Word HTML document or select Clean Up HTML from Word, the Clean Up Word HTML dialog box appears.

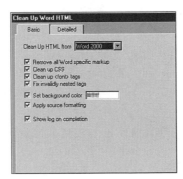

Dreamweaver should automatically detect which version of Word created the HTML file from tags that Word adds to the file. You can also choose the version manually with the Clean Up HTML from drop-down menu. The Clean Up Word HTML dialog box has two tabs—Basic and Detailed. Select from the following options on the Basic tab:

- *Remove All Word Specific Markup*—Removes all of the XML from the <html> tag, meta and link tags from the <head> section, Word XML markup, conditional tags, empty paragraphs, and margins. You can select each of these options individually using the Detailed tab, shown in Figure 23.14.

FIGURE 23.14

The Detailed tab allows you finer control over the Remove All Word Specific Markup and the Clean Up CSS options.

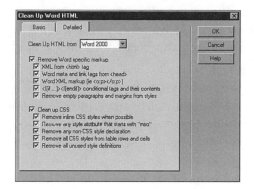

- *Clean Up CSS*—Removes the extra CSS styles from the document. The styles removed are inline CSS styles, style attributes that begin with mso, non-CSS style declarations, CSS styles in table rows and cells, and unused styles. You can select the options individually using the Detailed tab.

- *Clean Up <font> Tags*—Removes those tags.

- *Fix Invalidly Nested Tags*—Fixes the tags, particularly font markup tags, that are in an incorrect place.

- *Set Background Color*—Enables you to specify the background color of the Web page. Dreamweaver's default is white, #ffffff.

- *Apply Source Formatting*—Applies the Code Formatting options that you have set in the Code Format category in Dreamweaver preferences.

- *Show Log On Completion*—Displays a dialog box with a summary of the changes that Dreamweaver made to the Web page.

After you select the options from either the Basic or the Detailed tabs, click OK. Dreamweaver will clean up the Web page. Your selected options will appear the next time you select the Clean Up HTML from Word command.

Debug JavaScript Code

You can use the JavaScript debugging capabilities of Dreamweaver to troubleshoot your client-side JavaScript code. The debugger will work with Microsoft Internet Explorer on the Windows operating system, as well as Netscape Navigator on both Windows and the Macintosh operating system. You access the debugger by launching the Debug in Browser command under the File menu.

Debugging is a programming term that means using techniques to track down errors in code. Dreamweaver will automatically check for syntax and logical errors in your JavaScript code. *Syntax errors* are naming errors, for instance misspelling a JavaScript method name. *Logical errors* are errors where your code is not producing the logical results that you want it to produce. Syntax errors are often easier to fix. To launch the debugger:

1. Select a browser from the Debug in Browser command in the File menu. The Debugger will immediately list any syntax errors in your Web page.

2. The JavaScript Debugger opens, as shown in Figure 23.15. You will need to agree to the Java Security dialog that appears when the browser is launched (select either the Grant or the Yes button). This enables the Dreamweaver Debugger to communicate with the browser.

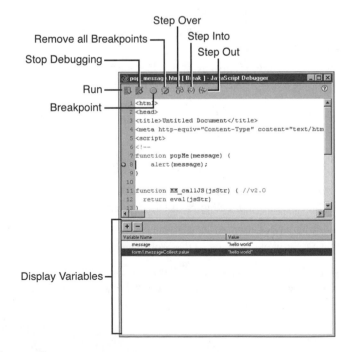

FIGURE 23.15
The JavaScript Debugger helps you troubleshoot problems with your JavaScript code.

3. To go directly to that code and fix the error, select errors in the JavaScript syntax error window.

You can set breakpoints in the JavaScript code where you want the code to stop running. A useful debugging technique is to stop the script at a certain point and check the values of variables to see if they are what you expect. Breakpoints can only be set between <script> tags. In the Debugger, to set a breakpoint

1. Place the insertion point in a line of code and select the Breakpoint button. Toggle the breakpoints on and off with the Breakpoint button or select the Remove All Breakpoints button.

2. Enter variable values to watch in the JavaScript Debugger by clicking the + button in the lower half of the JavaScript Debugger window.

3. Select the Run button to load the page. The page will stop at the breakpoint and you can see what the values of your variables are at that specific line of code.

You can also step through code function by function by using the Step Over, Step In, and Step Out buttons. Instead of using the Run button, use the appropriate Step buttons to either run the current function or step over the function to keep it from processing.

Launch an External HTML Editor

The Roundtrip HTML characteristics of Dreamweaver enable you to move your Web pages between Dreamweaver and text-based editors with little or no effect. Although Dreamweaver is a wonderful tool, it is sometimes easier to accomplish a task with an HTML editor other than Dreamweaver. Dreamweaver makes it extremely easy to go back and forth between Dreamweaver and other HTML editors.

Launch an external editor by selecting the Edit with command in the Edit menu. If you haven't set up an external editor yet, you'll see the Edit with External Editor command under the Edit menu. The first time you launch this command the File Types/Editors category of Dreamweaver preferences appears, as shown in Figure 23.16.

To set up an external HTML editor, select the Browse button, and navigate to the editor. You might want to select a simple text editor such as Notepad (Windows) or SimpleText (Macintosh). Or, select a program like HomeSite for Windows or BBEdit for the Macintosh.

FIGURE 23.16

The File Types/Editors category in Dreamweaver preferences enables you to link to your favorite external editor.

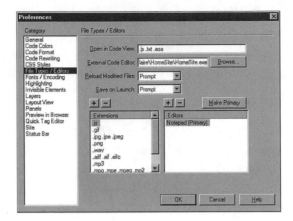

If you occasionally use NotePad, you'll love Edit Pad. This replacement for the Windows NotePad can open multiple files and do robust searches. This little application is great for quickly editing CSS files. You can download it by entering "Edit Pad" into the search at CINET's Download.com (http://www.download.com). The program is postcardware, meaning you send a nice postcard to the author if you like it!

Dreamweaver can detect whether you have made a change to the Web page in the external editor. Specify what you want Dreamweaver to do if it detects a change in the Reload Modified Files drop-down menu, shown in Figure 23.17. Dreamweaver can always reload the modified Web page, never reload the page, or prompt you to decide whether to reload the page. You can also set how Dreamweaver will save the Web page in the Save on Launch drop-down menu. Dreamweaver can either always save the Web page, never save the page, or prompt you to save the page.

I set Dreamweaver to prompt me to save my Web page before going to an external editor. In addition, I always save it. I also always reload the Web page when I return to Dreamweaver from the external editor (I like HomeSite). That way, I have the most recent version of the Web page open.

After you set up the external editor, Dreamweaver will open the external editor with the current Web page when you select the Edit with command under the Edit menu. The command reflects the external editor name so if you set up HomeSite as your external editor, the command will be named Edit with Homesite. The Web page will continue to be open in Dreamweaver and will be open in the external editor too. When you return to

Dreamweaver, the Web page will be reloaded depending on your choice in the Reload Modified Files drop-down menu in the External Editors preferences.

FIGURE 23.17
The Reload Modified File drop-down menu sets how Dreamweaver will deal with the Web page when you return from modifying it in another editor.

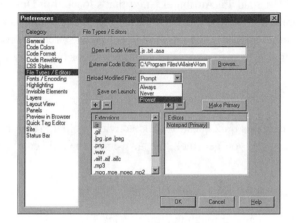

 Did you notice that you can configure other editors in the External Editors preferences? You can set up external editors for any objects that you might include in your Web pages. The external editors are associated with the file extension of a referenced file. For instance, you could set any .png files to open in Fireworks.

Summary

In this hour, you learned how to use the Quick Tag Editor and the Code inspector. You learned how to set preferences for HTML tag colors, formatting, and rewriting. You learned how to use the Clean Up HTML from Word command. You also learned how to use the JavaScript Debugger, and how to configure and use external editors with Dreamweaver.

Q&A

Q Why would I want to use an editor other than Dreamweaver?

A You might want to use an editor in addition to Dreamweaver to hand-code a certain section of your Web page, for instance adding JavaScript. Or, you might want to take advantage of some of the special features of the editor. For instance, HomeSite has features built in so that you can easily add CFML (ColdFusion Markup Language) to your Web pages.

Q Can I add attributes that don't appear in the Quick Tag Editor's tag drop-down menu?

A Edit the file called TagAttributeList.txt that's located in Dreamweaver's Configuration directory. You can edit the file in a text editor. This file controls the attributes that appear in the tag drop-down menu. Dreamweaver does not list every attribute that is available so there might be one or two that you might want to add.

Workshop

The Workshop contains quiz questions and activities to help reinforce what you've learned in this hour. If you get stuck, the answers to the quiz can be found following the questions.

Quiz

1. How do you toggle through the three Quick Tag Editor modes?
2. What does it mean when a tag appears highlighted in yellow in your Web page?
3. Does Dreamweaver automatically format the HTML that you type into the Code inspector?

Answers

1. You toggle through the Quick Tag Editor's three modes by pressing Ctrl+T for Windows or Command+T for the Macintosh.
2. When a tag appears highlighted in yellow in your Web page, it means that Dreamweaver thinks it is an invalid tag.
3. No, Dreamweaver does not automatically format the HTML that you type into the Code inspector. You can use the Apply Source Formatting command in any Web page.

Exercises

1. Experiment using the different Quick Tag Editor modes. Pay attention to how the Property inspector reflects selecting attributes in the Quick Tag Editor. Many of the same attributes are selectable in the Property inspector's radio buttons, text boxes, and check boxes.
2. Examine the HTML of a Web page in the Code inspector. First, select an object in the document window and then open the Code inspector. Do you see the HTML for the selected object?

Hour 24

Customizing Dreamweaver

The Dreamweaver *API* (Application Programming Interface) provides developers with the power to extend Dreamweaver's capabilities. A thorough understanding of HTML and JavaScript are required to develop custom behavior actions, floating panels, data translators, and other extensions. However, Dreamweaver enables all developers to create custom objects, customize the Object panel, and create new commands.

There are developers skilled in JavaScript who create Dreamweaver behaviors, objects, commands, and floating panels that you can download free from the Web. See Appendix B, "Internet Resources," for the URLs to some of these sites. When Dreamweaver doesn't seem to have a behavior, object, or command for what you are trying to accomplish in your Web page, search these Web sites and you might find just what you need. Macromedia has created a forum for you to find objects that extend the functionality of Dreamweaver at the Macromedia Dreamweaver Exchange (www.macromedia.com/exchange/dreamweaver).

In this hour, you will learn

- How to rearrange, edit, and add Dreamweaver objects to the Object panel
- How to use the History panel
- How to record and save steps as Dreamweaver commands
- How to edit Dreamweaver dialog boxes
- How to install third-party extensions with the Package Manager

Modify the Object Panel and Create Your Own Object

The Object panel, by default, has seven panels: Characters, Common, Forms, Frames, Head, Invisibles, and Special. If you open up the Dreamweaver directory, you will see the Configuration directory. Much of Dreamweaver structure is based on the file structure and content within the Configuration directory.

The Objects directory within the Configuration directory contains eight directories, shown in Figure 24.1: Characters, Common, Forms, Frames, Head, Invisibles, and Special, and Tools. Is it a coincidence that this directory contains sub-directories with the same names as the panels in the Object panel? No, the Object panel takes its structure from the sub-directories in Object directory.

FIGURE 24.1

The Objects directory configures the contents and structure of Dreamweaver's Object panel.

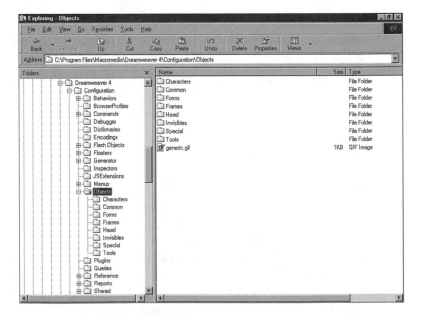

There is an additional directory in the Object directory called Tools. This directory holds the objects that display the objects at the bottom of the Object panel: the Standard and Layout views, Layout Table, and Layout Cell.

Open up one of the directories, such as the Characters directory shown in Figure 24.2. There are files with the same name as each object in the Characters panel of the Object panel. All of the files that pertain to a particular object must have the exact same name; only the file type and file extension differs.

- The GIF (.gif) file contains the icon image that appears in the Object panel.
- The HTML (.html) file contains the content that gets inserted in the Web page when you select the object or a form that enables you to format the object.
- An optional JavaScript (.js) file contains code that is necessary for the object.

24

FIGURE 24.2

Each object in the Object panel requires an icon image and an HTML file. Optionally, the object may also have a JavaScript file to complete the object's function.

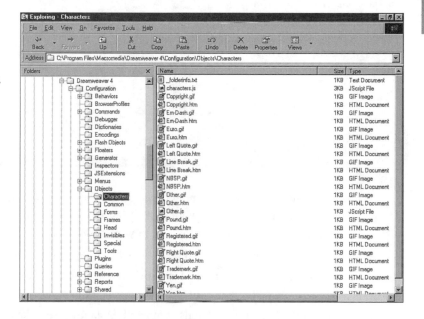

If you have installed Dreamweaver more than once, or have installed Macromedia CourseBuilder (see Appendix A, "CourseBuilder for Dreamweaver"), you may have more than one Configuration folder. Dreamweaver only uses the folder named Configuration. If you have prevous configurations, Dreamweaver renames the old folder Configuration-1, -2, and so on.

To create your own custom panels or rename the panels that already exist, simply modify the directory structure of the Configuration/Objects directory. For instance, create a new panel in the Object panel with objects that you commonly use:

1. Open the Configuration/Objects directory.

2. Create a new directory and name it what you would like the new panel in the Object panel to be named. An example is shown in Figure 24.3.

FIGURE 24.3

Add a new directory to the Configuration/Objects directory to create a new panel in the Object panel. The panel will have the same name as the directory.

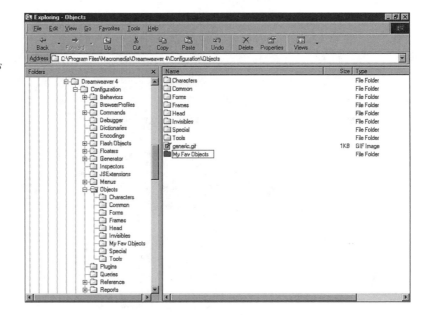

3. Either move or copy commonly used object files from the other panel directories. Make sure to move or copy all of the files, including JavaScript files that have the name of the object you are adding to your custom panel.

4. Return to Dreamweaver and open the Object panel, if it is not already displayed.

5. Ctrl+click the Object panel drop-down menu. The drop-down lists the existing panels plus the additional Reload Extensions command, as shown in Figure 24.4.

6. Select the Reload Extensions command. Dreamweaver takes a few seconds to reload the objects in the panel.

7. Select the Object panel drop-down menu again. Your new panel should be listed.

8. Select your new panel. It should appear with the Objects that you moved or copied into the panel directory, such as the example shown in Figure 24.5.

FIGURE 24.4

The Object panel drop-down menu displays an additional command, Reload Extensions, when you Ctrl+click it.

FIGURE 24.5

The Object panel displays the new panel and the objects it contains after the extensions are reloaded.

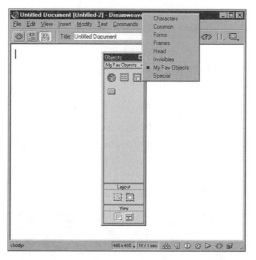

The Get More Objects command in the Insert menu launches your browser and takes you directly to the Macromedia Web site where you can download new objects for Dreamweaver. You will need to be connected to the Internet to use this command.

24

Don't see your new panel? Is the directory for your new panel in the Configuration/Objects directory? It can't be located inside of the directory for any of the other panels. Did you reload the Object panel following the instructions above? If you think you have done everything correctly but your panel still doesn't show up, try restarting Dreamweaver.

Edit an Object

You can open Dreamweaver objects and change them, if necessary. Make a backup copy of the object's files before you make your changes, in case you make a mistake and need to revert to the original files.

An example of an edit you might want to make is to modify the HTML of the Table object. When you select this object from the Object panel, the dialog box presents the table values three rows, three columns, 75 percent width, and a border of 1 as the default. What if you frequently create tables with attributes that are different from these? You can modify the Table object to reflect the settings you use most often. To modify the Table object:

1. Open the Table object HTML file, `table.htm`, in Dreamweaver. The file is located in the Configuration/Objects/Common directory.

2. Make a backup copy of `table.htm`. You can call it `table.bak`.

3. Make sure you have `table.htm` open and not `table.bak`. Check the file name in the Dreamweaver title bar. Notice that the dialog box that Dreamweaver presents for you to set up a table is actually an HTML form, shown in Figure 24.6.

Table.htm in the title bar

FIGURE 24.6

The Insert Table dialog box is actually a Web page containing an HTML form that you can edit in Dreamweaver.

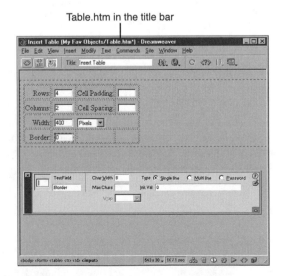

4. Change the initial value of the text fields for the rows, columns, and other attributes to values that you often use. Since this is a form, you might want to review Hour 16, "Creating and Using a Form to Collect Data," if you have any questions. Modify the initial value in the Init Val text box of the Property inspector when you have a text field selected.

5. Save and close the file.

6. Open a new window in Dreamweaver and insert a table. You should see the changes you made to the Table object reflected in the Insert Table dialog box.

Make a New Object

You can create your own simple object that inserts HTML into a Web page. For instance, you could create a formatted copyright statement as an object. Whenever you need to add the copyright to a Web page you can quickly select it from the Object panel. This is a powerful feature that enables you to create snippets of HTML that are easily accessed from the Object panel and that you can use repeatedly.

To create a simple object:

1. Open a new window in Dreamweaver.

2. Enter the text or objects that you want in your custom object, as shown in Figure 24.7.

FIGURE 24.7

A copyright statement is formatted in Dreamweaver and saved as an object in the Object panel.

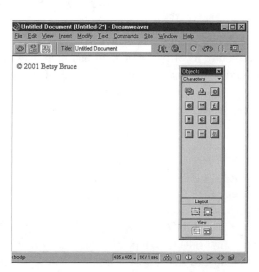

3. Give the Web page a title. The title appears as a tooltip when you place your cursor over the custom object in the Object panel.

4. Save the Web page into one of the panel directories in the Configuration/Objects directory. You can name the object with either the `.htm` or `.html` file extension.

5. Ctrl+click the Object panel drop-down menu and select the Reload Extensions command. Your new object appears with the default object icon as its icon. Select the object in the Object panel, and it is inserted into your document.

> You can create a GIF image for a custom icon in an image-editing program like Fireworks. The icon needs to be 18×18 pixels. Save the icon with the same name as the object HTML file and in the same directory. You might need to restart Dreamweaver to see your new icon.

Make a Menu Command

Dreamweaver enables you to record and save a step or set of steps as a command. There are two different ways to accomplish this:

- Record a set of steps as you perform them and then play them back.
- Select a step or set of steps from the History panel and save them as a command.

Record a Command

Dreamweaver enables you to record a set of steps and then play back the steps. Dreamweaver can record a single set of steps in this way. Once you record a new set of steps, the previous set will be replaced. In addition, the recorded command is lost when you close Dreamweaver. You'll explore how to save a recorded set of steps in a few minutes.

> Dreamweaver keeps you from recording steps that are not reproducible by Dreamweaver.

To record a set of steps, first select the type of object that you will be applying your steps to. You will not be able to select objects while recording. Select the Start Recording command from the Commands menu. The cursor changes to a little cassette as shown in Figure 24.8. Perform the steps to record and then select the Stop Recording command from the Commands menu.

Recording cursor

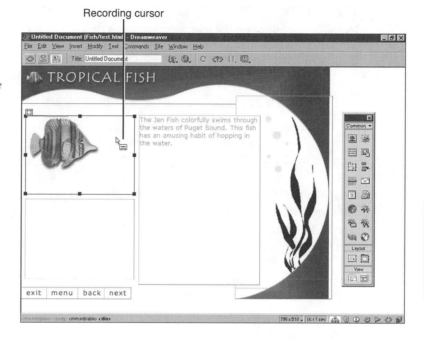

FIGURE 24.8
While recording steps in Dreamweaver, the cursor becomes a little cassette.

Apply the recorded command by selecting an object and then selecting Play Recorded Command from the Commands menu. Dreamweaver will perform the steps that you previously recorded. You can continue to use this command until you either replace it with another command or close Dreamweaver.

Save a Command from the History Panel

The History panel, shown in Figure 24.9, displays all of the steps you've performed on the current document since you opened it. The History panel enables you to undo certain steps, copy steps to the clipboard and apply them to different Web pages, and save a set of steps as a command.

FIGURE 24.9
The History panel records and displays all the steps you've performed on the current Web page.

You can set the number of steps that Dreamweaver displays in the History panel in the General category of Dreamweaver preferences. The default for the Maximum Number of History Steps setting is 50.

You can clear all of the currently listed steps by selecting the Clear History command from the History panel drop-down menu.

The steps in the History panel are listed in the order you performed them, with the most recent step at the bottom of the list. Undo steps by moving the slider up, as shown in Figure 24.10. Notice that the steps dim after they have been undone. To redo the steps, move the slider back down.

FIGURE 24.10

Move the slider in the History panel to undo steps. The steps dim when they are undone. Move the slider back down to redo the steps.

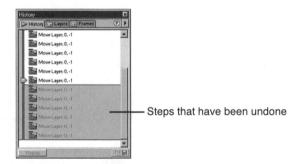

————— Steps that have been undone

To save a command that you have already recorded, select the Play Recorded Command. A step called Run Command appears in the History panel list. Select the Run Command step and click the Save As Command button. The Save As Command dialog box appears, as shown in Figure 24.11. Enter a name for the command.

FIGURE 24.11

Save a recorded command to the Commands menu using the History panel's Save As Command button. Name the command in the Save As Command dialog box.

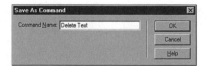

Custom commands appear at the bottom of the Commands menu. To run your custom commands, select them from the menu. Use the Edit Command List command to launch the Edit Command List dialog box, shown in Figure 24.12. This is where you can rename a command by selecting it in the list or delete the command completely by clicking on the Delete button.

FIGURE 24.12

Rename or delete custom commands in the Edit Command List dialog box.

24

You can also save a set of steps from the History panel as a command. Select the steps in the panel by dragging the cursor over them. Select the Save As Command button and name the command the same as you just did for your recorded command. The commands that you create are saved as JavaScript files in the Configuration/Commands directory.

Get More Commands in the Commands menu launches your browser and takes you directly to the Macromedia Web site where you can download new commands for Dreamweaver. You will need to be connected to the Internet before you use this command.

Edit a Behavior Action

You might want to edit the way a behavior action dialog box appears in your copy of Dreamweaver. Do this the same way you edited the Table object above. The behavior actions HTML files are stored in the Configuration/Behaviors/Actions directory. They each have at least one associated JavaScript file that sets up the behavior. Again, you'll want to save a backup copy before you make any changes to these files.

I like the Show-Hide Layers dialog box to be a little wider so I can easily view the names of nested layers. To edit this action, open Show-Hide Layer.htm in Dreamweaver. Select the menu list, shown in Figure 24.13. Click the List Values button and add an additional * before and after the text "no layers found". This forces the list to be wider. Save the Web page and you'll see the change the next time you use the Show-Hide Layer behavior.

FIGURE 24.13

*Widen the Show-Hide Layer list box by adding an extra * to the first item.*

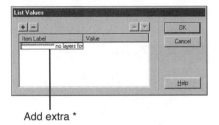

Add extra *

There are a number of useful behaviors available on the Web. Check the sites sited in Appendix B for useful behaviors.

Manage Extensions

You can easily install third-party extensions to Dreamweaver by using the Manage Extensions command under the Command menu. This command launches the Macromedia Package Manager, enabling you to automatically install and uninstall extensions that have been packaged in a standard Macromedia Extensions format. There are many extensions available to extend Dreamweaver's functionality at the Macromedia Dreamweaver Exchange. Extensions can be commands, objects, suites, or behaviors.

To use the Package Manager to install third-party extensions:

1. Download an extension file from the Dreamweaver Exchange Web site. The file has the `.mxp` file extension.

2. Select the Manage Extensions command from Dreamweaver's Command menu. The Package Manager appears, as shown in Figure 24.14.

3. Select the Install New Package button in the Package Manager. The Select Package to Install dialog box appears.

4. Browse to the directory where you saved the file you downloaded. Select the file and click the Install button.

5. Accept the disclaimer by selecting the Accept button.

6. The extension is installed into Dreamweaver. The appropriate icons and commands are added automatically.

Remove Package button

FIGURE 24.14

The Package Manager enables you to install third-party extensions automatically into Dreamweaver.

Install New
Package button

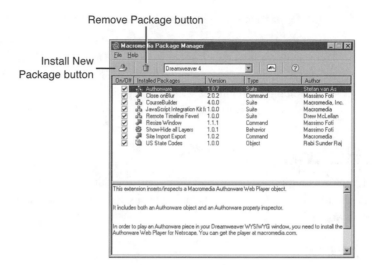

You can disable an extension by unchecking the check box next to the extension name under the On/Off column of the Package Manager. This does not uninstall the extension but simply makes it unavailable in Dreamweaver. To uninstall an extension, select the extension name and click on the Remove Package button in the Package Manager.

Summary

In this hour, you learned how the structure and content of Dreamweaver's Configuration directory influences Dreamweaver's interface. You learned how to create your own objects and panels in the Object panel. You also learned how to record steps as commands and use the History panel. You learned how to edit the appearance of dialog boxes for Dreamweaver objects and behavior actions. You also installed third-party extensions with the Package Manager.

Q&A

Q If all of the objects in the Object panel are listed in the Insert menu, is there a way I can add custom objects to the menu?

A Dreamweaver automatically lists the custom object at the bottom of the Insert menu after you issue the Reload Extensions command.

Q Where can I get more information on extending Dreamweaver?

A Select the Extending Dreamweaver command under the Help menu to see the Dreamweaver help pages about extending Dreamweaver. You can also get lots of information about Dreamweaver at the Web sites listed in Appendix B and at Macromedia's Dreamweaver Exchange site, `www.macromedia.com/exchange/dreamweaver/`.

Workshop

The Workshop contains quiz questions and activities to help reinforce what you've learned in this hour. If you get stuck, the answers to the quiz can be found following the questions.

Quiz

1. How do you create a new panel in the Object panel?
2. How can you undo steps in the current document using the History panel?
3. Where do you launch custom commands from?

Answers

1. Create a new panel in the Object panel by adding a directory to the Configuration/Objects directory.
2. Move the slider in the History panel up to undo steps in the current document.
3. Launch custom commands from the bottom of the Commands menu.

Exercises

1. Make your own custom panel in the Object panel with the objects that you need most often. Or, you can create a project specific panel. For instance, if you are working on a site working with many Flash movies and other media you could create a panel called Media.
2. Create a custom object that inserts a last modified date into a Web page. Use the Date object and set it to update automatically.

APPENDIX A

CourseBuilder for Dreamweaver

CourseBuilder for Dreamweaver, formerly called Attain Objects for Dreamweaver, provides a number of pre-built interactions that you can customize for your Web pages. Use CourseBuilder to deliver HTML-based, cross-platform, cross-browser interactions that can be viewed without plug-ins. CourseBuilder isn't a separate application; it's an add-in application to Dreamweaver.

You can learn more about CourseBuilder for Dreamweaver at the Macromedia CourseBuilder for Dreamweaver support site, www.macromedia.com/support/coursebuilder/. Macromedia also provides a CourseBuilder newsgroup at news://forums.macromedia.com/macromedia.dreamweaver.coursebuilder.

CourseBuilder Interactions

CourseBuilder adds a number of items to the Dreamweaver interface. Insert a CourseBuilder Interaction with the CourseBuilder Interaction icon from the Learning panel of the Object panel, shown in Figure A.1. Inserting the object launches the CourseBuilder Interaction Gallery, enabling you to choose an interaction type. There are additional commands added to the Modify menu when CourseBuilder is installed.

FIGURE A.1

After you install CourseBuilder for Dreamweaver, you will have an additional icon available in the Object panel to insert CourseBuilder Interactions in your Web page.

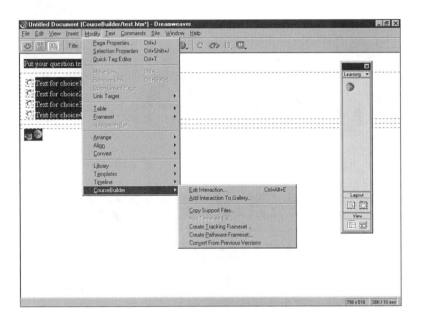

You need to save your Web page before inserting a CourseBuilder Interaction. CourseBuilder needs to copy script and image files to directories relative to your Web page. CourseBuilder will add a directory, called Images, with all of the images necessary for any of the CourseBuilder Interaction types. CourseBuilder also creates a directory called Scripts that contains all of the scripts (JavaScript) that are required to run the interactions.

After you have saved the Web page, the CourseBuilder Interaction Gallery appears. You can choose either 3.0 or 4.0+ browsers as your target browsers. If you select 3.0 browsers, you will be limited to only multiple-choice and text entry questions. You have access to all of the different interactions when you choose 4.0+ browsers.

The Gallery shows visual representations of the various interactions. You select the various categories and then click on one of the interaction types to insert it into your page. CourseBuilder includes a number of different types of interactions:

- Multiple choice questions
- Drag-and-drop questions
- Explore interactions
- Buttons
- Text entry questions
- Timers
- Sliders
- The Action Manager (used for custom coding)

After you select an interaction in the Gallery, additional tabs appear at the bottom of the CourseBuilder Interaction dialog box. These tabs vary according to which interaction you've selected. To set up your interaction, select each of the tabs and fill out the information.

The *Action Manager* is the final tab on every interaction type. The Action Manager enables you to set up conditions and segments that trigger actions including all of the Dreamweaver behaviors. For instance, if the answer is correct (a condition) then place text in a layer (a behavior). This extremely powerful part of CourseBuilder enables you to judge interactions and provide feedback.

 CourseBuilder Interactions work in both Internet Explorer and Netscape, but there are a few limitations. Check the browser compatibility chart in the CourseBuilder documentation for an overview of what you can expect.

You can track interaction scores to a frame, a *Learning Management System* or *LMS*, or a database application. CourseBuilder includes a command under the CourseBuilder sub-menu (in the Modify menu) that creates tracking framesets. You can create a tracking frameset for Pathware, a LMS, or a plain tracking frameset. The frameset captures scores from multiple Web pages and then sends the final score back to the CMI or a database, or simply displays it for the user.

You can save your own custom interaction templates to the gallery with the Add Interaction to Gallery command. Using an existing template as a base, you can modify the template and then save in the configuration that you prefer.

Multiple Choice Questions

Multiple choice question interactions, shown in Figure A.2, enable you to set up radio buttons, check boxes, or custom graphics for the user to click on. Use these interactions to create tests, assessments, surveys, or other learning activities.

 You can total the score of several multiple choice interactions on one page by adding an Action Manager interaction to the Web page.

FIGURE A.2
These multiple choice question types are available in CourseBuilder.

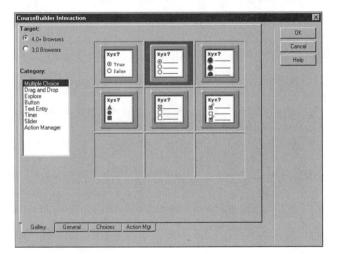

Drag-and-Drop Questions

Drag-and-drop interactions, shown in Figure A.3, enable the user to position objects on the screen and receive feedback. The interactions consist of draggable objects and targets. You can set up the interaction to allow objects to be dragged only to targets or allow targets to be dragged to the objects, too. Objects can snap back to the original position if the user drops them in an incorrect place.

FIGURE A.3
These drag-and-drop question types are available in CourseBuilder.

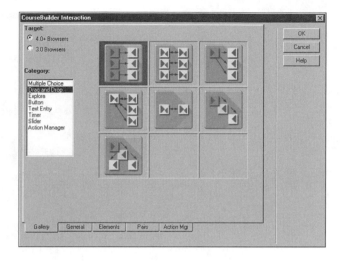

Explore Interactions

Explore interactions, shown in Figure A.4, let users click on hot-areas and receive feedback. You position the hot-area over a portion of the screen. The hot area can contain text or images, or can be invisible.

A

FIGURE A.4
These explore interaction types are available in CourseBuilder.

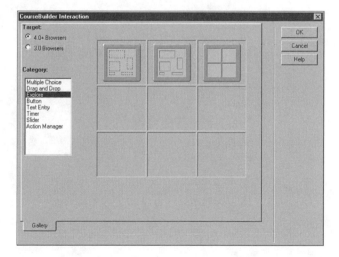

Buttons

You can add a button, shown in Figure A.5, to your Web page and use the Action Manager to capture a button click. You may want to add a button to a page to trigger judging a question or popping up a new browser window with additional information.

FIGURE A.5

These buttons are available in CourseBuilder.

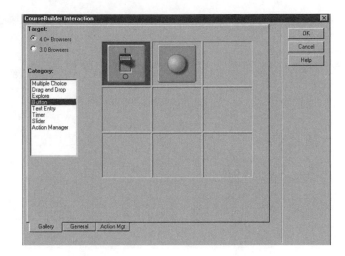

Text Entry Questions

Text entry interactions, shown in Figure A.6, capture short text responses, single words, or phrases from the user. The interaction displays a single- or multiple-line text input box.

FIGURE A.6

These text entry question types are available in CourseBuilder.

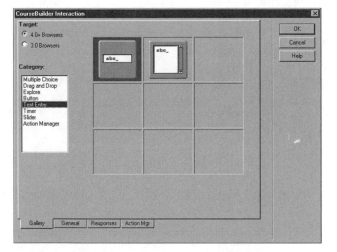

Timers

Add a timer, shown in Figure A.7, to another CourseBuilder Interaction to trigger events over time. For instance, you may want to warn the user that they only have a few more seconds to complete a timed interaction. You can also set a trigger to disable the interaction if the user hasn't completed a question in the allotted time.

A

FIGURE A.7

These timers are available in CourseBuilder.

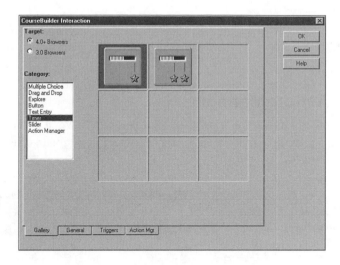

 There are different timer images that come with CourseBuilder, including an hourglass, a clapboard, raising bars, and others.

Sliders

Add a slider, shown in Figure A.8, to your Web page to allow the user to select a choice in a range of values. You might want the user to use the slider to answer a question. You could also make an object on the Web page move according to the position of the slider.

FIGURE A.8

These sliders are available in CourseBuilder.

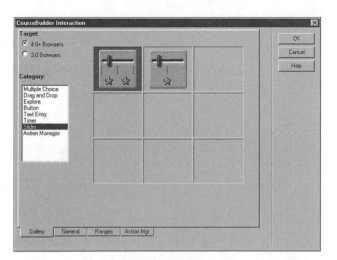

There are different slider images that come with CourseBuilder, including sliders of different colors that are either horizontal or vertical.

The Action Manager

Each different interaction has the Action Manager, shown in Figure A.9, available on the final tab. You can also insert an Action Manager interaction to affect other interactions on the Web page.

FIGURE A.9

The Action Manager interaction controls other CourseBuilder Interactions on the Web page.

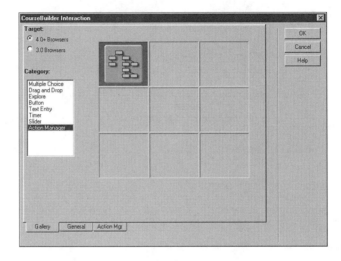

APPENDIX B

Internet Resources

You are in luck! You are learning about an information delivery medium—the World Wide Web—that contains a ton of information about itself. There are many, many helpful Web sites on topics that interest Web developers. You may even get inspired to create your own Web site to share your knowledge with others.

Web sites move and change quickly, so I apologize if some of these links are already out-of-date. Also, be aware that not all of the information you get from the Web is accurate. It's a good idea to get information from trusted sources or find sources to confirm the information you get from unknown sources.

Dreamweaver Development

Macromedia's Dreamweaver Support Center
www.macromedia.com/support/dreamweaver/

Dreamweaver Depot
weblogs.userland.com/dreamweaver/

Hava Site
www.hava.com/

Macromedia's CourseBuilder for Dreamweaver Support Center
www.macromedia.com/support/coursebuilder/

Dreamweaver Resources
www.arrakis.es/%7Eandrewc/downloads/dream.htm

Bren's Dreamweaver Lounge
www3.subnet.co.uk/brendan/dreamweaver/

Dreamweaver News and Information
www.owlnet.net/dwnews/

DynamicDream
www.beyond-design.com/dreamweaver/

General Web Development

CNET Builder.com
www.builder.com/

Webmonkey
www.webmonkey.com/

SiteExperts
www.siteexperts.com/

Web Developer's Virtual Library
www.wdvl.com/

World Wide Web Consortium (W3C)
www.w3.org/

About.com HTML
www.about.com/compute/html/cs/dreamweaver/

Netscape's DevEdge
devedge.netscape.com/

Microsoft's MSDN Online Web Workshop
msdn.microsoft.com/workshop/

Webreview.com-Cross Training for Web Teams
www.webreview.com/

ProjectCool
www.projectcool.com/

The Spot for Web Site Builders
thespot.i-depth.com/

Dynamic HTML (DHTML)

Dynamic HTML Zone
www.dhtmlzone.com/

The Web Standards Project
www.webstandards.org/dhtml.html

Dynamic Drive
www.dynamicdrive.com/

The Dynamic Duo-Cross Browser DHTML
www.dansteinman.com/dynduo/

Dreamweaver Extensions

Macromedia Exchange
www.macromedia.com/exchange/dreamweaver/

Massimo's Corner
www.massimocorner.com/

Yaro's Yaromat
www.yaromat.com/dw/

Rabi's Extensions
www.geocities.com/SiliconValley/Garage/2001/dreamweaver/

Dreamweaver Extensions
www.cascade.org.uk/software/dreamweaver/index.html

Dreamweaver Supply Bin
home.att.net/%7EJCB.BEI/Dreamweaver/

B

Scripting Resources: CGI, JavaScript, ASP, PHP, and CFML

CGI

FreeScripts: Free CGI Scripts Written in Perl
`www.freescripts.com/`

Matt's Script Archive
`www.worldwidemart.com/scripts/`

Free Stuff Center: Free Webmaster Tools
`www.freestuffcenter.com/sub/webmastertop.html`

JavaScript

JavaScript Tricks
`home.thezone.net/~rbennett/utility/javahead.htm`

Webmonkey JavaScript Code Library
`hotwired.lycos.com/webmonkey/reference/javascript_code_library/`

ASP (Microsoft Active Server Pages)

Macromedia Dreamweaver UltraDev
`www.macromedia.com/software/ultradev/`

ASPHole-ASP Resources for Web Professionals
`www.asphole.com/asphole/`

PHP

PHP-Hypertext Preprocessor
`www.php.net/`

PHP Builder
`www.phpbuilder.com/`

CFML (ColdFusion)

ColdFusion Developer's Center
`www.allaire.com/developer/referenceDesk/`

CFAdvisor
`www.cfadvisor.com/`

Accessibility

Bobby-Web Site Analyzer
www.cast.org/bobby/

Anybrowser.org Accessible Site Design
www.anybrowser.org/campaign/abdesign.shtml

useit.com: Jakob Nielsen's Website
www.useit.com/

Downloads

JavaWebSpigots
www.demon.co.uk/davidg/spigots.htm

CNET Download.com
www.download.com/

Chank Fonts
www.chank.com/free/

CoolGraphics-Free Cool Graphics
www.coolgraphics.com/

Browsers

Netscape Navigator
home.netscape.com/browsers/index.html

Microsoft Internet Explorer
www.microsoft.com/windows/ie/

Opera
www.opera.com/

BrowserWatch
browserwatch.internet.com/

CNET's Browsers Topic Center
www.browsers.com/

B

Organizations

HTML Writer's Guild
www.hwg.org/

Webgrrls International
www.webgrrls.com/wexplorer.htm

Digital Eve
www.digitaleve.com/

Macromedia User Groups
www.macromedia.com/support/programs/usergroups/

INDEX